AF720471

THE HISTORY AND THEORY
OF INTERNATIONAL LAW

General Editors

NEHAL BHUTA
ANTHONY PAGDEN
BENJAMIN STRAUMANN

The Laws of War in International Thought

THE HISTORY AND THEORY OF INTERNATIONAL LAW

General Editors

NEHAL BHUTA
Chair of Public International Law, University of Edinburgh

ANTHONY PAGDEN
Distinguished Professor, University of California Los Angeles

BENJAMIN STRAUMANN
Alberico Gentili Senior Fellow, New York University School of Law

In the past few decades the understanding of the relationship between nations has undergone a radical transformation. The role of the traditional nation-state is diminishing, along with many of the traditional vocabularies which were once used to describe what has been called, ever since Jeremy Bentham coined the phrase in 1780, 'international law'. The older boundaries between states are growing ever more fluid, new conceptions and new languages have emerged which are slowly coming to replace the image of a world of sovereign independent nation states which has dominated the study of international relations since the early nineteenth century. This redefinition of the international arena demands a new understanding of classical and contemporary questions in international and legal theory. It is the editors' conviction that the best way to achieve this is by bridging the traditional divide between international legal theory, intellectual history, and legal and political history. The aim of the series, therefore, is to provide a forum for historical studies, from classical antiquity to the twenty-first century, that are theoretically-informed and for philosophical work that is historically conscious, in the hope that a new vision of the rapidly evolving international world, its past and its possible future, may emerge.

PREVIOUSLY PUBLISHED IN THIS SERIES

The Battle for International Law
South-North Perspectives on the Decolonization Era
Edited by Jochen von Bernstorff and Philipp Dann

Rewriting the History of the Law of Nations
How James Brown Scott Made Francisco de Vitoria the Founder of International Law
Paolo Amorosa

To Reform the World
International Organizations and the Making of Modern States
Guy Fiti Sinclair

The New Histories of International Criminal Law
Retrials
Edited by Immi Tallgren and Thomas Skouteris

Sovereignty
A Contribution to the Theory of Public and International Law
Hermann Heller, edited and introduced by David Dyzenhaus

Law and the Political Economy of Hunger
Anna Chadwick

The Laws of War in International Thought

PABLO KALMANOVITZ

Research Professor, Centro de Investigación y Docencia Económicas (CIDE)

OXFORD
UNIVERSITY PRESS

OXFORD
UNIVERSITY PRESS

Great Clarendon Street, Oxford, OX2 6DP,
United Kingdom

Oxford University Press is a department of the University of Oxford.
It furthers the University's objective of excellence in research, scholarship,
and education by publishing worldwide. Oxford is a registered trade mark of
Oxford University Press in the UK and in certain other countries

© Pablo Kalmanovitz 2020

The moral rights of the author have been asserted

First Edition published in 2020
Impression: 1

All rights reserved. No part of this publication may be reproduced, stored in
a retrieval system, or transmitted, in any form or by any means, without the
prior permission in writing of Oxford University Press, or as expressly permitted
by law, by licence or under terms agreed with the appropriate reprographics
rights organization. Enquiries concerning reproduction outside the scope of the
above should be sent to the Rights Department, Oxford University Press, at the
address above

You must not circulate this work in any other form
and you must impose this same condition on any acquirer

Crown copyright material is reproduced under Class Licence
Number C01P0000148 with the permission of OPSI
and the Queen's Printer for Scotland

Published in the United States of America by Oxford University Press
198 Madison Avenue, New York, NY 10016, United States of America

British Library Cataloguing in Publication Data
Data available

Library of Congress Control Number: 2020936724

ISBN 978–0–19–879025–9

Printed and bound by
CPI Group (UK) Ltd, Croydon, CR0 4YY

Links to third party websites are provided by Oxford in good faith and
for information only. Oxford disclaims any responsibility for the materials
contained in any third party website referenced in this work.

Para Aurora

Series Editors' Preface

The three decades since the end of the Cold War have seen the rise, and partial ebb, of interest in just war as a normative idea and cosmopolitan standard from which to evaluate the contemporary international law's framework for inter-state force, and the regulation of the conduct of armed conflict. Applied political philosophy's concern with the normative rightness of "the use of force" (in international law-speak) was likely provoked by an earlier set of motivating circumstances, framed by the American war in Vietnam and the rising tide of civil disobedience in the name of a refusal to participate in what was decried as an unjust war (both in respect of the purposes of the war, and its actual conduct). In the same period, the newly—and evanescently—ascendant "Third World" bloc of recently decolonized states were pressing for the recognition of the international belligerent rights of National Liberation Movements, a move denounced by Western powers as the revival of a dangerous concept of just war.

But cosmopolitan moral theory's just war would outstrip the anti-colonial states' vision of national liberation and (sometime) revolutionary wars as the road to self-determining sovereign statehood, and indeed turn against it. The justice of just war was increasingly argued as reducing ultimately to the protection of individuals and their human and democratic rights; state sovereignty was a mere means to such cosmopolitan ends, and was defeasible to those ends. Humanitarian and pro-democratic intervention went from controversial concepts tainted by Cold War rivalry and the odor of colonial police action to normative paradigms of just war with which the regrettably statist international legal order had failed to keep pace. The laws governing the conduct of hostilities—the laws of war—also did not escape scrutiny: their humanitarian ambition and symmetrical application between (state) belligerents, irrespective of the relative justness of each party's cause, was indicted as another normative failure. At the heart of this contemporary cosmopolitan vision of just war and its conduct, was not only a methodological individualism which accorded only instrumental and second order value to state sovereignty, but also a strong rejection of any dualism of relevant principles of justice as they might apply within states *and* between them.

In this volume, Dr. Pablo Kalmanovitz develops an erudite and concise argument which takes aim at founding assumptions of contemporary just war theory by carefully recovering and elegantly exposing the logic of early modern just war thought and its successor, the notion of "legal" or "regular" war. His contextually informed readings of Vitoria, Suarez, Molina, Grotius, Wolff, Vattel, and nineteenth-century writers such as Lieber are theoretical reconstructions of the "problem-situation"[1] they confronted in articulating a framework for the justness of organized armed violence by sovereigns, against each other and against other kinds of political communities. He finds that early modern just war thought—exemplified in the writings of scholastics and humanists—maintained a high tolerance for extensive violence against populations and property, while nonetheless insisting on the real existence of a moral and legal order that is universal, both substantively and positively. Embedded in these understandings of just war was a consequentialist logic which grasped sovereign power and a pacified civil state as an indispensable condition for human co-existence, to the extent that *ratio status* authorized and even required considerable violence to defend it. But the rationalization of this violence was founded not on a worship of the state as person or thing, but in a casuistic reason of state which, on the one hand construed the state as necessary for the attainment of the highest human good, while on the other, conceived of it as founded upon and acting within natural and human reasons that empower and restrain its bellicose potential. Law stands both above and beneath the state: providing (highly permissive) rules for its relations with other political orders, which conduce toward convergence on an understanding of both the inevitability and dangers of violence *inter se*; and establishing the supremacy and necessity of internal orders of justice that *require* law and the accordance of legal right between subjects (however free or unfree) as the *sine qua non* of the unity that defines sovereign power.

The transition from early modern just war, to "solemn" war, to eighteenth-century "legal" war, is traced by Kalmanovitz through Grotius to Wolff and Vattel. He describes the emergence of a coherent concept of "regular" war between public powers, which at once permitted war as a legal right, but also sought to constrain enmity within a logic of consequences underpinning the permissions and proscriptions of "the voluntary law of nations." The domain of natural law, if it was not to become an excuse for constant unlimited war against enemies deemed criminals, had to be adapted to the reality of a society of states, each rationally pursuing their own well-being. In such a society, the greatest threat is not conflict, but hegemony and any attempt by one state to constitute itself as a universal monarchy. The moral logic of the voluntary law

[1] See Straumann 2019.

of nations is one of prudence, balance, restraint, and reciprocity, all the while maintaining the possibility of war as policy and instrument. Kalmanovitz recovers the political theory underlying this idea of "legal" war, and its associated conventions such as "war declarations." He makes the acute observation that the logic of "regular" war was underpinned by civilizational ideas such as the *jus publicum europaeum* and the inter-connected monarchical courts of European capitals. With its ideals of disciplined and aristocratic conduct of war, and the reciprocity of treatment between equal states, the concept of "legal" and "regular" war informed the nineteenth-century codification of the laws and customs of war, even as the humanitarianism and pacifism of the late nineteenth-century codification movement stood in tension with the military ethos of the increasingly professionalized officer corps.

The logic of "regular" war never completely receded from our arguments about international law and the use of force; its logic of prudence found affinities in post-war international relations realism, but also in the idea that the relative justness of a state's *casus belli* did not mitigate its duties under the laws of war. Even as the cosmopolitan dimensions of international law enlarged, most obviously with the expansion of human rights law and the strengthening of the humanitarian and criminal law rules applicable to organized violence within and between states, the international legal order's debt to the "regular" war tradition remains considerable. Dr. Kalmanovitz's study will surely help us settle our accounts.

Nehal Bhuta,
Edinburgh, May 2020

Acknowledgments

This book has been long in the making. Being able to thank many of those who have contributed to its writing and completion is one of the greatest satisfactions of having it published.

The book's distant ancestor is a doctoral dissertation that I wrote in the political science department at Columbia University and defended in 2010. I am grateful to Jon Elster, my dissertation advisor, for his always incisive feedback and for encouraging me to pursue my own intellectual path, even when it steered away from his interests in transitional justice and *ius post bellum*. Thanks to Jon I spent two wonderful summers during my doctorate as guest researcher at the International Peace Research Institute in Oslo (PRIO), where my interests in international law and its history were sparked by conversations with Greg Reichberg and Morten Bergsmo. Financial support during my Ph.D. from Columbia University, PRIO, and the Harry Frank Guggenheim Foundation are gratefully acknowledged.

The book took its current shape while I was postdoctoral fellow at Yale University, from 2011 to 2013, and the European University Institute (EUI) in Florence, from 2013 to 2015. At Yale I would like to thank specially Bryan Garsten and Ian Shapiro for their hospitality, and the lively theory community for many stimulating conversations and events. Thanks also to the fantastic students in my seminar on the history of international political thought, who helped me get a clearer sense of the core sources in the book, and to the American Council of Learned Societies (ACLS) for funding my time at Yale.

Without Nehal Bhuta's generous mentoring, insight, and support at EUI this book would not exist. His working group on the history of international law, and the cosmopolitan and intellectually diverse community at EUI, were ideal environments for thinking about the intellectual history of the laws of war.

My life as a postdoctoral nomad ended when I took permanent academic positions, first as associate professor in political theory at the Universidad de los Andes, in Bogotá, and currently as research professor in international studies at the Centro de Investigación y Docencia Económicas (CIDE) in Mexico City. I am grateful to both institutions for their support. My interest in the book was nourished in Bogotá by many conversations with Iván Orozco and Julieta Lemaitre, and by the students in my class *Guerra, Justicia y Derecho* at los Andes. CIDE gave me the great privilege of time to write and finish the manuscript. I want to thank specially my colleagues in the international studies division for their good spirits while I was immersed in the last stages of writing, and Mark Aspinwall in particular for being such a congenial chair.

I have had the good fortune of presenting draft chapters and receiving comments in multiple academic fora over the past years, of which I would like to highlight two. Benedict Kingsbury and Tony Anghie were graceful hosts and fantastic interlocutors in a workshop-retreat at the University of Utah in 2014, where I presented a first version of the book prospectus. Martti Koskenniemi's reactions to the prospectus and subsequent conversations were brilliant, kind and extremely helpful. Catherine Lu generously invited me to spend time at McGill University in the summer of 2017, where I presented an overview of the book and a first version of the last chapter before the Research Group on Global Justice at the Yan P. Lin Centre. I am grateful to Catherine for her support and for many priceless conversations in many places over the years.

Draft book chapters were presented at (in chronological order): the 2011 annual conference of the Association for Political Theory at the University of Notre Dame; the workshop on "The Neutral Third Party in Conflict Resolution" at the *Collége de France*; the political theory workshop at Yale University; the Stockholm Centre for the Ethics of War and Peace; the 2014 Global International Studies Conference in Frankfurt; the International Relations colloquium at Hebrew University in Jerusalem; the legal theory working group at EUI; the workshop on "The History of International Law" at EUI; the 2015 conference of the European Consortium for Political Research (ECPR) in Montreal; the 2016 meeting of the International Studies Association (ISA) in Atlanta; the workshop on "Just and Unjust Norms of Warfare" at Sciences Po in Paris; the conference on "Critical, Historical, and Comparative Perspectives on International Humanitarian Law" at the University of Wisconsin, Madison; the conference on "Philosophical Foundations of International Criminal Law" organized by the Centre for International Law Research and Policy (CILRAP) and held in New Delhi in 2017; the 2018 annual ISA meeting in San Francisco and the 2019 annual ISA meeting in Toronto.

In these and other occasions, I have been supported, encouraged, and enlightened by many people, and would like to thank in particular Arash Abizadeh, Or Bassok, Arnulf Becker-Lorca, Richard Bellamy, Seyla Benhabib, Lauren Benton, Eyal Benvenisti, Annabel Brett, Amandine Catala, Ariel Colonomos, Neta Crawford, Tom Donahue, Michael Doyle, Marcela Echeverri, Stefan Eich, Karen Engle, Pablo Gilabert, Javier Habib, Casiano Hacker-Cordon, Sergio Jaramillo, David Johnston, Hent Kalmo, Helen Kinsella, Carrie A. Lee, Doreen

Lustig, Reidar Maliks, Carlos Manrique, Karuna Mantena, Giovanni Mantilla, Fred Mégret, Sam Moyn, Mauricio Nieto, Paulina Ochoa-Espejo, Liliana Obregón, Thomas Pogge, Stefano Recchia, Mark Rigstad, Daniel Schwartz, Melissa Schwartzberg, Steve Smith, Annie Stilz, Luke Thompson, Ann Thomson, Daniel Viehoff, Jennifer Welsh, and Yves Winter. I am also thankful to three anonymous reviewers for OUP who helped me see more clearly what this book was about, to Merel Alstein for her editorial insight, and to Jordan Burke and the editorial team at OUP for their great patience.

My greatest debt of all is to Aurora Pellizzi, who has heard me talk about this book far more than she would like, and who in the long process of writing has unfailingly supported me in the downs and encouraged me to celebrate the ups. Her love and companionship have meant more than I could ever express or thank for. May our son Lucio live in a world where war and its laws have fallen into desuetude.

Table of Contents

List of Abbreviations xvii

Introduction 1

1. Political Theology, *Ius Gentium*, and Just War in Spanish Scholasticism 17
   - 1.1 Sovereignty, law, and war in the order of nature 20
   - 1.2 *Ius gentium* and moral conscience 25
   - 1.3 Belligerent inequality 31
   - 1.4 Partiality in adjudication and good conscience 36
   - 1.5 Execution of just war: *ius in bello* and *ius post bellum* 40
2. Hugo Grotius on Solemn War and the Difference Sovereignty Makes 45
   - 2.1 Grotius's doctrine of solemn war 48
   - 2.2 Natural law and the external law of nations 53
   - 2.3 Why might can make right 57
   - 2.4. *Temperamenta belli* 65
3. Regular War and Resort to Force in the Enlightenment 69
   - 3.1 State sovereignty in international society 73
   - 3.2 Voluntary law of nations and belligerent equality 78
   - 3.3 War declarations and manifestoes 86
   - 3.4 Belligerent status 93
4. Enlightenment Ideals of Limited Warfare 97
   - 4.1 Critique of *ius in bello* in just wars 100
   - 4.2 Regulars, irregulars, barbarians 103
   - 4.3 Immunity of noncombatants and neutrals 111
   - 4.4 Law enforcement 118
   - 4.5 Peace treaties and *post bellum* rights 122
5. Humanizing War in the Nineteenth Century 127
   - 5.1 Regular war in the nineteenth century 128
   - 5.2 Civilization, progress, and legal cosmopolitanism 136
   - 5.3 Sovereignty and human rights in war 139
   - 5.4 The humanitarians' dilemma 142
   - 5.5 The two faces of the laws of war 148

Epilogue 153

References 159
Index 175

List of Abbreviations

AI Francisco de Vitoria. 1991 [1539]. "On the American Indians." In *Francisco de Vitoria: Political Writings*, edited by Anthony Pagden and Jeremy Lawrance. Cambridge: Cambridge University Press.

CP Francisco de Vitoria. 1991 [1528]. "On Civil Power." In *Francisco de Vitoria: Political Writings*, edited by Anthony Pagden and Jeremy Lawrance. Cambridge: Cambridge University Press.

IDNG Christian Wolff and Elie Luzac. 1772. *Institutions du Droit de la Nature et des Gens*. Leiden.

JG Christian Wolff. 1934 [1749]. *Jus Gentium Methodo Scientifica Pertractatum*, translated by Joseph H. Drake. Oxford: Clarendon Press.

LGL Francisco Suárez. 1944 [1612]. „A Treatise on Laws and God the Lawgiver." In Francisco Suárez, *Selections from Three Works*, edited by James Brown Scott. Washington: Carnegie Endowment for International Peace.

LN Emer de Vattel. 2006 [1758]. *The Law of Nations*, edited by Béla Kapossy and Richard Whatmore. Indianapolis: Liberty Fund.

LPB Hugo Grotius. 2006 [1603]. *Commentary on the Law of Prize and Booty*, edited by Martine Julia van Ittersum. Indianapolis: Liberty Fund.

LW Francisco de Vitoria. 1991 [1539]. "On the Law of War." In *Francisco de Vitoria: Political Writings*, edited by Anthony Pagden and Jeremy Lawrance. Cambridge: Cambridge University Press.

OJR Luis de Molina. 1947 [1602]. *De Iustitia et Iure*, disputations 98–124. In Manuel Fraga Iribarne, *Luis de Molina y el Derecho de Guerra*. Madrid: Consejo Superior de Investigaciones Científicas.

OST Francisco de Vitoria. 1934 [1537]. "On St. Thomas Aquinas, *Summa Theologica* Question 40: On War." In *The Spanish Origins of International Law*, edited by James Brown Scott. Oxford: Clarendon Press.

OW Francisco Suárez. 1944 [1621]. "Disputation XIII: On Charity [*De bello*]." In Francisco Suárez, *Selections from Three Works*, edited by James Brown Scott. Washington: Carnegie Endowment for International Peace.

RWP Hugo Grotius. 1925 [1646]. *The Rights of War and Peace*, translated by Francis Kelsey. Oxford: Clarendon Press.

SC Jean-Jacques Rousseau. 1997 [1762]. "On the Social Contract." In *Rousseau: The Social Contract and Other Later Political Writings*, edited by Victor Gourevitch. Cambridge: Cambridge University Press.

TJD Domingo Soto. 1922 [1556]. *Tratado de la Justicia y el Derecho*. Madrid: Editorial Reus.

Introduction

Why are soldiers who kill during hostilities usually deemed innocent of murder? What would make violence perpetrated by regular state forces special and different from violence perpetrated by other groups or individuals? It is a central element of the concept of sovereignty, and of the international laws of armed conflict, that recourse to violence by state agents during war has a special status. As many contemporary war ethicists have denounced, such claim to special status is far from straightforward. It appears not just unclear but untrue that soldiers who kill under the command of an aggressive state should be treated as innocent of murder. At the very least, if they are not liable for murder in criminal law, anyone with the power to stop their aggression should be permitted to do so, just as anyone is permitted to use force in self-defense against an armed thief in a dark alley.[1]

And yet the law of armed conflict does not permit civilians to attack soldiers, even those who fight for aggressive states. On the contrary, as the exclusive holders of belligerent privileges in international law, states can permissibly kill those who directly attack their soldiers.[2] Belligerent privileges thus appear to have the troubling implication that aggressive states can create the conditions under which they may lawfully use force against innocent people.[3] To avoid this troubling implication, it has been argued that all permissions associated with the conduct of hostilities should be conditional on having a just cause for war. Those who fight in self-defense or in defense of innocent people have done nothing to forfeit their rights to life, physical integrity, and more. States should not be allowed to use force against them, regardless of whether they are soldiers or civilians. Many war ethicists are well aware of the great practical challenges

[1] This line of questioning, which denies that there is anything morally distinctive in the practice of war, has been at the center of "revisionist" approaches to war ethics, which have now generated a vast literature. See most influentially Rodin 2004; McMahan 2009; Lazar 2009; Fabre 2012. Seminal contributions to the debate between "revisionist" and "traditional" approaches to war ethics can be found in Rodin and Shue 2008.

[2] Art. 50(3) of Additional Protocol I defines civilian negatively as those who are not members of the armed forces of a Party to the conflict, not members of militias or volunteer corps, and do not spontaneously take up arms against the enemy state. Those who take up arms against the state can be permissibly targeted.

[3] As noted by McMahan 2004, 699.

The Laws of War in International Thought. Pablo Kalmanovitz, Oxford University Press (2020). © Pablo Kalmanovitz.
DOI: 10.1093/oso/9780198790259.001.0001.

of legal reform in this direction, but they nonetheless sustain that moral duties may override legal ones, and that in principle and progressively the laws of war should become more discriminating between aggressors and defenders.[4]

Perplexity about the nature of belligerent privileges in international law has not been confined to war ethicists. Legal commentators have debated whether the law of armed conflict actually confers rights to belligerents; whether it merely "suffers [belligerents] to take certain actions" without adverse legal consequences; or whether it is an eminently restrictive and prohibitive regime.[5] If we take as our baseline the full set of human rights protections in peacetime, plainly the law of armed conflict contains more than restrictions. All its restrictions in fact operate within a far more permissive background than what states are allowed to do under the rule of human rights in peacetime. The First Additional Protocol to the Geneva Convention registers this permission when it states that "combatants . . . have the right to participate directly in hostilities" (art. 43.2). This liberty right in state forces has enormous consequences for those within range of the destructive impact of hostilities. So why should state forces—and only they—have the right to use the most destructive means of violence in the context of hostilities?

The question is all the more pressing given the contemporary prevalence of non-international armed conflicts. The main codified instruments of the law of armed conflict were created by states and devised largely for inter-state armed conflicts. Non-international armed conflicts are a residual category in these instruments, which have few norms addressed directly to their particular dynamics. Non-international armed conflicts not only fail to sustain the reciprocity dynamics that historically made the laws of war a largely self-enforcing regime, but contemporary international law does not treat the parties in these conflicts as equals in legal privileges and obligations, a condition which is arguably a requisite for the efficacy of legal regulation.[6]

Commentators have been rightly troubled by these developments. Under current conditions, the law of armed conflict threatens to suppress individual

[4] McMahan 2009, 14–16. See in a similar vein McMahan 2008; Rodin 2008, 2011; Lazar 2012. By far the most nuanced and sophisticated effort to bring recent war ethics scholarship into conversation with the contemporary law of armed conflict is Haque 2017.

[5] The quoted phrase appears in Roberts 2008, 935. The position that the law of armed conflict is an exclusively prohibitive regime is defended in Haque 2016, 2019. For an informative overview of legal debates about the nature of the powers conferred by the law of armed conflict, see Sassòli 2019, 486–95.

[6] The standard position in contemporary international law is that belligerent privileges apply only to state forces (Henckaerts and Doswald-Beck 2009, 11; cf. Kress and Mégret 2014). On the role of reciprocity in the laws of war ("an unstated but necessary norm underlying the laws of war") see Morrow 2014, 62, passim; Posner 2013; Peeler 2019. The claim that belligerent equality is a precondition for the efficacy of laws of war is defended in Walzer 1977, 41; Bull 1966, 71; Lauterpacht 1953.

judgment and responsibility and to become a predominantly authorizing and permissive regime, oriented more toward sanctioning and legitimating than limiting the use of force.[7] According to some, under current conditions the law of armed conflict may no longer be a viable legal regime at all.[8] Others, by contrast, have heralded the progressive "humanization of the laws of war" through its "convergence" with human rights and international criminal law, the common purpose of which is to protect civilians and ultimately to safeguard the dignity of the human person.[9]

The aim of this book is neither to settle these debates nor to provide the best answers to the questions that have puzzled contemporary war ethicists. Rather, it is to look at the historical arguments and conceptual creations that brought these debates and puzzles into our time. The book is a study of the intellectual history of the laws of war before their codification, that is, of the basic elements that came to constitute them as an authoritative discourse up to the first acts of codification in the second half of the nineteenth century. The study undertaken here aims to explore the foundations of the laws of war in the sense of examining historically important theoretical contributions to the laws of war's constitutive vocabularies and forms of legitimization; this is different from the sense of providing a rational foundation and critique of these laws derived from first principles of justice, individual rights and immunities, or "liability to attack." In the course of its historical and theoretical analysis, the book does reconstruct and analyze answers given by past legal and political theorists to questions often surprisingly similar to those raised by contemporary war ethicists and legal commentators. But the purpose of this reconstruction is not to recover "lessons from the past" for the present, but rather to show how those answers contributed to create the particular vocabularies of the laws of war, and how certain norms and conceptions of war came to be legitimized, incorporated into law, and put at the service of various forms of political action.[10]

[7] Kennedy 2006, 141–50; Koskenniemi 2002b, 167–71.

[8] Lamp 2011; Clark et al. 2018.

[9] Teitel 2011; Walzer 2004, 3–22; Meron 2000; Cançado Trindade 2001.

[10] In this way, my approach has been guided by methodological principles of the contextualist school of intellectual history, a central concern of which has been precisely with the production of normative languages and practices of legitimization. As Quentin Skinner observed in his study of the republican conception of liberty, "what it is possible to do in politics is generally limited by what it is possible to legitimize. What you can hope to legitimize, however, depends on what courses of action you can plausibly range under existing normative principles." Historically available conceptual framings "shape and limit" the lines of action that agents can pursue (Skinner 1998, 105). In particular, the concept of the state is inherently "performative," associated by construction to specific political practices, understandings, and ideals of political rule (Bhuta 2017). This book shows how the laws of war have been a singularly important arena of political construction and legitimization of state practices of violence.

In its particular orientation, the book belongs in the overlapping area of three fields of intellectual inquiry: contextualist histories of international political thought, critical histories of international law, and ideational and critical approaches to the study of norms in International Relations.

The theorists of the laws of war I examine created concepts and vocabularies to articulate abstract and general accounts of norms and value. I approach their works as sources of distinct ways of speaking and thinking about the law of nations and the coercive powers of the state. To access the meaning and significance of these sources, I have borne in mind their specific sites of production in space and time, for which I have profited greatly from a growing literature that provides richly contextualized studies of most of my sources.[11] One the other hand, if all contributions to intellectual history must strike some balance between its theoretical and historical dimensions, my own approach has leaned toward theory.[12] I have been particularly attentive to reconstructing key conceptual distinctions and argumentative moves made in historically important texts, and have attempted to explain their broader theoretical significance and implications for political and legal practices of war making.

This book belongs to *international* intellectual history in the sense that it situates the creation of general accounts of the laws of war within a broader field of intellectual inquiry into the international political arena. Beginning in early modernity, this arena was populated not only by well-established states—monarchies and republics—but also by more or less loose federations, nations under suzerainty, colonial enclaves, business and religious corporations, and individuals in the state of nature. Notwithstanding this great variety, the book looks specifically at the construction and legitimization of the coercive power of *states*, that is, the exclusive sovereign privilege to wage war against other states, corporate bodies, or individuals who are not their subjects or claim not to be.[13] One of the central tasks of this book is to show how the intellectual

[11] For a classic statement of the research program of intellectual history as a study of political languages and vocabularies, see Pocock 1987. An updated version of Skinner's plea for contextualized histories of political ideologies appears in Skinner 2002 [1969].

[12] The case for the irreducibility of the theoretical and historical dimensions in intellectual history, and the necessity of striking a balance, is made by Brett 2002b, 114, 126–8. Raymond Geuss suggestively sees in genealogy a necessary complement to history and theory in intellectual history. Genealogy is all the better "the more detailed and illuminating an account it could give," and the further back it can go into, "the history and origin of contemporary political terms and theories and set this in the context of power struggles between individuals, institutions, and social movements in the recent past" (Geuss 2001, 12). This book may be seen as a contribution to the larger project of presenting a deep genealogy of the laws of war, for which a clear understanding of past theoretical articulations is a necessary part.

[13] Armitage 2012, 7, 4. For a rich historical account of the manifold political entities that populated the international—or rather extra- or trans-national—realm since early modernity, and of the complex legal fabric that wove their interactions together, see Benton 2010.

construction of the laws of war was a central part of the intellectual project that from early modernity spelled out the nature, function, and powers of state sovereignty.

My approach has also benefited from a surge of scholarly interest in the history of international law over the past two decades, which itself has been influenced by the historiography of the contextualist school.[14] Rather than looking anachronistically to past legal texts as anticipations or approximations to contemporary legal understandings, this scholarship has emphasized the need to understand law as a historically and socially situated political discourse, which can be mobilized more or less effectively to serve or undermine the interest of agents pursuing various agendas.[15] On the other hand, however, legal scholars have also underscored the specificities of legal language. Legal systems have a cumulative character that most other political vocabularies lack because legal precedents, which are pieces of legal history, can have legal force in the present. The law can keep alive within itself its conceptual and doctrinal past.[16] Also distinctive of recent legal scholarship has been its interest in using history as a basis for contemporary critique. By looking at the production of international legal concepts in time and space, a better sense is gained of the political uses of law, in particular of its roles in legitimizing and enabling practices of domination and hegemonic power.[17]

This interest in critique has sometimes put legal scholars at odds with more strictly contextualist intellectual historians. Historians have cautioned that, by orienting their approach to history by contemporary legal and critical concerns, legal scholars can easily fall into the trap of anachronism and presentist distortion of the past.[18] On the other hand, legal scholars have observed that identifying the relevant context in any exploration of historical sources requires a judgment that cannot be determined by the sources themselves. Historians must always make choices about what constitutes the relevant context, and these must necessarily depend on how they interrogate the past from the present.[19]

Overall, this book has leaned toward theory and critique. One of its central purposes is to unearth and elucidate the historical roots of contemporary

[14] An important collection of the fruits of this research agenda can be found in Fassbender and Peters 2012.

[15] Koskenniemi 2013a, 226–8. On the reasons for the reluctance of lawyers to undertake properly historical investigations, see Kennedy 1996; Lesaffer 2007a; Craven 2007.

[16] Orford 2013, 170–7.

[17] Anghie 2007; Pitts 2015; Koskenniemi 2013. Valuable studies of the laws of war from this perspective include Berman 2004; Kennedy 2006; Kinsella 2011; Mégret 2006.

[18] Hunter 2013; Lesaffer 2007.

[19] Orford 2013, 170–7; Koskenniemi 2014, 123–9.

predicaments associated with the law of armed conflict. When I look at my sources, I do bear in mind contemporary legal categories that were not always available to these sources. Perhaps the best illustration is the principle of distinction between "combatant" and "civilian," which is at the heart of the law of armed conflict but the contemporary definition of which was introduced only in 1979 in the Additional Protocols to the Geneva Convention. While my sources did not have these terms and concepts, they did have related conceptual pairs and terms, such as "combatant" and "noncombatant," "enemy" and "neutral," "guilt" and "innocence," "regular" and "irregular." My interest in how these forms of discrimination were constructed historically comes largely from the centrality of the principle of distinction in contemporary law. It is also motivated by a critical awareness of the political implications of the legal privilege to use force as a facilitator and legitimizer of violence.[20] A strictly contextualist examination of my sources—whatever that might mean—would have foreclosed the kind of theoretical enrichment and critique of the present that I want this book to generate.

Like many legal scholars and political theorists, I am interested in using intellectual history as a way to interrogate and denaturalize contemporary ways of understanding. It is my hope that, after looking at the intellectual history of the laws of war, the reader will come out with a sharper sense of doubt about the legitimacy of legally sanctioned state violence today. For that purpose, I have been particularly interested in recovering a sense of the dilemmas and misgivings that beset theorists and made them hesitate in the historical process of articulating the language of the modern laws of war. Many of these doubts and misgivings are largely lost to contemporary commentaries on the law of armed conflict, which have mostly stayed within the bounds of its intricate internal logic.[21]

In its focus on ideational and normative elements of international politics, this book is also indebted to a growing body of literature in International Relations that has taken seriously both the relevance of legal concepts and ideas for international politics and the critical pay-offs of historical work. This literature takes off from a fuller appreciation of the relevance of law for international

[20] Berman 2004; Kinsella 2011.

[21] Mégret 2016. If we grant that the laws of war can embody some values, then we can follow Skinner's invitation to exploit the critical power of intellectual history. As he writes, "the intellectual historian can help us to appreciate how far the values embodied in our present way of life, and our present ways of thinking about those values, reflect a series of choices made at different times between different possible worlds. This awareness can help to liberate us from the grip of any one hegemonic account of those values and how they should be interpreted and understood" (Skinner 1998, 116–17). This book does not try to recover alternative accounts of value in the laws of war but rather to elucidate what would be required of us—what sort of normative commitments—to grant that the laws of war can embody the values it claims to embody.

politics, which has to do not only with strategic interests in cooperation and association, but also with the multiple ways in which the law can constitute identities, enable some actors to do things which are otherwise proscribed or inaccessible, and mobilize social pressures for action and change.[22] The old realist cliché that international law is only epiphenomenal on state power is professed now by a vanishingly small minority in the discipline.

It is one of the founding myths of the laws of war that they began with the first international codifications of the 1860s—the 1864 Geneva Convention and the 1868 Saint Petersburg Declaration—which kicked off the various episodes of codification that culminated with the great codification at the Hague in 1899. This myth cannot be accurate, however, because these early codifications already presupposed and indeed required a shared vocabulary within which diplomats, military officers, and lawyers could negotiate, dispute, and ultimately draft their legal codes. The first diplomatic conferences that negotiated codified instruments of the laws of war made frequent references to prevailing laws and customs of war among civilized nations. While the negotiations over what these customs were or meant precisely were central to the political enterprise of codification, their vocabulary and shared understandings were in the making long before these diplomatic efforts. Like many other elements of international politics, their origins can be traced back to early modernity, when mostly protestant jurists and philosophers borrowed and transformed concepts and principles found in Roman law in order to give meaning and conceptual order to the emerging realities of inter-state conflict in Europe.

When looking at the early modern neo-Roman contributions to the laws of war, it is already possible to see how inextricably linked the languages of sovereignty, law, and justice have been in the history of the laws of war. The concept of sovereignty allowed the most articulate producers of the language of the laws of war to overcome acute moral doubts and dilemmas. Far more than the result of positive codification, or the pragmatic embodiment of a universal imperative of humanitarian protection, the vocabulary of the laws of war has been a practical and concrete expression of highly complex theoretically conceptions of the relationship between state sovereignty, law, and justice.

It is therefore a remarkable and puzzling aspect of most recent work in the ethics of war that state sovereignty barely makes an appearance. It is as if, due

[22] Valuable recent studies that have brought together the strategic, identitarian, and legitimizing dimensions of the laws of war include Crawford 2013; Dill 2015; Fazal 2018; Jo 2015; Kinsella 2011; Stanton 2016.

to its deep connection to war and law, the state could somehow disappear from view and be taken as a fixed parameter in ethical theorizing. War ethicists have come to understand themselves as engaged in a "cosmopolitan" enterprise that is separable from both international law and politics. Along these lines, in order to establish the basis of legitimacy of the laws of war, one needs to start from individual rights, which set the terms on the basis of which force can be justified or condemned. Those who violate rights are aggressors, those who protect rights are defenders, and any justification of killing must reflect this core duality. But even though aggression is usually defined in this literature as the grave infringement of individual rights, the fundamental question of adjudication—who is to decide if an action is an infringement of rights—is barely raised or theorized. Depoliticized and detached from law, ethical reflection on war has removed itself from much of the actual practice of state violence and its most prevalent and influential form of legitimation.[23]

By contrast, adjudication has arguably been the most pressing and central concern in the intellectual history of the modern laws of war. The overwhelming answer given by jurists and political theorists writing on the laws of war since early modernity has been the sovereign is to judge. This is ultimately why sovereignty has made such a fundamental difference when it comes to assigning the legal privilege to kill in war and establishing the legal governance of war and its aftermath. The intellectual history presented in this book shows how the laws of war were created and evolved as a powerful device to administer the effects of sovereign decisions on the use of force. The conundrum of how to balance or mediate conflicts among sovereign authorities, and between claims of authority and claims of right, is at the heart of virtually all theorizing on the laws of war before their codification.

The constitutive role and centrality of state sovereignty in the laws of war may not be so evident today. Since the 1990s, the law of armed conflict has increasingly come to be associated with its mitigating and protective dimensions, as the widespread use of the term "international humanitarian law" as opposed to "international law of armed conflict" revealingly signals.[24] By contrast, the intellectual history of the laws of war shows clearly the enduring and problematic

[23] I offer a fuller critique of this approach to war ethics for its de-politicization and lack of a theory of adjudication in Kalmanovitz 2015a.

[24] David Luban speaks of "two cultures of military law" which reflect this process (Luban 2013). One culture belongs to military lawyers, who tend to use the term "law of armed conflict," while the other is made of humanitarian lawyers who tend to use "humanitarian law." Their differences are not just terminological but hinge also on their contrasting understandings of military necessity and hence ultimately on the scope of sovereign decision. On the re-emergence of the humanitarian language in the 1990s, along with the postulate of convergence between human rights and humanitarian law, see further Alexander 2015.

centrality of state sovereignty in the project of regulating war through law. When the infliction of grave violence during war is seen to be permissible because it is consistent with the laws of war, there is necessarily a deference to state authority (or to claims of authority from actors not recognized as states), that is to say, typically, to the decisions of elites in control of the coercive apparatus of a state. Prohibition, amelioration, and mitigation of harm as prescribed by the laws of war are certainly valuable, but they are possible only because, during the special condition of war, states are understood to be permitted to use means of violence that far exceed what would be permissible in peacetime.

Once we recognize the centrality of state authority for the legitimizing power of the laws of war, we are in a better place to see the various ways in which the laws of war can operate politically as a legitimizing tool. To illustrate with a broad distinction, when the status of sovereignty is reserved to a small club of elites, then the laws of war become a predominantly *reactionary project*. The laws tend to reflect and favor the interests of established strong powers, and as such tend to entrench the *status quo* and legitimize their violence vis-à-vis weaker states and non-state actors. But when the status of sovereignty is conceived more ecumenically, as by republicans in the eighteenth century and nationalists in the nineteenth century who did not restrict statehood to a selective club but rather conceived of it as earnable by popular or national struggle, then the laws of war can be mobilized as part of an *emancipatory project*.[25] In this latter case, compliance with the laws of war can be used to signal the capacity of aspiring public powers to act as sovereigns, that is, to command and use force responsibly and in accordance with maxims of good statesmanship. This latter effect is now largely irretrievable due to developments in weapons technology and the doctrine of recognition in international law, but its sheer historical existence can shed a contrasting light on the present.[26]

Historically, there has been contention and deep disagreements among states when drafting and applying the laws of war in specific areas. Different specifications and understandings of the laws of war distribute tactical

[25] Benvenisti and Lustig persuasively interpret the first codifications in the nineteenth century as a product of the reactionary project of preserving the power of the Holy Alliance in Europe and suppressing nationalist movements that lacked recognized sovereign standing (Benvenisti and Lustig 2020). On the other hand, Vattel's republicanism and Francis Lieber's nationalism point to more emancipatory uses of the laws of war (see Chapter 3 below, in particular section 3.4, below.)

[26] The last emancipatory moment for the laws of war was arguably the inclusion of national liberation movements as qualifying for belligerent status in the 1977 Additional Protocols to the Geneva Conventions. This was made possible by the politics of an enlarged state system, which included a large number of socialist and global south states supportive of the national liberation movement (Kinsella 2017; Mantilla 2019).

advantages and disadvantages differently among states and non-state actors. To mention a well-known case, the proscription of privateers in the second half of the nineteenth century was promoted and accomplished by established naval powers. It was defended as a valuable restriction on naval warfare, not inaccurately, but it created serious disadvantages for states that lacked large navies and relied on private ships in naval warfare.[27] Fascinating as these disputes are—and revealing of the political makings of the laws of war—my interest in this book has been to reconstruct the development over the long run of the common language in which they were framed and negotiated.

Political contestation over norms has been motivated by competing interests and varying strengths among contestants, among other things, but they were articulated within common vocabularies and under shared notions of legitimacy. And while military, diplomatic, religious, commercial, and other social and discursive practices also contributed to produce the distinctive language of the laws of war, this book focuses mostly on some of the "great texts" in legal and political thought that have been devoted to the systematic conceptual articulation and justification (or condemnation) of state violence.[28] My approach has been to select and read closely a few theorists whose texts came to be recognized by peers, diplomats, political stakeholders, students, and the broader public as authoritative presentations of the law of nations and its foundations. The selection of texts is far from exhaustive, but I hope the book's lack of breadth is compensated by the depth of its excavations. Two criteria have guided my choice of authors: their influence as historical figures—their being widely perceived as authoritative exponents of the laws of war—and their theoretical sophistication and richness.

By looking at a few selected authors whose works span over four centuries, the book is necessarily a study of both continuity and discontinuities. On the one hand, the authors I examine can plausibly be seen as taking part in a common project within the long tradition of natural law and the law of nations, namely, the regulation of state force in the law of nations. Reflecting this long tradition of thought, my working conception of the laws of war is broad and corresponds roughly to what the early moderns termed *ius belli*. It encompasses

[27] Witt 2012, 133–6.

[28] As Annabel Brett has argued, while "great texts" and "great authors" do not by themselves invent the vocabularies they display, they are exemplary in the complexity and systematicity with which they can convey these vocabularies (Brett 2002b, 118, 127–128). "Great authors" can moreover be approached as particularly revealing "specimens" of a historical type or tendency, which accounts for the enduring value of examining individual contributions to the history of international legal thought (Koskenniemi 2012a, 965–8). Alternatively, great texts can be seen as particularly able producers of "theory-dependent notions," which shape the political and legal reality in which they are subsequently read and used (Bhuta 2017).

not only matters of *ius in bello* (the laws governing hostilities, which is how international lawyers now usually understand the term "law of armed conflict") but also matters of *ius ad bellum* (the law of resort of force) and *ius post bellum* (the law of transition to peace). On the other hand, there are fundamental discontinuities and deep ruptures within this tradition, which reflect fundamental divergences on how best to conceive of the project of regulating war in the law of nations. These ruptures and discontinuities are central to the story I want to tell in this book.

Chapter 1 is devoted to Spanish scholasticism in the early modern period. It focuses mainly on the two towering figures that mark the beginning and end of the great Spanish school of natural law, the Dominican Francisco de Vitoria (1483–1546) and the Jesuit Francisco Suárez (1548–1617). The main goal of the chapter is to examine how the scholastics used the vocabulary of the Roman *ius gentium* in their discussions of the justice of war making. The chapter takes seriously their role as Catholic theologians and advisors to the Spanish crown, and situates their theoretical writings on war and law within the broader context of their political theology of international order.

The chapter highlights the centrality of the problem of conscience to their whole theoretical enterprise, that is, the problem of establishing whether and how war could be fought and concluded without committing mortal sins. While their theoretical work was meant to provide guidance for religious practices of confession, the scholastics did not separate the problem of conscience from that of legality. On the contrary, law, in particular the law of nations, is at the heart of their solution to the problem of conscience. They argued that war is not sinful if waged as a legal trial or authoritative response to an *injuria*, a violation of right in the law of nations (*iura gentium*). Only sovereign or "supreme" public powers had the authority to establish whether an injury that merited war has been committed, and they could permissibly command soldiers to fight to redress the injury.

But while law was central to their solution to the problem of conscience, the scholastics were not primarily concerned with providing juridical solutions to political problems. This is manifest in their relative indifference to what may be called the problem of partiality, which was built into their conception of just war. By presenting just war as a form of legal trial, they assigned to rulers simultaneously the roles of judge and plaintiff in disputes that led to war. As they themselves acknowledged, this was problematic from the perspective of natural law and raised doubts about the potential of just wars to be true vehicles of justice. Later jurists in the natural law tradition thought this problem was serious enough to require a fundamental re-orientation of how the legality of state force was to be understood. In the case of the Spanish theologians, by contrast, partiality does not affect their solution to the problem of conscience, and they did not think it was serious enough to merit a major revision of their broadly Thomistic views.

Against the background of Spanish scholasticism, Chapter 2 turns to the work of Hugo Grotius (1583–1645) and looks at the neglected concept of "solemn war" (*bellum solenne*) which he introduced in his great work *De iure belli ac pacis* (1625) alongside the scholastic concept of just war. The chapter situates Grotius's ideas on solemn war within a neo-Roman tradition of thought about war, to which Grotius was indebted and which the Spanish scholastics explicitly rejected. Solemn wars do not result from a public power of adjudication but rather from a privilege to engage in hostilities which peoples constituted as political communities have. To be legally valid, solemn wars only have to be formally declared by legitimate rulers, and very few restrictions apply to their conduct and conclusion.

The chapter reconstructs the reasons why Grotius thought it was necessary to introduce the concept of solemn war, in particular why he thought only sovereign powers should have the privilege to declare and wage them. It shows that Grotius drew the normative force of the doctrine of solemn war from the moral imperative to pursue the lesser evil. If ideals of just war were placed in the "external" law of nations, he argued, then wars would be longer, more frequent, and more lethal, because adjudication of international disputes should always be expected to be contested and hard to disentangle. While private actors in the state of nature could lawfully wage just wars, the privilege to wage solemn war should be exclusive of sovereign states. States embody jural communities, which can be trusted to administer justice fairly and to infrequently abuse their belligerent powers. In the interest of civic peace, they should in general have a monopoly over the power of the sword.

The chapter argues that neither just war nor solemn war has primacy in Grotius's legal system; they coexist in now theoretically unfamiliar ways. Each belongs to a separate and seemingly inconsistent strand in the law of nations, and ultimately reflects incompatible forms of justice. Just wars must be fought in keeping with "internal justice" and solemn wars with "external justice." This legal distinction reflects a profound fracture between the spheres of statecraft and soulcraft. In the interest of avoiding bad consequences, Grotius argued, there must be a purely external law of nations that regulates hostilities but is agnostic about the justice of the sovereigns' cause. Nonetheless, each law has its own place within Grotius's broad conception of legal science. He gave relatively little weight to the external law of nations. It was a pragmatic and regrettable response to the dynamics of political power in international society, but not something for the keeping of which Christian rulers could be commended, nor something Christian soldiers should ever be proud of doing.

Chapters 3 and 4 turn to two of the most important and influential heirs of Grotius in the Enlightenment, Christian Wolff (1679–1754) and Emer de Vattel (1714–1767). Chapter 3 focuses on their re-articulation and theoretical expansion of Grotius's concepts of solemn war and external law of nations into what they called "regular war" and "voluntary law of nations." Far from grounding these concepts on the principle of lesser evil, they conceived of the voluntary law as an embodiment of the conditions of possibility of a society of equal states, where each state has an equal right to decide autonomously on what its own security and pursuit of rights requires. The voluntary law of nation they conceived neither in opposition to nor as a constraint on the practice of reason of state—or "civil prudence," as Wolff called it—but rather as instrumental, deferent, and generative of practices of diplomacy and sound statesmanship.

Chapter 3 looks specifically at the doctrine of legitimate resort to force in the theory of regular war (*ius ad bellum*). Again in contrast to Grotius, for whom war declarations were purely formal speech acts, Wolff and Vattel produced the theoretical bases for a legal doctrine of war publication, which they articulated around the obligation of states to publish "war manifestoes" stating their reasons for waging war. Their public reasons should display their respect for the sovereignty of other states and their recognition of the binding force of the law of nations. Other sovereigns, its own citizens, and the European public at large were tasked with assessing the plausibility of their justificatory claims and responding accordingly. Typically, both sides in regular wars could offer plausible reasons for war and as such appeared as equals before the laws of wars. States that failed to offer reasons, or that just barely provided pretexts, were labeled "enemies of mankind," their *in bello* privileges could be suspended, and all states were called to join forces against them.

Extending the analysis in Chapter 3, Chapter 4 looks at how the Enlightenment theorists' deference to reason of state plays out in the doctrines of *ius in bello* and *ius post bellum* in regular wars. Generally speaking, if in the case of resort to force reason of state stands as an eminently permissive principle, at least relative to the stricter *ius ad bellum* of just wars, when it comes to the conduct of hostilities and conclusion of war, the limiting dimensions of reason of state stand out. The chapter's central contention is that for Wolff and Vattel the law of nations provides a vocabulary to articulate maxims of sound policy in the administration of a war's destructiveness. These maxims reflect a proper understanding of the economy of violence that all states should follow during war and in their transition to peace.

However, at the heart of the doctrine of *ius in bello* in regular wars there is a tension between two competing state interests. On the one hand, all states are assumed to have an interest in limiting the destructiveness of their clash of forces. In virtue of this general interest, states are taken to agree on certain limitations applicable to the conduct of war. On the other hand, however, states are also known to have short-term interests in using all available means to overcome their enemy, in particular illegal means if they provide tactical advantage. An important function of the law of nations is to mediate this core tension between shortsighted and crude reason of state and long-term enlightened self-interest in the practice of warfare.

The chapter looks at several areas in the practice of regular warfare, identifies the strategic logic behind the laws proposed by the Enlightenment theorists, and discusses how robust were their limiting effects. These areas include the definition of the status of regular forces, irregulars, and savages; the immunity of noncombatants during sieges and requisitions; the immunity of neutrals; the use of reprisals; and the conclusion of war in peace treaties. My discussion underscores how, in all these areas, limiting equilibria were practically possible but always precarious. They depend, first and foremost, on political and military leaders having a sound understanding of, and adhering to, enlightened long-term state interests, which often they did not. The task of the Enlightenment jurists, as they themselves understood it, was to help rulers and military officers better see what their best interests required.

The fifth and last chapter examines the emergence of humanitarianism in the late nineteenth century against the background of the Enlightenment theory of regular war. It focuses mainly on matters of *ius in bello*, and its sources include some of the lawyers and publicists who helped draft or promoted the first positive legal instruments governing the conduct of war. Foremost among these are Francis Lieber (1800–1872), who famously drafted Abraham Lincoln's "General Orders No. 100" during the American Civil War; his friend and Swiss colleague Johann Caspar Bluntschli (1808–1881), one of the foremost international legal publicist of the second half of the nineteenth century; and the Swiss philanthropist Gustave Moynier (1826–1910), also an international lawyer and co-founder of the International Committee of the Red Cross.

The chapter looks at various efforts to integrate the concept of humanity, along with its associated imperatives and norms, into the theory and doctrine of regular war. It portrays Lieber as a key continuator of the regular war tradition into the nineteenth century, and shows how Bluntschli and Moynier sought to incorporate claims of humanity and human rights into the conception of law and war they received from Lieber. If for Wolff and Vattel reason of state could be seen as a form of political prudence, and hence as a virtue, Bluntschli and Moynier were more skeptical and overall critical of the bellicose practices of European statesmen invoking national interests. The chapter examines the deep changes in international legal theory that enabled this fundamental transformation, and reconstructs some of the great dilemmas that it created for the project of codifying the laws and customs of war at the end of the nineteenth century. In particular, it shows how Moynier agonized over the prospect of humanitarianism becoming aider and abettor of European militarism by making war appear less appalling than it is. He thought that humanitarianism could be redeemed as a "secret weapon of pacification" because it would ultimately lead to pacifism.

The chapter concludes by showing how the channeling of humanitarian concerns through the law of nations in the second half of the nineteenth century produced a law of war with two opposing faces, which has often clouded proper understanding of its particular nature up to the present. The end of the nineteenth century is the origin of the contemporary idea of a necessary balance between the principles of necessity and humanity.

Overall, I hope my historical examination will help the reader identify a remarkable dialectic. If the Spanish scholastics validated war before the tribunal of conscience only as a response to an injury that was adjudicated by the affected sovereign, Grotius sought to separate the realms of politics and moral conscience, as their conflation was ill fitting for a society of sovereign states plagued with religious contention and political discord. From the perspective of this opposition, Grotius's theory of solemn war appears as the only path toward a politically viable law of nations, and scholastic just war as a dangerous and over-demanding account of the laws of war. Vattel and Wolff followed Grotius in this direction, but rejected the permissiveness and formal proceduralism of his solemn wars. According to them, there is a distinctive wisdom in the exercise of sovereignty that dictates certain rules of limitation in the conduct of hostilities. There are also obligations toward other sovereigns which require that resort to war be publicly justified. From these more limiting conceptions of sovereignty and international society they produced accounts of *ius ad bellum*, *ius in bello*, and *ius post bellum* that are more restrictive than Grotius's. The humanitarians of the nineteenth century, finally, sought to create a space of neutrality and de-politicization within which initiatives of rescue, succor, and amelioration could unfold. In so proceeding, they were far less inclined to defer to state sovereignty than their Enlightenment predecessors, and less hopeful about the limiting effects of reason of state. The laws of war must care directly for individual human beings, including combatants *hors de combat*, noncombatants, and neutrals.

While a product of history and contingency, the three central elements in this dialectic—moral conscience, deference to sovereign invocations of military necessity, and claims of humanity—correspond to layers that exist still today in or around the laws of war. Knowledge of the history of their constitution and internal tensions can help us get a clearer sense of the nature of the contemporary laws of armed conflict.

1

Political Theology, *Ius Gentium*, and Just War in Spanish Scholasticism

The many contributions of Spanish scholasticism to early modern political and legal thought—in particular those made by theologians and jurists in the "School of Salamanca"—have not lacked appreciation by intellectual historians. Their accounts of natural law and the law of nations have been considered a central source for the modern theory of individual rights, and their social contractarian account of state authority has been deemed comparable to John Locke's, even though it was made over one century before.[1] Their contributions to the Christian "just war tradition" have been well appreciated for a long time.[2] They have also been widely recognized as early contributors to—if not "founders" of—the distinctive vocabulary of international law, which they employed to assess the validity of Spanish empire and its relation to other sovereigns in the sixteenth and seventeenth centuries.[3] In addition to these intellectual contributions, the Spanish "schoolmen" were closely involved in the highest politics of Spain. They were active participants in the most algid political and theological polemics of their time, including the justice of the Spanish conquest of America and the Philippines; the relationship between Europe and the Ottoman Empire; religious conflict in Europe; slavery and the slave trade, and much else.[4]

[1] For valuable overviews of the "School of Salamanca," see Pereña 1981; Pagden 1982; Skinner 1978, 135–73;, Höpfl 2006; Hamilton 1963. On the theory of subjective rights, see Brett 1997, 123–64; Tierney 1997, 288–315. The comparison with Locke's social contractualism appears in Skinner 1978, 155–66.

[2] See e.g. Vanderpol 1919; Regout 1935; Fraga Iribarne 1947; Pereña 1954; more recently Schwartz 2018.

[3] Koskenniemi 2011; Pagden 1990, 2012b.

[4] The founder of the School, the Dominican theologian Francisco Vitoria, taught thousands of students and was regularly consulted by the Spanish Emperor Charles V on matters of state, including famously the legitimacy of Spanish rule in Mexico. Vitoria's pupil Domingo de Soto (1495–1560) was confessor of Charles V, participant at the Council of Trento, and holder of the Prime Chair of Theology in Salamanca, to which he was nominated by the Emperor himself. Francisco Suárez (1548–1617) held the prestigious Chair of Theology in the Jesuit College in Rome and was appointed by King Phillip II to the Prime Chair of Theology in Coimbra. Like Vitoria, Suárez was regularly consulted by the king; he produced a defense of Philip II's right to the Portuguese throne and a polemic attack against James I of England, which defended the permissibility of his assassination (Hamilton 1963, 171–88).

The Laws of War in International Thought. Pablo Kalmanovitz, Oxford University Press (2020). © Pablo Kalmanovitz.
DOI: 10.1093/oso/9780198790259.001.0001.

There is no question that the Spanish scholastics recognized early the reality of a distinctively international realm of politics. In fact they were defenders of this realm, which they saw as a reflection of the will of God and the nature of man. They followed Aristotle in believing that the natural *telos* of man dictates that he join political societies, but made the further point that the world would inexorably be organized as a society of "perfect," nearly independent political units. Political units at the international level could have various constitutional forms—they could also be stateless groups of individuals, or corporations such as the Catholic Church—but each constituted an agent with legal standing vis-à-vis other such units. As units, they shared an interest in cooperation and could have commerce among themselves, but they could also come into conflict and in the extreme case to war.

My main goal in this chapter is to examine how the scholastics used the vocabulary of the Roman *ius gentium* in their discussions of war-making.[5] I begin by summarily discussing some of the theological and metaphysical premises on which they built their more properly legal arguments. I underscore how central for their whole theoretical enterprise was the *problem of conscience*, that is, the problem of establishing whether war can be waged without committing mortal sins, and what is sinful and what permissible in the conduct of warfare. A great deal of their work was meant to provide guidance for priests administering the sacrament of confession. And yet the scholastics did not separate the question of conscience from that of legality; on the contrary, law, and the law of nations in particular, is central to their solution to the problem of conscience.

There are two large groups of contemporary commentaries on the scholastics' writings on war, neither of which has paid a great deal of attention to their political theology. One belongs to the genre of disciplinary histories of international law. It has reconstructed in detail the Spanish scholastics' general views on the law of nations, and the laws of war in particular, with an eye to detecting contrasts with, and anticipations of, modern international law. In these commentaries, the metaphysical and theological underpinnings of scholastic legal thought are largely of antiquarian interest.[6] The second group consists of students of the Christian just war tradition, and more broadly of just

[5] I focus selectively on a few of the best-known figures of the School, mainly on Vitoria and Suárez and to a lesser extent on Soto and Molina, and characterize broadly their views on war, law, and the state. The School of Salamanca in fact includes a large number of scholars, not all of whom were theologians. However, there appears to be a great deal of consistency within the School on the subject of war and law, which may be a consequence of their method of close commentary on Isidore and Aquinas (Schwartz 2018). In virtue of the very nature of their craft, the scholastics stayed relatively cohesively within the frame of some fundamental Aristotelian and Thomistic premises relative to law and political order (Hamilton 1963, 5–7; Bain 2013; Höpfl 2006).

[6] The *locus classicus* of this genre is Scott 1934. See also e.g. Meron 1991; Cavallar 2002, 90–8.

war theory and the ethics of war. In these commentaries, the scholastics tend to be read as moral theorists. Their general and abstract theses, conceptual precision, and argumentantive craftsmanship, have met the high standards of contemporary analytical ethics. However, neither the specific role of *ius gentium* in their theory of just war, nor the theological orientation of their moral theses, has been of much interest in this literature.[7]

And yet the Spanish scholastics were first and foremost theologians, albeit theologians with a breathtakingly broad understanding of the order of considerations that their scholarly work required. Many of them were trained in law and saw great theological significance in the law, not only canon but also civil and of nations. In this chapter I take seriously the scholastics' self-understanding and read them as theologians and metaphysicians who were deeply preoccupied with the practical consequences of war for the human soul.[8]

The key to my reading can be found in Vitoria's introduction to his *relectio* on the American Indians (1539), were he lays down the reasons why he entered the polemic on the legitimacy of Spanish rule in America. As a theologian, he writes at the outset of the *relectio*, he must ponder the justice of Spanish conquest because failure to do so would lead to "unpardonable wrongdoing." Theology and divine law are necessary to establish on first principles the law that regulates war because the Indians are not Spanish subjects, hence Spanish law does not apply, and because the justice of conquest poses a "case of conscience" and as such is "the business of priests and the Church."[9] Vitoria's own framing of his *relectio* aside, there is the absolutely central political-theological thesis that the coercive power of states—their right to use force, punitive and military—must have divine origins because individual human beings do not have the power to kill fellow human beings. Life belongs to God and only God can take it, and therefore only a divinely created public power can resort to war. The power to punish and wage offensive wars cannot be "founded in positive law" but must come from natural and divine law.[10]

Political theology and pastoral care are at the heart of the scholastics' engagement with war and its regulation. The project of disciplining the consciences

[7] For this approach to the Spanish scholastics, see e.g. Schwartz 2018; Reichberg 2007, 2008; Bellamy 2018. There are striking resemblances between some of the scholastic theses and contemporary "revisionist" war ethics. This may explain some of the renewed interest in historical figures among contemporary just war theorists (see e.g. McMahan 2009, 33–4, 61–2, 111–15).

[8] The crucial importance of theology for Spanish legal thought has been emphasized by Schmitt 2003, 101–25; Koskenniemi 2011; Bain 2013; Schröder 2010.

[9] AI, 235, 238.

[10] Vitoria CP, q1a4, 11–12. Also Suárez LGL III.3.2–3. Suárez reconstructs the lineage of this thesis to include Cajetan, Covarrubias, Vitoria, and Soto. The modern natural law tradition, beginning with Grotius, rejected this line of argument.

of military men and political leaders produced a lexicon to classify the sins and crimes committed by soldiers on the battlefield, a process in which Jesuit theologians and military chaplains were particularly involved.[11] But the broader context of this confessional task is set by the idea that the coercive power of public authority is an element in the order that God and nature have willed for human beings. It cannot to be denounced or rejected, as pacifists mistakenly do, but it has to be managed, regulated in the *ius gentium*, and supervised by theologians. Commenting on Aquinas's discussion of "whether or not it is always a sin to wage war," Vitoria denounced "certain newly arisen heretics"—Luther—and the early Christian pacifist Tertullian for denying that Christians could permissibly wage war at all. It is clear from Scripture and the authority of the Church Fathers that rulers can wage war, Vitoria argued, because they are entrusted with the protection of subjects and the common good against internal and external foes. Even though war is certain to bring about "innumerable sins," and may appear contrary to the Christian imperatives of charity, love of one's enemies, and forgiveness of injuries, the evils of just war are less serious than those that would result if rulers refrained from waging just war.[12]

1.1 Sovereignty, law, and war in the order of nature

It was a shared view among Spanish scholastics that, as a matter of natural necessity, in the postlapsarian world there must be a multiplicity of political communities, each ruled by a supreme public power that recognizes no superior in temporal affairs. Given the natural division of the world into separate *civitates*, each endowed with the power of the sword, war is both a necessary instrument of political rule and a perennial if regrettable feature of human affairs.[13]

Vitoria's early discussion in his *relectio* "On Civil Power" (1528) set the basic terms of discussion of the state in the Spanish school.[14] Following Aristotelian and Thomistic premises, he argued that the final cause of commonwealths—the

[11] Lavenia 2014, 456; Höpfl 2004, 15–18. On the practical effects of theological doctrine in the context of the Spanish conquest of America, see Hanke 1949, 133–46; Pagden 2012a.

[12] Vitoria OST, cxvi–cxvii; LW q1a1, 296–8. See similarly Molina OJR Disp 99, 251–65, and Suárez OW I.2–4.

[13] With this internationalist postulate, the scholastics famously rejected claims by the Spanish crown and Pope to universal empire (Tuck 1999, 68–77; Pagden 2012b).

[14] Valuable commentary on the scholastic theory of the state includes Pagden 1982, 68–77; Skinner 1978, 148–66; Gierke and Barker 1934, 44–8, 241–3; Hamilton 1963, 30–58.

natural *telos* of political rule—is to help human beings have good lives.[15] As social animals dependent on association for survival and flourishing, human beings are "compelled by nature" to seek others. They come together in families to form cities, and eventually associate in political communities which ultimately achieve "self-sufficiency" as a characteristic mark of their completion or "perfection." Like natural organisms, commonwealths realize their nature when they become self-legislating and largely autarchic, giving themselves a self-sustaining social order which is separate and independent from that of other commonwealths.[16]

Cities and commonwealths are therefore devices "implanted by nature in man for his own safety and survival," not contingent human creations. They are necessary both for bare life and for having a good life, and as such cannot be freely renounced. While things may have been different in the age of innocence, the precariousness of human life after the fall of man forced people to come together in political society and appoint rulers.[17]

The world, then, is organized by nature not as a single empire—there can be no "lord of the whole world"—but rather as holding a multiplicity of nearly self-sufficient or "perfect" polities. They are not completely self-sufficient, nor can they exist in complete isolation from each other, but they engage in relations of various sorts, including commerce, war, and mutual aid. In a famous passage of "On Civil Power," Vitoria declared that the "whole world" (*totius orbis*) is "in a sense a commonwealth," governed by principles of natural law and the positive laws of *ius gentium*. Far from insular or exclusively self-legislating, polities interact in a global community governed by universal rules, without thereby losing their independent character.[18] Suárez clarified that polities cannot be wholly autonomous because, "when standing alone they are never so self-sufficient that they do not require some mutual assistance, association, and intercourse, at times for their own greater welfare and advantage,

[15] CP q1a2, 6–10.

[16] Vitoria LW q1a2, 301–2. Similarly Suárez LGL III.1.3–5; Soto TJD I.ii.1.

[17] Vitoria CP q1a2 and q1a7. It should be noted that the extent to which individual freedom can mediate the constitution of states for the scholastics has been disputed in contemporary commentaries. According to the traditional Aristotelian-Thomistic line, coming together in a state is not a matter of free choice, nor the result of individual assessments of the best means of protection in a hostile world, but rather the result of a natural impulse or, as Anthony Pagden puts it, a "response to a psychological law of motion" (Pagden 1982, 69). Tierney and Brett, by contrast, have argued that for Vitoria and others the natural imperative to associate politically is not overwhelming, and freedom and choice do mediate the constitution of a state (Brett 1997, 124–37; Tierney 1997, 292–301).

[18] Vitoria CP q3a4, 40. Contrasting assessments of the significance of the concept of community of mankind are offered by Tuck 1999, 74–7; and Haggenmacher 1983, 334–41. According to Tuck, Vitoria's references to a "community of mankind" are isolated and ill-fitting within his Aristotelian framework. Haggenmacher more persuasively argues that such references are not isolated but rather a central element in Vitoria's theoretical project of universalizing the *ius gentium*.

but at other times because also of some moral necessity or need."[19] In order to regulate these relations of assistance, association, commerce, and war, states require "special rules of law" which develop organically from their practices, and which are more precise and concrete than the general principles of natural law. This is the specific function of the *ius gentium* or law of nations.

While it is a matter of natural necessity that independent commonwealths coexist and interact in the world, the specific and particular distribution of their jurisdictions, and the particular form of their political constitutions, is the contingent result of human choice, custom, and accident. Natural law directs human beings to associate in commonwealths and to set up rulers, but it does not designate specific rulers, define territorial boundaries, or determine the constitutional form of polities.

The scholastics brought together accounts of state formation in the Roman *ius gentium* and biblical history to explain the concrete division of the world into multiple commonwealths. Beginning with the great grandsons of Noah, who "divided in their land and after their nations," multiple commonwealths were created through acts of incorporation and "succession." The "methods of succession," by which existing commonwealths could be transformed, included inheritance, custom (*usucapio*), and just war.[20] Thus, the natural imperative of political creation was actualized and made concrete in and through the *ius gentium*, which gave legal sanction both to constitutive acts of consent and first occupation (building, fortification) as well as transformations in territorial rights through military conquest and division.[21] The actual territorial divisions of the world—the boundaries of dominium rights and their associated forms of jurisdiction—are creatures of *ius gentium*, which is both constitutive of a world in which supreme rulers can have and dispute rights, and stipulative of the procedures at their disposal to adjudicate and enforce these rights.

The determinations of the *ius gentium* are positive and contingent, not transcendental or divinely mandated. Since no particular human being has been designated to rule by God or nature, rulers must initially be appointed directly by members of the political body, and the terms of their appointment are to some extent contingent and "dependent upon human choice." Only in virtue of consent can the natural liberty and equality of human beings be abandoned, and subjection to a particular ruler come into being.[22]

[19] LGL II.xix.9, 349.

[20] Vitoria AI q2a1, 255–7. A similar account can be found in Suárez LGL III.ii.5, III.iv.2–4. For further discussion of the legal implications of the biblical history of origins, see Brett 2011, 196–8.

[21] Vitoria OST, cxii; Suárez LGL II.xviii.3–4, 7.

[22] Vitoria CP q1a4, 11; Suárez LGL III.2.3, 373. "Men as individuals," wrote Suárez, "possess to a partial extent the faculty of establishing, or creating, a perfect community" (LGL III.iv.1, 382–3). However,

However, what comes into existence upon the constitution of a political body is not only a contract between individuals and ruler, but also the actualization of nature's and ultimately God's transcendental plans for human beings. This divine and natural design is activated by the will of individuals to share a life in common—in *this* particular place and among *this* particular people—but not created by it. Suárez referred to the medieval theory of the corporation and the mystical body of the Christian Church to illustrate the peculiar character of this activation. When human beings are considered separately, as a "multitude of them collected . . . confusedly, in a disorderly manner," no political power exists. But once the "mystical body" of a political association comes into being through the consent of its members, public power emerges "without delay and by the force of natural reason," and most importantly, "already constituted with just the mode of being [that it has] and not otherwise." Its specific mode of being is that of *suprema potestas* or sovereignty, which has "power over itself and the faculty of self-government," including the powers of legislation over its members, and of jurisdiction and coercion over its subjects within and enemies without.[23]

In sum, while perfect political communities come into existence by consent, their essential features do not depend on consent but are already and necessarily in place upon their constitution. These include having a single head, because commonwealths must be able to act as a single body and seek the common good in *consortium*. Upon incorporation, *civitates* become integrated as political bodies under a ruler, which is set above all its members and has the power to "compel and coerce" its own limbs. As Vitoria put it, "if all members of society were equal and subject to no higher power, each man would pull in his own direction as opinion or whim directed, and the commonwealth would necessarily be torn apart."[24]

Building further on this transcendental line of argument, Suárez identified three inherent powers of sovereignty: legislation, jurisdiction, and coercion.[25]

while there is choice about the particular form of the constitution, there is no choice about the distinctive powers of sovereignty. In contrast to the modern social contractarians, for Suárez and other scholastics sovereign powers are neither transferred by subjects nor established in a social pact. On this see further Tierney 1997, 311–15; Brett 1997, 124–37; Wilenius 1963, 75–86; Lloyd 1991, 292–7.

[23] LGL III.3.6, 380. The constitution of the mystical body of the state is not an act of free will, but there is will when it comes to which rulers are appointed and in what terms. Baker suggests an analogy with marriage: the consent of husband and wife is necessary for marriage to exist, but the general terms of marriage, in particular that the man is head of household, do not result from agreement but from the nature of, and "divine scheme" behind their union (Gierke and Barker 1934, 241–3).

[24] See respectively Vitoria CP q1a4, 11 and CP q1a4, 9.

[25] LGL III.1.6–10.

Because law is necessary for political rule, the state must have legislative power; and because passing sentence is necessary for making laws particular and concrete, it must also have the power of jurisdiction. Furthermore, since particular sentences must be accompanied by the threat of coercion because "directive without coercive force has no value," the state must have the power to enforce its rulings. It is impossible, Suárez concluded, that the power of coercion (*merum imperium*) "should exist apart from the power of jurisdiction, just as, conversely, it is impossible for jurisdiction to exist apart from every element of sovereignty."[26]

When the power of the sword is turned outwards, then there is war. The scholastics followed Aquinas in drawing a strong analogy between inward and outward exercises of the power of the sword. In his seminal formulation, Aquinas held that "offensive war" is a power of jurisdiction applied to "enemies from without" (*exterioribus hostibus*), who although normally outside the jurisdiction of the just belligerent, during war become subjects by reason of their wrongdoing. Similarly for Vitoria, a warring prince "acts the part of the judge in the contention which is the cause of war."[27] His right to judge outside of his jurisdictional boundaries, and to enforce his ruling against his enemies, derives from having suffered an injury. Only on such grounds could foreigners be "deserving of punishment and subject to an alien jurisdiction."[28]

When introducing this conception of just war, the scholastics followed a long-standing distinction between strictly defensive and "offensive" wars (*bellum aggressivum*, as opposed to *bellum defensivum*).[29] While defensive war is a universal right, not limited to public authorities, its scope of application is defined by two narrow conditions. First, defenders must be undergoing a wrongful attack, such that they would die or suffer serious injury unless they use force; and secondly, only force necessary to stop and repel the attack is permissible, not further force to punish or reclaim a right that was violated during the attack. Offensive wars, by contrast, seek not just to defend against a wrongful attack but also to punish and exact reparations for injuries suffered. As a form of administration of justice, they must necessarily include rights and permissions far wider than those of strict self-defense, in particular to exact reparations and punish the guilty in the enemy state. Strictly speaking, only

[26] LGL III.1.9–10, 369.

[27] LW q1a4, 304. For Aquinas's formulation, see *Summa Theologica* II-II q 40 (Aquinas and Dyson 2004, 240).

[28] Suárez OW IV.1, 816. See similarly Molina OJR Disp 103, §5 and Disp 105, §7.

[29] On the history of the distinction, see Reichberg 2012, 342–8; Keen 1965, 68–70. Scholastic accounts of defensive war appear in Vitoria OST, cxvi; CP q1a4, 11–12; LW q1a1, q1a2, 298–300; Soto TJD V.i.8; Molina OJR Disp 102 §1; Suárez OW I.4–7.

offensive wars can be labeled just or unjust, because only they are concerned with the administration of justice and the vindication of rights. In contrast to defensive wars, they are a privilege of sovereign rulers because only public powers can administer justice, and subordinate public powers must appeal to their superiors for justice instead of waging war.

The scholastics understood the power to wage offensive war to have practical implications beyond the vindication of a commonwealth's own particular rights. It is in effect the cornerstone of a system of international justice, law, and order. Given that no superior in temporal affairs exists with the standing and capacity to protect rights, more than strictly defensive force is necessary to secure rights in international politics. Among sovereigns, Vitoria argued, "defensive wars could not conveniently be waged unless there was also vengeance inflicted on the enemy." Without the fear of punishment, "the enemy would simply grow more bold about invading a second time." The threat of just war deters not only deters aggressors but also all potential injurers, and as such protects all the commonwealths in the world.[30]

1.2 *Ius gentium* and moral conscience

That coercive power in the hands of multiple supreme rulers is a reflection of the order of nature does not mean that nature would transparently indicate when force is justified. The scholastics emphasized that it is one of the gravest responsibilities of rulers to decide whether it is safe and just to use the public powers that God has willed, nature has created, and the people has bestowed on them. At stake is not only the subsistence of the commonwealth, but also the good conscience and eternal damnation of its ruler and subjects. We will see in this and the following sections that the scholastic solution to the problem of good conscience was articulated largely in the vocabulary of the Roman *ius gentium*. Law and moral conscience—statecraft and soulcraft—appear inextricably linked in their writings. The *ius gentium* both provided the language in which the justification of war is articulated and defined the procedures that were to be followed for war to be waged in good conscience.

When discussing the *ius gentium*, the scholastics drew from a rich array of sources in Roman and canon law, including Isidore's *Eymologies*, the Roman *corpus iuris civilis*, and Gratian's *Decretum*, as well as Aquinas's discussions in

[30] Vitoria LW q1a1, 298. On the general deterrent effect of just wars, see further Vitoria OST, cxvii; Suárez OW IV.5, 818; I.5, 804; IV.7, 819.

the *Summa*.[31] But far from simply reproducing the received wisdom of Roman law, they essentially built a novel account of *ius gentium* that fit their own preoccupations. As several commentators have recently highlighted, a central purpose of their revisionist work was to make the *ius gentium* an effective and practical tool for managing contemporary political and moral problems of extra-national character, first and foremost the overseas projection of power by the Spanish empire.[32] Their skilled re-articulation of *ius gentium* turned it into a powerful instrument for universalizing and legitimizing particular forms of political ordering and control around the world. At the center of the scholastics' engagement with the *ius gentium* was their interest in persuading rulers and the public of the need for theological supervision over this projection power.

The first step in their re-articulation of *ius gentium* was to distinguish it analytically from natural law. Classical Roman law and Aquinas made no significant distinction. While the *ius gentium* was thought to apply exclusively to human beings, and the *ius naturale* to all living creatures, in substance they were essentially coextensive. For Aquinas, things that belong to the *ius gentium* were established on the basis of natural reason, and therefore "do not need to be enacted in any specific way, because they are indicated by natural reason itself."[33] Most Spanish scholastics challenged this view and followed Vitoria in arguing that the laws of *ius gentium* are human and positively enacted, and as such could not be inferred directly or solely from reason.[34]

As we saw in the previous section, the *iura* that were established on the basis of *ius gentium*, and the practices it regulates, include particular and historically contingent ways of organizing society, and reflect practices and customs that develop and change with time. Slavery and ambassadorships, which figure prominently in the *Digest* (I.1.4), were manifestly contingent and mutable, as were also dominium rights. Given their contingent and changing character, the rights and rules of *ius gentium* could not be part of the eternal and unchanging natural law.[35] Vitoria concluded on this basis that the *ius gentium*

[31] On the Roman law sources of the scholastics, and particularly on the influence of the Roman *ius gentium* in their political and legal thought, see further Haggenmacher 1983, 311–20; Stein 1999, 41, 67, 94–6. Also of great importance were Gratian's *Decretum*, the twelfth-century compendium of canon law, and its subsequent commentaries in the *Decretals*, on which see Tierney 2007, 102–5.

[32] This aspect of scholastic legal thought was emphasized by Michel Villey and more recently by Anthony Anghie and Martti Koskenniemi (Villey 2013 [1975], 340–4; Koskenniemi 2012, 13–31, 2011; Anghie 2004, 13–31).

[33] *Summa Theologica* II-II q57a3 (Aquinas and Dyson 2004, 164–5), citing Ulpian in *Digest* I.1.1.

[34] Soto is the notable exception. For him the law of nations was part of the law of nature, but it had to be inferred by more intricate chains of reasoning (Soto TJD I.v.4, and compare Suárez's rejoinder in LGL II.xvii.8, 331). On Soto's views on *ius gentium*, see Brett 2011, 23–5; Todescan 2013, 138–41.

[35] According to Pagden, an important trigger for the scholastics' departure from the traditional Thomistic line on *ius gentium* was precisely the perceived gradual erosion in Europe of the old practice of taking slaves during war (Pagden 1981). More generally, for the scholastics the *ius gentium* was a law

had no intrinsic rational necessity or goodness but was only a "relative good," established by "agreement among men" and as such "to be placed more under positive law than under natural law."[36]

This somewhat ambiguous formulation indicates a second crucial step in the scholastic re-articulation of *ius gentium*. While Vitoria was keen to emphasize that it was positive and contingent, he also argued that it was practically indispensable for the realization of natural law. As he wrote in his later commentaries on Aquinas, *ius gentium* is "nearly necessary" for the preservation of natural law, indeed it "so closely approaches to the natural law that the natural law cannot be preserved without it."[37] The *ius gentium* consequently has a hybrid or dual character: it is positive law but also part of the natural order, albeit a flexible and contingent part.

Suárez provided the most sophisticated attempt to clarify the hybrid character of the law of nations, or, as he wrote, its being "an intermediate form between natural and human law."[38] *Ius gentium* could in a sense be inferred from natural law, as Aquinas had held, but only through a peculiar form of derivation: not by purely rational and "manifest conclusion" but by "an inference less certain," which is "dependent upon the intervention of human free will and of moral expediency."[39] Expediency and free will intervene to make natural legal principles concrete, or to actualize them in practice through and in the *ius gentium*.[40] However, the intervening human will, even though free, is not arbitrary nor are its determinations purely optional, as they could be in certain areas of municipal law. Rather, they are and must be essentially oriented by consideration of "the welfare of all nature, as well as conformity to her primary and universal principles."[41] In this way, *ius gentium* is a necessary if somewhat flexible supplement to general principles of natural law.

While Vitoria simply referred to the Roman *corpus iuris* to support his treatment of certain rights as *iura gentium*, Suárez went further and sought to explain the nature of *ius gentium* in general terms. His explication opened the way for the inclusion of new rules in the law of nations, beyond those appearing in the old *corpus iuris civilis*. What distinguishes *ius gentium* from

of contingent territorial divisions among peoples "on the move, seeking, settling, and dividing lands," and as such inherently dynamic and changing (Brett 2011, 196–8).

36 OST, cxii.
37 OST, cxiii.
38 LGL II.xvii.1, 325.
39 LGL II.xvii.9, 333.
40 LGL II.xviii.7.
41 LGL II.xx.2, 352.

both *ius naturale* and *ius civile*, he proposed, is that it is a universal form of customary law.[42] Generally speaking, customary laws are generated by regular and sustained habits or modes of conduct within a community, most of whose members have the intention that such practices become law.[43] In the case of *ius gentium*, the community in question is the world or mankind as a whole, and most importantly the community of sovereign states, which habitually follow particular modes of intercourse which they deem to have binding force.[44] It is consequently more apt to speak in Suárez of *ius inter gentes*, rather than *ius gentium*, because for him the *ius gentium* was properly speaking "the law which all the various peoples and nations ought to observe in their relations with each other."[45]

There are two ways in which the law of nations bears on the moral conscience of individuals and the salvation or condemnation of Christians. Firstly, as is the case for all legitimate positive law, the laws of *ius gentium* are binding not only *in foro externo*—enforceable through coercive means—but also *in foro conscientiae*. "Whoever transgresses [the laws of secular rulers] is guilty of a crime in the court of conscience," taught Vitoria, which for Christians could amount to a mortal sin.[46] While for polemical reasons Vitoria and his followers emphasized this claim in the context of municipal laws, it also applies to the laws of *ius gentium*. Those who break the law of nations, "whether in peace or in war, are committing mortal crimes, at any rate in the case of the graver transgressions such as violating the immunities of ambassadors."[47]

Along similar lines, Suárez clarified that only customs that are compatible with the law of nature are fit to be part of *ius gentium*; otherwise, they are not candidates for law but rather corrupt mores that must be eradicated.[48] On the other hand, the customary norms of *ius gentium* could in themselves be morally indifferent, for instance whether a territorial border is drawn here or there. As he wrote, the practices constitutive of *ius genium* do not "prescribe anything as being of itself necessary for righteous conduct" nor "forbid anything as being of itself and intrinsically evil (*intrinsece malum*)."[49] But while not necessarily *indicative* of what is inherently evil, the rules of *ius gentium*

[42] LGL II.xix.6–9; VII.iii.7; VII.iv.4–8. For illuminating discussion of this crucial aspect of Suárez's international legal theory, see Tierney 2007, 114–24.

[43] LGL VII.i.4; VII.xii.11; VII.xiv.6.

[44] LGL II.xix.9; VII.iii.7; II.xix.8.

[45] LGL II.xix, 347.

[46] Vitoria CP q3, 32.

[47] Vitoria CP q3a4, 40. See further Hamilton 1963, 50–2, and for the crucial importance of Reformation polemics in this context, Skinner 1978, 135–73.

[48] LGL VII.iv.4.

[49] LGL II.xvii.8–9, 333.

are *constitutive* of evil: "[*ius gentium*] does not forbid evil acts on the ground that they are evil, but renders [certain] acts evil by prohibiting them."[50] Once a custom crystallizes into a norm of *ius gentium*, it is no longer morally neutral but acquires the moral valence of any valid legality. A legally sanctioned border, even though defined in arbitrary ways, must be respected as delimiting the space of a recognized and hence rightful political *dominium*.

The second way in which *ius gentium* bears on moral conscience is that actions forbidden by *ius gentium* can be deemed morally wrong and sinful because of their close connection to natural law.[51] Even though the two types of law are distinguishable analytically, substantively they are deeply enmeshed, as we have seen. On the one hand, natural law gives *ius gentium* its particular orientation. On the other hand, the enactment of subjective *iura gentium* and other institutions of *ius gentium* can create obligations in natural law that are binding as a matter not of custom but of necessity. The paradigmatic case is the obligation to abstain from another's property. Property is a positive institution which ultimately derives from custom, but once created it has the implication that theft is morally wrong, and that restitution for wrong is morally, not customarily, obligatory.[52]

Suárez further illustrated this fundamental point by reference to two central elements of *ius gentium*: ambassadorships and war. Ambassadors do not exist by nature or necessity. Conceivably human communities could exist and live well without appointing or receiving them. However, once the institution of ambassadorships was created, violating their immunity became a "sign of enmity" that was contrary to "justice and good faith."[53] Strictly speaking, to reject ambassadors is not contrary to reason, but once diplomacy is established in pursuit of the natural imperative of seeking peace and concord among political communities, doing so becomes an expression of hostility and a breach of natural duty.

Similarly, war is an institution of *ius gentium* and as such both contingent and source of natural obligations. War is not necessary in virtue of natural reason because "men could have established some other mode of inflicting

[50] LGL II.xix.2, 342.

[51] Suárez, LGL II.xviii.3; II.xviii.7; VII.iii.7.

[52] Suárez explained that there is no general principle of natural law that mandates the exclusive allocation of goods in persons, much less any particular division of property (LGL II.xviii.3–4). As a nearly universal practice, private property is part of *ius gentium* but it is only permitted not mandated by natural law. Conceivably, human beings could exist and have good lives under schemes of common use or limited possession. But once private property is instituted, some natural rights and obligations do follow, most importantly the obligations to abstain from another's property and to make restitution for wrongful taking (see further Tully 1993, 105–7).

[53] LGL II.xix.7, 347.

vengeance, or entrusted that power to some third prince and quasi-arbitrator with coercive power." However, because just war is "easier and more in conformity with nature," it is an institution of *ius gentium* and as such "may not be rightfully resisted."[54] The doctrine of just war cannot be established solely from reason, as it presupposes particular and historically changing institutional arrangements, for instance "the division of fields or lands and of dwelling places, and the settlement of common boundaries."[55] But once instituted, the laws of war generate permissions and restrictions that have morally binding force and universal application.

One might react to this dual character of the law of nations—its being both morally indifferent and the source of universally binding moral rights and obligations—with perplexity. Contemporary commentaries have often considered it an expression of scholastic confusion about the nature of international law.[56] It is more illuminating to see it, I submit, as the result of a deliberate and indeed historically unprecedented move to capture and reflect in the *ius gentium* concrete practices of political and social life, while tying them to moral standards of universally binding force. The violation of these standards could amount for Christians to mortal sin and for all human beings to condemnable and punishable moral wrongs.

Under this light, one can better see how the law of nations' dual character allowed the Spanish scholastics to give universal sanction to European practices and modes of order. In particular, resort to war could be justified for the protection and universal spread of particular and contingent practices and modes of political ordering. In the extreme case of Vitoria, the whole world appears as a commonwealth not only in the sense of having the power to produce *iura gentium* but also in that people should be able to move freely, settle, and trade globally. Coercion and war could be justified in order to uphold the "natural partnership and communication" that should exist globally, that is, to ensure that the whole world remained open to travelling, trading, and settling. In the case of America, if the American Indians denied Spaniards entry to their lands; or refused trade; or did not extract and prevent others from extracting underground minerals, then they could be attacked and forced to open their borders to visitors, trade, and extraction.[57] Vitoria's followers in the Spanish school were quick to point out that this radical vision of global openness did

[54] LGL II.xix.8, 348. As we shall see below in section 1.4, elsewhere Suárez argued that arbitration was unfeasible in practice.

[55] II.xviii.3, 336.

[56] See e.g. Skinner 1978, 152–3; Hamilton 1963, 98–109; Tierney 2007, 110–12.

[57] AI q3a1, 278–80.

not reflect European practice and was problematic in multiple ways.[58] Suárez offered a more limited, state-centric, and indeed recognizably modern vision of world order with a correspondingly narrower set of *iura gentium*, the violation of which could constitute a cause for war.[59]

But while Vitoria and his followers disagreed on the catalogue and scope of the *iura gentium* that could justify war, their views on the role of *ius gentium* in justifying force were largely aligned. *Ius gentium* is the source of particular yet universally enforceable obligations in matters of navigation, trade, and territorial and property rights. The doctrine of just war is all about how such enforcement should take place. Its universal force rests not only on the "will of mankind" but also on its close association with natural law. This was made explicit by Vitoria when he argued that the American Indians could be forced to obey *ius gentium* even though they could not possibly have consented to it, because "the consent of the greater part of the world is enough to make [*ius gentium*] binding, especially when it is for the common good of all men."[60]

1.3 Belligerent inequality

One of the central principles in the scholastic doctrine of just war—one which distinguishes it from classic Roman accounts of *bellum iustum*—is that in a just war only one side can have justice. This follows from the very nature of the

[58] It implied, for instance, that France could enter Spanish territory to dig in for unexploited precious minerals. Soto and Molina denied that foreigners could freely appropriate *res nullius* within the territory of constituted commonwealths. Unexploited underground minerals are "common possession" not universally but only relative to the members of the commonwealth under the territory of which they lay. Soto also argued that the right to travel and dwell was valid only for legitimate purposes, not in cases of vagrancy (Brett 2011, 25–36, 201–2).

[59] Suárez summarized his narrower view on the *iura* the violation of which could justify war under three heads: "One of the heads would be the seizure by a prince of another's property, and his refusal to restore it. Another head would be his denial, without reasonable cause, of the common rights of nations (*communia iura gentium*), such as the right of transit over highways, trading in common, &c. The third would be any grave injury to one's reputation or honour . . . it is a sufficient cause for war if an injury of this kind be inflicted either upon a prince himself or upon his subjects; for the prince is guardian of his state and also of his subjects" (OW IV.3, 817).

[60] AI q3a1, 280. Suárez, it should be noted, was less assertive than Vitoria on the universality of *ius gentium*. He wrote in *De Legibus* that the law of nations "is not observed always, and by all nations, but [only] as a general rule, and by almost all . . . hence that which is held among some peoples to be *ius gentium*, may elsewhere and without fault fail to be observed" (LGL II.xix.2, 342.) He noted in particular that failure to observe the rules of *ius gentium* within a commonwealth could be lawful, as in the case of a prince prohibiting slavery in his realm (LGL VII.iv.8). However, for public acts contrary to *ius gentium* to be valid, they could not affect foreigners or other states: "a custom [or a statute] contrary to the *ius gentium* can be approved and tolerated in the case of one people, in such fashion that it does not result in serious harm or prejudice to another people" (LGL VII.iv.7, 466). Like Vitoria, Suárez also held that it was enough for a custom to become law that only a majority of the community followed it (LGL VII.ix.12).

rights that justify war. To use contemporary language, these *iura gentium* are claim rights, and as such create duties in others to abstain from obstructing the right-holder's exercise of his right. It is consequently "entirely absurd," Suárez argued, that "two mutually conflicting rights both be just."[61] In just war the injurer is consequently "forbidden to defend himself; for he is bound to render obedience and to give up to that other party that which is the latter's right."[62] The notion that in war both sides could be just entails a logical contradiction, as it implies that both sides are innocent and as such not liable to be attacked. Just wars are by necessity asymmetrical affairs: only one side can have justice, while the other side is necessarily legally delinquent.[63]

Vitoria somewhat mitigated the radical and disruptive effects of this principle of belligerent inequality by introducing his famous doctrine of excuses, which goes again to show how central the question of sin or guilt was in his engagement with the *ius gentium* and war problematique. In cases of "invincible error," he argued, when those fighting unjustly could not possibly know that they were doing wrong, neither moral nor criminal liability for violating rights applies.[64] War is still justified against such innocent enemies, but moderation should be observed in the use of force.[65] Furthermore, soldiers should in general be excused for the injustice of their war because they should normally defer to their ruler's judgment in matters of *ius ad bellum*. Otherwise, "if subjects were unable to fight until they understood the justice of the war, the safety of the commonwealth would be gravely endangered."[66] In general, soldiers should be assumed to be fighting in good faith; if they fight unjust wars, they should be treated not as criminals deserving death but rather as innocent wrongdoers, who are immersed in unjust war-making without fault. Typically, Vitoria concluded, it is *licit* for soldiers on both sides at war to fight, even though objectively speaking—"in itself" or as a matter of "true justice"—only one side can have justice.[67]

[61] OW IV.1, 816.

[62] LGL II.xviii.4, 338. The formal logic of subjective claim rights aside, in scholasticism these *iura gentium* were tied to objective forms of *ius* that excluded in principle the possibility of contradictory claims of right having simultaneous validity (Tuck 1979, 45–50; Fernández-Santamaría 1977, 107, 113). At most one side can have justice in disputes over rights because subjective rights are necessarily tied to this objective order.

[63] Further statements of the logical contradiction in the idea of bilaterally just wars appear in Vitoria LW q1a3, 303; q2a1, 307; q2a4; Molina OJR Disp 103 §10, 105 §7.

[64] LW q2a4, 313.

[65] Molina OLJ Disp 102 §§2–6.

[66] Vitoria LW q2a3, 311. See further Vitoria LW q2a2, 308; LW q3a5, 321; Soto TJD V.iii.3; Molina OJR Disp 113 §§3–4; Suárez OW VII.15.

[67] LW q2a4, 313. Pagden and Lawrance translate this passage as "the subjects on both sides are *justified* in fighting" (emphasis added) but the Latin reads "*et sic ex utraque parte subditi licite pugnant.*" *Licite pugnant* is weaker than justification, as *licet* refers only to something being permissible or free

In this way, the scholastics were able to simultaneously uphold the image of war as law enforcement while sustaining the old Roman distinction between war and crime, enemy (*hostis*) and brigand (*latro*). It does not imply, however, that all soldiers in war have equal legal or moral standing, or that their wars have "simultaneous ostensible justice." They are still unequal in one fundamental respect: those fighting for the just side do no wrong when they attack their enemies, whereas those fighting for the unjust side virtually always do wrong, even though usually faultlessly.[68]

Furthermore, the category of "faultless wrong" is unstable in practice, as Vitoria's discussion of American Indians illustrates so well. When ignorance is a consequence of a refusal to listen—or, as he said, a "refusal to believe what one has heard"—it can no longer be qualified as invincible.[69] And while the American Indians may initially have been innocent—"by nature cowardly, foolish, and ignorant"—through their sustained and stubborn reluctance to heed to Spanish demands, they turned into "wicked" and "treacherous foes," and as such became liable to the most extreme acts of war, including "plunder, enslavement, deposition of their old masters, and the institution of new ones."[70] As Molina pointed out, generally speaking it is rare that a just ruler's adversary remain innocent once the injustice of his case had been explained to him.[71] Once enemies are shown—by the just side—that they are in the wrong, they must change their ways, for otherwise their "contumacy" is established and they become liable to the full war powers of the just side.[72] In practice, invincible ignorance and deference to one's ruler can easily turn into recalcitrance and contumacy.

To highlight the distinctiveness and particular form of this scholastic construction of just war, several important contrasts may be noted with the laws

from penalty, not to rightful title to something (Brett 1997, 134) Soldiers fighting unjust wars in good faith do not sin and should be immune to punishment, but they do not fight justly.

[68] Contrast in this regard James Turner Johnson's influential reading of this crucial passage in Vitoria, which concludes that Vitoria defended the equal standing of soldiers during war on the basis of their "simultaneous ostensible justice." As we have seen, in Vitoria there is a (defeasible) presumption that all soldiers at war fight in good faith, and as such are innocent, which does not amount to equal standing or ostensive equality of justice (cf. Turner Johnson 1975, 185–203). It is also problematic to suggest that upholding the sovereign privilege of belligerence had similar downstream effects in Vitoria and Gentili because in both deference to sovereign authority equalizes enemy soldiers (cf. Schröder 2010, 169; Lesaffer 2010, 222). As will be seen below, Gentili's principle of sovereign belligerent equality has a fundamentally different basis from Vitoria's presumption of soldiers' innocence.

[69] AI q2a4, 268, 270–1.

[70] AI q3a1, 282–3.

[71] Molina OJR Disp 102 §6.

[72] Suárez OW IV.7, 819.

and practice of *bellum iustum* in the Roman *ius gentium*.[73] First and most importantly, the Roman *bellum iustum* was not a form of administration of justice. True, Cicero influentially affirmed that Roman wars should be undertaken only so that "we may live without injustice," and gave as proof of the righteousness of Roman warfare the practice of fetial priests of demanding restitution for injuries in formal declarations of war.[74] But vindication of injuries was not the only form of *bellum iustum* for Cicero or in Roman practice. "Contests for honour and standing" among rival empires were also legitimate, as was also the pre-emption of potential attacks by declared or potential enemies.[75] Overall, the criteria of lawful resort to war in Roman sources were far more permissive and indeed political than those in Spanish scholasticism. Enemies of Rome were those that *could* undermine its rule or its allies', as it was considered justified to wage war preventively, against a known rival or an emerging threat that had not yet caused an injury. Rome may have considered itself superior to all other peoples, but it did not try to constitute itself as their judge in virtue of their wrongs.

Also importantly for present purposes, in Roman practice enemies were not seen as legally delinquent or morally evil. On the contrary, the Roman *ius gentium* recognized special legal privileges in legitimate enemies (*iustus hostis*), including the right to appropriate Roman property taken during war. As Cicero noted, true enemies are "just and legitimate," as such equals under *ius genitum* and covered by the protections of fetial and other common rules, unlike pirates and bandits.[76] In fact, enemies of Rome who fought bravely were praised, and their claims against Rome could be considered valid without this implying that Rome's own claims would be any less valid. Enemies who were admired and had valid claims could nonetheless be fought and killed. Instead of just cause and unilateral justice, bilateral justice and emphasis on status are distinctive aspects of the Roman conception of *bellum iustum*.[77]

By contrast, the Spanish scholastics flatly condemned the "wars of the gentiles" precisely on this latter basis. Enlargement of empire cannot be a just cause for war, Vitoria argued, because if it were, "both parties in a war would

[73] The following relies on Brunt 1990, 305–14; Riggsby 2006, 157–89; Ando 2010, as well as Carl Schmitt's seminal discussion (Schmitt 2003, 152–162).

[74] *De Officiis* I.34–36 (Cicero, Griffin, and Atkins 1991, 14–15).

[75] *De Officiis* I.36 (Cicero, Griffin, and Atkins 1991, 17).

[76] *De Officiis* III.107 (Cicero, Griffin, and Atkins 1991, 141–2). The equality of lawful enemies is affirmed in *Digest* 48.15.5, which puzzled medieval and Renaissance commentators (Haggenmacher 1983, 203–6, 284–6; Tuck 1999, 32–3).

[77] See further Tuck 1999, 31–4; Brunt 1990, 314.

have equally just cause to fight, and both would be innocent."[78] Similarly Suárez argued that the ancient Roman claim that war could be waged for the sake of "ambition, avarice, and even vainglory or a display of ferocity" was "entirely absurd," as it would imply that "a war would be just on both sides, essentially and apart from any element of ignorance."[79] Pre-emptive wars were unjust because only an injury could make someone the legitimate target of attack.

It is worth noting, finally, that this scholastic condemnation of the wars of the gentiles made sense as critique because of the re-appropriations of the Roman conception of *bellum iustum* by Renaissance and early modern jurists working in the civil law tradition. Perhaps the most famous contributor to this neo-Roman conception of war is the Italian jurist Alberico Gentili, who wrote at the beginning of his treatise *De Iure Belli* (1612) that "it is the nature of wars for both sides to maintain that they are supporting a just cause," and since human reason is too weak to discern the justice of the cause, identical rights and obligations must be granted to all sides at war.[80] Gentili credited the Renaissance civilist Rafael Fulgosius and the legal humanist Andrea Alciatus as precursors of this idea.[81] In a commentary on *Digest* I.1.5, written at the beginning of the fifteenth century, Fulgosius had held that the absence of a judge with standing to adjudicate conflicts among supreme rulers made justice indeterminable in practice, and war itself an adjudication procedure. As long as they were sovereign, both parties at war had the same legal standing, and their disputed rights were settled through their contest of force. Alciatus, an early and influential advocate of the exclusive jurisdiction of *princeps* in temporal affairs, argued that since disputes among supreme rulers were inherently intricate and complex, *princeps* should be assumed to have equally valid claims of justice at the outset of war.[82] On this basis, equality of rights, privileges, and obligations should be the legal principle governing both *ius in bello* and *ius post bellum*.[83]

[78] LW q1a3, 303.

[79] OW IV.1, 816; equally Molina OJR Disp 105 §7.

[80] In international politics, he further wrote in *De iure belli* (I.vi), "we see everything dimly, and are not cognizant of that purest and truest form of justice" (Rolfe and Phillipson 1933, 31–3).

[81] *De iure belli* I.vi (Rolfe and Phillipson 1933, 31).

[82] On Alciatus's views on war, see Haggenmacher 1983, 203–6, and for his defence of the exclusive jurisdiction of *princeps* with no superior in temporal affairs, see Lee 2016, 98–120; Kelley 1994, 75–80.

[83] This was also the prevalent view in the *practice*, if not the legal doctrine, of late medieval and early modern European warfare. Even though since the late Middle Ages the principle that only one side in war could be truly just was widely accepted, in practice it was generally assumed that both sides in war had valid claims and fought lawfully as long as they were authorized by legitimate—typically supreme—public authorities (Keen 1965, 63–71).

1.4 Partiality in adjudication and good conscience

By conceiving of just war as a power of jurisdiction, and legitimate resort to force as an act of authoritative adjudication, the scholastics produced a hard theoretical and practical conundrum that the ancient Romans did not have. For when they argued that war is just only in response to a violation of right, they designated the (allegedly!) injured sovereign to adjudicate the case. Sovereigns stand therefore as both judge and party in disputes that escalate to war. However, if war is justified only as a necessary instrument of legal enforcement and administration of justice in the postlapsarian world, then rulers' partiality in adjudication undermines the institution's central justification. It is doubtful that wars can be true instruments of justice if judges are by constitution partial.

Suárez conceded this much. He admitted that a situation in which "the same party in one and the same case is both plaintiff and judge" is problematic and contrary to natural law. Just war is a second-best option that must be accepted only because the domestic ideal of adjudication by impartial judges is unavailable among states—and rightly so.[84] Similarly, Molina recognized that it is very difficult to reach truth and justice when the interests of the judge are involved in the case. Both Vitoria and Molina granted that both sides at war should normally be expected to claim that justice is on their side.[85] And since by definition they have no superior to settle their dispute, contradictory claims would have equal formal standing in the law of nations. The problem is further compounded by the complexity and politically and emotionally charged character of disputes that lead to war. When it comes to establishing the justice of a war, Vitoria recognized, "it is difficult to hit on the true and just course of actions." Rulers can be led by passions and make mistakes, "to the detriment and the ruin of the many."[86]

While the scholastics were well aware of the problem of having rulers act as both judge and party in the adjudication of *casus belli*, for virtually all of them the problem was not serious enough to require fundamental doctrinal revisions.[87] This may not be so surprising if one bears in mind that their

[84] OW IV.6–7, 819.

[85] Molina OJR Disp 103 §1, 304, Vitoria LW q2 a1.

[86] LW q2a1; q2a2, 306, 308. Similarly for Suárez, "human affairs are more frequently governed by conjecture than by any sure reasons" (OW VI.5, 830).

[87] An arguable exception is the theologian Gabriel Vásquez, Suárez's near contemporary and fellow Jesuit. Vásquez appealed to the Roman law of choice of adjudication fora to avoid sovereign jurisdictional overlaps (Schwartz 2013). His concern was not strictly speaking with partiality but rather with the prospect of having wars allegedly just on both sides. His construction nonetheless shows both that alternative conceptualizations of *ius gentium* were available to the scholastics that avoided the problem of partiality, and that such conceptualizations were utterly unappealing in high political circles. Molina

fundamental preoccupation was with matters of faith and salvation, over and above providing sound juristic solutions to political problems. This is indeed one fundamental aspect in which their views are incomprehensible if they are read as jurists or moralists rather than theologians. As we will see below, partiality in adjudication was by no means an obstacle to finding a solution to the problem of good conscience, which was their first and foremost concern. Christians, they showed, could wage allegedly just wars in good conscience even if rulers were mistaken about justice.

In fairness to Vitoria, he did discuss various ways to mitigate the dangers of partiality. He emphasized the obligation to listen to one's counterpart and be ready to negotiate, as well as to consult "reliable and wise men who can speak with freedom and without anger or hate or greed" about the alleged *casus belli*. War should be declared only when negotiation was impossible and "on the opinion of the wise and reliable," which in addition to theologians should include members of the royal council, "senators and territorial magnates," whose advice could temper the "influence of some passion" and help avoid errors.[88] Potentially limiting as these consultations could be, however, they do not address the problem of partiality. Councilors, senators, and territorial magnates are all subordinate to their ruler and can be expected to be partial to their own commonwealth in disputes with foreign powers. They may be wise when it comes to assessing whether war is conducive to the public good of their commonwealth, but they should be expected to favor their own commonwealth over a foreign enemy.

The problem is starker in Suárez who, although aligned with Vitoria in affirming the duty of rulers to make consultations and examine justice diligently, went much further in defending the sovereign privilege to decide on the justification of war. In international disputes, he wrote, a sovereign is "not bound by the decision of those whom he himself has no constituted as judges," in particular not by the types of checks to which Vitoria appealed.[89] He rejected on this basis the idea that rulers had an obligation to appoint arbitrators to adjudicate disputes; it may be desirable that they do, circumstances permitting, but circumstances will often not permit.

rejects Vásquez's proposal in OJR Disp 103 §14 with the formal argument that a sovereign is supreme and as such can never be subject to another sovereign's jurisdiction.

[88] LW q2a1, 306–7; q2a2, 308.

[89] See respectively OW VI.1, 828, and OW VI.7, 831. On the Jesuit defense of absolutism and reason of state, to which Suárez contributed fundamentally, see Höpfl 2004, 84–111; Pereña 1954, 129–57.

Suárez's skeptical discussion of the duty to appoint arbitrators shows how little concern he had for the problem of partiality. Appealing to a standard scholastic distinction between speculative and practical knowledge, he distinguished two steps in the process of adjudication.[90] The first is properly speaking a matter of juridical science and consists in the elucidation of specific claims of right, which involves establishing both the law and facts of the case. The second step requires jurisdiction and consists in the authoritative sanction of the conclusion reached at the first stage. Only the ruler or his appointees, not legal experts, have sanctioning power. Notwithstanding Suárez's admission that partiality in adjudication is problematic, he argued that arbitrators were superfluous in the first stage and deficient in the second. They were superfluous because, when it came to "acquaintance with the rights of both sides," only "knowledge and discretion" are necessary, and the sovereign's councilors were as capable as foreign arbitrators to elucidate the rights in dispute.[91] They are deficient in adjudication because their sanctioning power could only come from a sovereigns' delegation, and yet "very frequently one or other of the princes holds the foreign judges in suspicion," and consequently arbitration is "a most rare occurrence." Since there is no shared trust among sovereigns on third parties that could adjudicate their disputes, arbitration is unfeasible in practice.[92]

The risks of partiality and injustice are augmented in Suárez by his argument that, if the justice of a case is debatable—if both sides had plausible reasons—then the ruler need not abstain from war but could consider whether the reasons weighing in his favor were "more probably true" than his opponents'. In virtue of an assessment of probabilities—the weight of the various reasons and authorities brought to bear on a question—speculative uncertainty need not imply practical certainty; a ruler's higher speculative probability in a dispute could give him practical certainty.[93] In contrast to Vitoria, then, for whom

[90] OW VI.1.

[91] OW VI.6, 831.

[92] If there is so much distrust *among* sovereigns, one is left to wonder why the scholastics thought sovereigns could be trusted with unilateral adjudication. A valuable discussion of Suárez's views on arbitration can be found in Pereña 1954, 251–60. The historical record of arbitration in Europe was in fact quite strong up to the sixteenth century, but by the time of Suárez's writing it had declined sharply. Grewe provides a large list of arbitration cases between the thirteenth and sixteenth centuries, and concludes that, during this period, "the overall picture of this institution and the number of arbitral settlements, which through peaceful means eliminated a great deal of conflict, remain impressive" (Grewe 2000, 98–9, 104).

[93] On "probabilism" in Jesuit thought, see Maryks 2008, 83–126; Schwartz 2013. Suárez's use of probable reasons here would put him in the camp of what Maryks calls "probabiliorism," because for Suárez only if a ruler had more probable reasons than his opponent could he legitimately wage war. For probabilists, just having probable reasons was enough for practical certainty.

rulers must abstain from fighting when justice is debatable—"when both parties seem to have convincing reasons on their side"—Suárez lowered the cognitive bar in the assessment of *casus belli* and amplified the universe of cases in which sovereigns could take themselves to be justified in waging war.[94]

It is clear, at any rate, that the scholastics did not have a solution to the problem of partiality. The problem results from a deep tension in their theory, which simultaneously upholds principles of natural law and corrective justice while defending the exclusive power of sovereigns to adjudicate disputes. From this construction it follows, on the one hand, that in virtue of the logic of claim rights, only one side can have *iusta causa*, but, on the other hand, that each side in a conflict will decide the case. Since no binding mechanism exists or was posited that could impartially adjudicate conflicting sovereign decisions, the contradiction between sovereign decision and the objectivity of just cause remains unsolved. To bring up another illuminating contrast with the Roman account of *bellum iustum*, there the authority and expansion of Rome has clear priority over the imperative of avoiding injustice. True, in the procedure of declaring war, fetial priests demanded satisfaction for an injury received, but consideration of whether such demands were equitable or just was neither part of the practice nor a serious concern. *Rerum repetitio* was essentially a formality because the Romans did not regulate war in order to make it an instrument of justice, but rather a legitimate means of preserving and expanding their empire.[95]

Now, to recall, the reason why the scholastics adhered so firmly to the requirement of *iusta causa* is eminently theological: life belongs to God and only God can take it. Human public powers can be ministers of God's coercive power but in principle only by reason of guilt. The theological problem of conscience is how to reconcile the fact that war is a necessary institution in the order of nature with the knowledge that its uncertainties and countless horrors could bring eternal damnation to soldiers and rulers.

Their solution to this problem has two components. First, there is the proposition that a ruler's judicious examination of a potential *casus belli*, if done in good faith and following consultations with the wise and learned, exculpates him from sin *even if it is in fact mistaken*.[96] Diligence in examination brings "security of conscience," which means one can follow the practical conclusion of one's deliberation safely, regardless of whether it is actually correct. In fact, Vitoria argued, one *must* follow the opinion of wise men "even though they

94 Vitoria LW q2a3, 309.

95 This aspect of the Roman *ius ad bellum* is emphasized by Ando 2010; also Brunt 1990, 306–7.

96 Vitoria AI Introduction, 235–7.

may judge wrongly." Striving in good faith to grasp what justice objectively requires—rather than accurately establishing justice—is enough for salvation. Secondly, during war subordinates to the ruler, soldiers in particular, are free from sin if they obey superiors in good faith *even if their judgment is mistaken.* Obedience to authority in good faith is enough for salvation, unless the injustice of the ruler's act is so plain and manifest that soldiers have a clear obligation to abstain. In general, however, lesser subjects should obey and need not examine closely the justice of the wars they are called to fight.[97]

Note that the opinion of the "wise and learned" carries a great deal of weight in this solution. Who the wise are Vitoria states at the outset of his *relectio* on American Indians: "those whom the Church has appointed as teachers," whose verdict in doubtful cases is law.[98] In a sense, then, the scholastics did ultimately give priority to the authority criterion, but not to the political authority of the sovereign but rather to that of "prelates, preachers, confessors, and jurists versed in divine and human law."[99] During confession, under the shadow of eternal damnation and with the assistance of his confessor, the sovereign had to determine in *foro conscientiae* whether a serious injury had in fact been inflicted that merited war.

The contrast with the wars of the Romans is again illustrative. While in Rome it was assumed that, upon performance of the formalities of the fetial rituals, the gods were in line with the Roman designs, the scholastics did not entertain such confidence.[100] The Jesuits may have weakened the strictures of confession, but the *foro conscientiae* was still a tribunal before which rulers had to appear and be held accountable. This was for the scholastics the ultimate check on the sovereign power to wage war, and the best assurance one could possibly have that just wars were in effect instruments of justice.

1.5 Execution of just war: *ius in bello* and *ius post bellum*

This theological perspective on the problem of partiality in adjudication also sheds light on the nature and distinctive character of the scholastic accounts of the two stages in the execution of a just war. The first stage is the realm of hostilities or, as Vitoria put it, of the "actual conflict of battle" (*actuali conflictu*

[97] Vitoria LW q2a2; Suárez OW VI.8.
[98] AI Introduction, 235.
[99] Vitoria AI Introduction, 236. Suárez, however, moved in a more political direction by giving the sovereign the power to appoint his own councilors.
[100] Brunt 1990, 308; Riggsby 2006, 167–8.

proelii), which is now commonly labeled *ius in bello*.[101] The second stage is the aftermath of war, nowadays termed *ius post bellum*, the defining task of which is the administration of justice in the aftermath of war and future peace by the just victor.[102]

It is common and tempting to read these accounts as simply drawing the logical implications of the idea of just war as a vindication of rights. Strictly speaking, as a matter of law only the just side can avail itself to any *in bello* and *post bellum* rights and permissions. Suárez even held that military actions undertaken by unjust soldiers would only add to their record of injustice.[103] Even if unjust soldiers or their rulers could be excused for waging unjust war, this does not eliminate their injustice. They are not entitled to exact reparations, punish, or to depose enemy rulers after war, even if they may be excused for waging war.

Alternatively, one could read the scholastics' accounts of *ius in bello* and *ius post bellum* as providing directives for the good moral conscience of soldiers and rulers while they execute the sovereign decision to resort to war. These directives presuppose that rulers have assessed the justice of their war in the best possible way and have resorted to force in good conscience. Keeping the precepts of justice in the course and at the end of war protects the ruler and his subjects from eternal damnation. Whether or not he is in fact correct about justice is a separate matter, which may require remedial action at a later point but is not itself sinful.[104] The doctrines, then, do not make all *in bello* and *post bellum* rights strictly conditional on *ad bellum* justice, but rather start from the premise that a fallible but good faith assessment has been made on the justice of resort.

In this last section, I want to discuss briefly some of the adaptations and re-articulations that the scholastics made to principles of natural and Roman civil law in order to fit what they perceived to be the practical realities and limitations of just war-making. For even though just wars were understood to be instruments of justice, they were also known to be highly imperfect instruments. In contrast to the administration of justice within commonwealths, in war rulers are highly constrained; and while principles of natural and civil law gave

[101] LW q3a5, 319.

[102] Even though the scholastics did not use the terms *ius ad bellum*, *ius in bello*, and *ius post bellum*, their discussion fits naturally into these categories (on the origin of the terms *jus in bello* and *jus ad bellum* in the twentieth century, see Kolb 1997). Suárez, for instance, distinguished the three moments clearly in his *Disputatio* on war: "three periods must be distinguished [with respect to every war]: its inception; its prosecution, before victory is gained; and the period after victory . . ." (OW VII.1, 836).

[103] OW VII.4.

[104] Vitoria discusses such remedial actions briefly in LW q2a5.

just war doctrine its fundamental orientation, they embodied ideals that just belligerents could aspire to attain only imperfectly. Acts that would constitute crimes outside of war—sometimes the most egregious possible crimes—could be justified or excused before the court of conscience for having been done "under the rights of war."[105]

The most important adjustment concerns the principle that only the guilty may be deliberately harmed in the process of vindicating rights. To kill the innocent deliberately is wrong and sinful because "no one may be deprived of his life save by reason of his own guilt."[106] The guilty in war are those who "shared in the crime [that justifies the war] or in the unjust war," whereas those who did not consent or give assistance in any way are innocent and should in principle be spared.[107]

The immunity of the innocent was qualified in two important ways. First, and minimally, actions that are contrary to justice in peacetime are nonetheless permissible during war if without them war could not be undertaken at all. Such is the case of the innocent who are *per accidens* but foreseeably killed during sieges or in the storming of cities. If such foreseeable killings were prohibited, said Vitoria, it would be "impossible to wage war against the guilty, thereby preventing the just side from fighting."[108] For this same reason, enemy soldiers could be permissibly killed even though they fought faultlessly, since "combatants cannot very well wage war without eliminating their opponents."[109] Furthermore, argued Suárez, since during war it is often impossible to establish accurately who is a fighter and who is not, it may safely be assumed that all males able to carry weapons are fighters and as such liable to attack.[110]

A second way in which the immunity principle was qualified is that harm to the innocent could be permissible if necessary to achieve victory in a just cause. Vitoria defended the lawfulness of means of war that would be manifestly unlawful outside of war, including the burning and ravaging of innocent farmers' crops and livestock.[111] In a wrenching line of argument, he argued

105 The quoted phrase comes from Keen. As he notes, also before courts of law the fact that acts were committed during hostilities could exculpate for murder, grant the right to ask for ransom, and give legal title over goods taken in the course of battle (Keen 1965, 64–5).

106 Suárez OW VII.15, 845.

107 Suárez OW VII.15, 845–6; Molina OJR Disp 115 §1.

108 LW q3a1, 315. Suárez argued that the innocent could be slain because their killing is not "intrinsic" but only contingent in the pursuit of a justified aim, i.e. the just side's victory. Their death is only an "incidental consequence," not voluntary, and "allowed by one who is making use of his right in a time of necessity" (OW VII.17, 848).

109 Vitoria LW q3a5, 319.

110 OW VII.10, 843.

111 LW q3a2, 317.

that *in extremis* soldiers could be allowed to sack cities, even though this would predictably produce all kinds of "inhuman savagery and cruelty," including "murdering and torturing of the innocent, deflowering young girls, raping women, and pillaging churches." Nonetheless, "if necessity decrees, it is not unlawful, even if the probability is that the soldiery will commit crimes of this kind."[112]

If the central principle of *ius in bello* is the (highly qualified) immunity of the innocent, in *ius post bellum* it is commutative justice. The unjust side has the obligation to compensate the just side at the end of war, but post-war compensation cannot go above the ceiling of "complete satisfaction," which is set by the injury that justifies the war, the costs of the war, and proportional punitive damages if applicable.[113] While in principle only those responsible for unjust takings or destruction should carry the burden of compensating the just side, if the goods of the guilty in the enemy side are insufficient for complete satisfaction, then the goods of the innocent could be taken too. Taking more, however, would be wrong, even a just cause of war for the other side. This limiting principle of *ius post bellum* ran contrary to the rules and practice of ancient Roman *bellum iustum*, to the principles laid out by earlier civil and canon lawyers, and to customary practice in European medieval warfare, which recognized virtually unlimited rights in belligerents to the spoils of war.[114]

The scholastics introduced another important qualification to the principle of complete satisfaction that was closer to Roman sources, namely, the imperative of preserving future peace. Property and territory—in particular "cities and forts"—could be taken not only on the basis of corrective justice but also for the sake of future peace.[115] It could be permissible to "supplant princes" or even to "take over government," argued Vitoria, when "security and peace cannot otherwise be ensured, when failure to do so would cause a dangerous threat to the commonwealth."[116] Along these lines, he justified the right of conquest in order to civilize American Indians and change traditional practices

[112] Vitoria LW q3a7, 323. Similarly Suárez OW VII.6, 840.

[113] Suárez OW VII.5, 839; Vitoria LW q3a7. Molina held that in cases of invincible ignorance the costs of war should not be paid by the unjust side, but otherwise followed this same line (OJR Disp 102 §6).

[114] On the practice of lawful spoilage during war up to the fifteenth century, see Keen 1965, 137–55. Vitoria's revisionism was ambivalent, however. In his *relectio* 'On the Laws of War', he upheld limits to legitimate spoliation on grounds of corrective justice, explicitly opposing standard rules of Roman *ius gentium* (LW q3a7, 322–3), but in 'On the American Indians' he supported those very same rules (AI q3a1, 283). Suárez did endorse the traditional *ius gentium* permissions in OW VII.7.

[115] Vitoria LW q3a7, 324; also Suárez OW VII.20, 850.

[116] Vitoria LW q3a9, 326.

which were contrary to natural law, in particular cannibalism and human sacrifices.[117]

Despite their various pragmatic qualifications, the scholastic doctrines of *ius in bello* and *ius post bellum* ultimately reflect the Thomistic conception of just war as an act of adjudication and vindication of rights. On the basis of this conception, the Spanish scholastics opposed the classical Roman understanding of *bellum iustum* and revised the norms in the Roman *ius gentium* that regulate hostilities and the conclusion of war. While the Roman *ius gentium* was an important source in their articulation of the doctrine of just war, it was adjusted and subordinated to their central preoccupation with the problem of good conscience and their commitment to Aristotelian and Thomistic premises. From a juridical point of view, their combination of Roman and scholastic sources was problematic to the extent that it could not resolve the problem of partiality in adjudication. This problem was not particularly troubling to the Spanish theologians, but it was to become a central concern for later intellectual figures in the modern tradition of natural law and the law of nations, as the following chapters will show.

[117] AI q3a8; rejected by Molina in OJR Disp 105 §8.

2
Hugo Grotius on Solemn War and the Difference Sovereignty Makes

In the previous chapter we identified two contrasting normative conceptions of war, one belonging to the scholastic teachings on just war, the other derived from Roman law and re-articulated by civil lawyers in the Renaissance. Both conceptions were available to Hugo Grotius when he set out to work on his first treatise on natural law and the law of nations, *De jure praedae* (completed in 1605 but published only in 1868). On the one hand, there was the scholastic conception of just war as a public act of jurisdiction and adjudication, to which the Spanish scholastics theologians contributed so greatly. On the other hand, there was the conception drawn from Roman law and practice by Renaissance and early modern civilists and legal humanists—notably Fulgosius, Alciatus, Ayala, and Gentili—which understands just war not as a form of adjudication but rather as a contest between public enemies, which during war recognize each other as equals and bearers of identical belligerent privileges and obligations derived from *ius gentium*.

Grotius's own position relative to these two conceptions of war cannot be inferred easily from contemporary commentaries on his works. On the one hand, given Grotius's upbringing in the humanist tradition and his interest in the autonomy and independence of sovereign states, we may expect him to be a resolute adherent to the Roman conception of war, and as such ideologically closer to Gentili than to Spanish scholasticism.[1] Grotius himself declared that, "the Romans are more worthy of consideration in respect to their examples in a degree commensurate with their superiority to the other nations in the art of war."[2] According to this reading, Grotius would have accomplished the seemingly impossible task of reframing humanist ideals of reason of state in

[1] Richard Tuck has made the strongest case for the importance of humanism—and lack of importance of Spanish scholasticism—in Grotius's thought: "far from being an heir to the tradition of Vitoria and Suárez, as was assumed by writers at the beginning of the century, he was in fact an heir to the tradition Vitoria most mistrusted, that of humanist jurisprudence" (Tuck 1999, 108, and further Tuck 1993, 154–201). Tuck, however, does not discuss specifically the place of the Roman conception of war in Grotius's thought.

[2] RWP III.vi.14, 675.

The Laws of War in International Thought. Pablo Kalmanovitz, Oxford University Press (2020). © Pablo Kalmanovitz.
DOI 10.1093/oso/9780198790259.001.0001.

the language of natural law, in the process departing radically from the law of nature and nations of Spanish scholasticism. His construction of the right to self-preservation may be seen as the cornerstone of a secular and properly modern system of natural rights, as well as a powerful rendering in natural law language of Renaissance imperatives of reason of state. The Roman conception of war would appear to fit best this re-articulation of natural law, flexible and deferent to sovereign decision as it is.[3]

On the other hand, however, even a superficial reading of *De iure praedae* and *De jure belli ac paci* (1625) suffices to come across numerous claims and references that seem to indicate a close proximity to the scholastic conception of just war.[4] Most revealingly, in the latter work Grotius famously held that wars are like lawsuits because only in virtue of an injury could they be justified. "No other just cause for undertaking war can there be excepting injury received," and "the sources from which wars arise are as numerous as those from which lawsuits spring; for where judicial settlement fails, war begins."[5] In such passages, Grotius's debt to the scholastic conception of war seems unquestionable, and his opposition to the Roman conception is sometimes explicit.[6] And while Grotius used to great effect his humanistic training to articulate a doctrine of just causes of war on the basis of Roman civil law techniques, the resulting doctrine of *ius ad bellum* appears alien to the Roman conception of war. Arguably one of Grotius's central goals in *De jure belli ac pacis* was to articulate systematically a doctrine of *ius ad bellum* around a complete set of subjective rights. In this task, he did not have to choose between humanism and scholasticism but rather combined elements from both and other sources in characteristically eclectic and creative ways. Ultimately, however, he operated largely as a theorist of just war in the scholastic tradition.[7]

[3] Tuck 1999, 1–15; Hont 2005, 14–15; Armitage 2012, 156–8. Hont suggestively characterizes Grotius's jurisprudence as a form of "juridically reformatted reason of state" in which the universal imperative of state protection comes to shape decisively the form of the law of nature and nations.

[4] As attested by the frequent inclusion of Grotius as a central figure in the "just war tradition." See e.g. James Tuner Johnson's early influential discussion (Johnson 1975, 222–31) and more recently e.g. Onuma 1993; Neff 2005, 96–9; Bellamy 2006, 71–4; May 2007, 53–7, Hathaway and Shapiro 2017, 9–12.

[5] RWP II.i.1 and II.i.2 respectively, 170–1; similarly LPB 50, 102–5.

[6] Grotius explicitly rejected Gentili's defence of preemptive wars against growing and menacing powers because it transgressed the Thomistic axiom that war can be justified only in response to an injury (II.i.17, and cf. Gentili *De iure belli* I.14). Grotius's discussion of just causes in *De iure belli ac pacis* cites multiple Spanish sources, including Báñez, Vásquez, Soto, and Cajetan (RWP II.i-1–7). In contemporary commentary, by far the strongest account of Grotius's debt to Spanish scholasticism and the theological tradition of just war is Haggenmacher 1983. See also Tierney 1997, 316–42, which provides a detailed response to Tuck, and more recently Brett 2016, 35–6, 52–3.

[7] Haggenmacher 1990, 164. For valuable discussion of how Grotius used the structure of remedies in Roman civil law to articulate his doctrine of just causes for war, see Straumann 2015, 170–206.

Reflecting these various readings and multiple sources, Grotius has also been portrayed as an ambivalent and hesitant intellectual figure or, alternatively, as a pursuer of elusive middle ways.[8] According to the influential reading of the English School of International Relations, Grotius oscillated between the two extremes of political realism and natural law idealism. On the one hand, we have his expectation that there is enough sociability or "solidarity" among individuals and states, so that the just war conception can be put into practice. States can coordinate their use of force sufficiently well to make decentralized law enforcement a viable project in international society. But, on the other hand, there appears to be an unprecedented awareness in Grotius that the conception of war as law enforcement could undermine international society, in particular because states are unlikely to agree on the justice of their disputes. The dangers to international society generated by the scholastic just war conception led Grotius to give the law of nations a novel stabilizing role, and to produce the alternative normative account of "solemn wars" (*bellum solenne*).[9]

It will be my contention in this chapter that Grotius did not take sides, nor hesitated between the two competing conceptions of war, but rather incorporated and rearticulated both into a single system of law. Grotius used the term "solemn war" or "just war according to the law of nations" (*bellum iustum ex iure gentium*) to denote his own reformulation of the Roman conception.[10] He used the generic term "just war" (*bellum iustum*) to denote his own version of the scholastic conception. My central task in this chapter will be to recover the reasons why Grotius thought it was necessary to introduce the concept of solemn war alongside that of just war, and to elucidate how, according to him, the two conceptions could coexist in a single system of law.

[8] According to Carl Schmitt, Grotius is an "unsteady and uncertain" intellectual figure, who impossibly kept both the scholastic centrality of *iusta causa* and the legal humanist emphasis on *iustus hostis* (Schmitt 2003, 159–62; similarly Grewe 2000, 191–5). Pushing against this old dichotomous polemic, Brett discusses how, in Grotius's account of the state, the particular role of expediency signifies both a departure from reason of state (because normativity is central in the pursuit of self-interest) and a break with scholastic natural law (because of the unprecedented justifying power of will and utility) (Brett 2002a).

[9] As Hedley Bull puts it, "on the one hand Grotius embraces the notion that war is an act of law enforcement, substituting the idea of enforcement by particular members of society for that of enforcement by a central authority. But on the other hand he recognizes that war is a recurrent phenomenon; and that international society may be threatened by the way in which it is conducted as well as by the failure of the side representing the law to achieve victory" (Bull 1966, 64–5; on Bull's reading of Grotius, see further Kingsbury 1999). Steven Forde reads Grotius not so much as an ambivalent figure, but rather as successfully finding a middle path between the poles of just war idealism and political realism (Forde 1998). For both Bull and Forde, the law of nations plays a crucial role in mediating between these two extremes (Bull 1966, 58–9; Forde 1998, 646–7). In previous work, I also argued that Grotius was ambivalent between the just war and solemn war conceptions (Kalmanovitz 2015b) but see now section 2.4 below.

[10] RWP III.iii.11, 639.

Unlike his predecessors in the civil law tradition Fulgosius, Alciatus, Ayala, and Gentili, Grotius did produce a theoretical account of the nature and justification of solemn warfare, the theoretical sophistication of which has not been sufficiently appreciated in recent commentary.[11] My discussion will show that Grotius was neither a just war theorist, nor a defender of the Roman wars, nor ambivalent about the two conceptions, but rather found a place for each within his very broad conception of legal science. The two conceptions are for him complementary not rivals, and their inner tensions reflect real trade-offs and limitations in the project of enforcing rights in international society.[12]

2.1 Grotius's doctrine of solemn war

Grotius began book I of *De iure belli ac pacis* with an extremely broad definition of war as "the condition (*status*) of those contending by force, viewed simply as such."[13] Who those contending may be, or what their contention may be about, is left open at the outset of the book. As Grotius explained, this definitional breadth was necessary to avoid prejudging the question whether war can be justified, or who can permissibly wage it and on what grounds. In principle, contention by both private and public actors could count as war. Furthermore, war is not a contest, as Cicero had defined it, but rather a legal condition of contestation, in which particular laws apply.[14] Having defined war so broadly, Grotius proceeded to introduce two important distinctions. First, a war can be public, private, or mixed depending on the status of the contending parties: public wars are waged by public powers, private wars by private agents, and mixed wars have both. Secondly, public wars could be either formal or "less formal" depending on whether the contending public powers are sovereign and the war formally declared. It is for this latter type of war—formal public war—that Grotius reserved the term "solemn war."[15]

[11] The most complete and suggestive discussion of Grotius's theory of solemn war is still Haggenmacher 1983, 568–612. See also Remec 1960, 96–113; Tadashi 1993b; Brett 2016, 44–50, and for the appropriation and spread of Grotius's idea, Neff 2005, 95–113.

[12] Since the category of solemn war and its supporting apparatus were introduced only in *De iure belli ac pacis*, and are virtually absent from Grotius's earlier treatise *De iure praedae*, I will focus primarily on the former. Unless otherwise noted, subsequently all references to Grotius are to *De iure belli ac pacis* (RWP)..

[13] I.i.1, 33.

[14] Grotius held before Rousseau that a condition of war could exist even when the parties do not actually engage in physical contention; the particular laws that regulate their condition continue to apply even when they are not actually engaged in fighting (III.xxi.1).

[15] I.iii.1, I.iii.4, 97.

Having introduced the legal concept of solemn war, Grotius later indicated its most remarkable feature: a war could be solemn, and as such have legal effects before courts of law, and yet lack a just cause.[16] Somehow, the injustice of a solemn war did not dissolve the validity of its legal effects. Injuries could be the source of rights, and aggressors could lawfully profit from wrong. To solve this seeming contradiction with elemental tenets of justice and natural law, Grotius distinguished two different senses of *ius*.[17] The *ius* proper of just wars is that of subjective right, including the natural power over oneself and one's property, and rights acquired through contract or promise. By contrast, the sense of *ius* that belongs properly to solemn war is that of *lex* or positive enactment, which includes lawful command and positive legal procedure. There is no inconsistency in saying that a war could be lawful—"just" in the second sense—and unjust in the first sense, because a lawful command can violate subjective rights.[18]

Grotius's doctrine of just war can be read as a derivation of his theory of corrective justice. Central to both *De iure praedae* and *De iure belli ac pacis* is the thesis that, by nature, war is justified only as a proportional response to a serious injury imminent or received.[19] Keen on cataloguing the subjective rights violation of which would constitute a *casus belli*, Grotius devoted a great deal of book II of *De iure belli ac pacis* to discussing the forms of injury that could justify war. Like the Spanish scholastics, he argued that from the very nature of just war it followed that the parties have unequal legal standing.[20] Before the injury that justifies the war, they are equals before the law of nature and nations; after the injury and because of the injury, the victim comes to have jurisdiction over the injurer, in particular criminal jurisdiction when there is fault. Grotius quoted Vitoria when arguing that, strictly speaking, the aggressor has no right to use force, but soldiers may usually be excused for using unjust force in virtue of their subordination; superiors may also sometimes be excused due to invincible ignorance. But even when the unjust side is faultless, his war remains unjust, and his enemy is just and entitled to use force and claim reparations.[21]

[16] II.i.3, III.iv.3.

[17] I.i.3–9.

[18] Grotius used the concept of prescription in civil law to illustrate the distinction. A debtor cannot be forced to pay his debt once the legal term for filing claims prescribe, and in this sense he has a positive or "external" right not to pay the debt, but he continues to have an "internal" obligation to pay which originates in the natural law of property (III.vii.6). A debtor is at fault in conscience and before God if he fails to pay his debts, but legal prescription means that this obligation cannot be enforced by state courts.

[19] LPB 101–26; RWP II.i.1–6, II.ii.1.

[20] LPB 124–6; RWP II.i.18, II.xxiii.13.

[21] RWP II.xxvi.4; II.xxiii.13.

Grotius did introduce important changes to received scholastic accounts of just war. Most importantly, he argued that private agents could engage in what the scholastics called "offensive just war" when they were outside the jurisdiction of any state, particularly in the open seas and in vacant islands.[22] As was famously the case for Locke later on, Grotius held more generally that a private right to punish could and had to exist in the state of nature because only in this way could sovereigns come to have it. "Just as every right of the magistrate comes to him from the state, so has the same right come to the state from private individuals."[23] By contrast, as we saw in the previous chapter, for the Spanish scholastics the right to punish was bestowed directly by God through the law of nature on public powers, and only on them.

This amounts, as has often been noted, to a momentous rupture with the scholastic account of public power, but in the specific context of the laws of war, arguably Grotius's most radical break with scholasticism lies in the introduction of the theory and doctrine of solemn warfare. The starting place for that doctrine, Grotius tells us, is not corrective justice but rather the Roman definition of enmity, in particular Pomponius's definition in the *Digest*, according to which enemies are "those who in the name of the state declare war upon us."[24] Wars formally declared between two peoples have peculiar legal effects that do not follow from "the nature of war itself" but in virtue of their status as peoples and their formal declaration of war.[25] There are only two conditions of *ius ad bellum* in solemn wars: belligerents must be sovereign and their decision to wage war must be publicly declared. Without these formalities, a war cannot have the legal effects of solemnity, just as without proper formalities legal wills and marriages are empty of legal effect.[26]

The main reason why war must be publicly declared, Grotius held, is that only public declarations can show that it is in effect a sovereign that resorts to war.[27] Declarations are eminently formal procedures and were modeled after the Roman practice of *rerum repetitio*. Their function is to constitute a formal condition of war, in which the particular laws of solemn war come into effect.

[22] LPB 104–5, 128–42; RWP I.iii.2, II.xx.6. On the novelty, motives, and historical significance of this move, see further Tuck 1999, 78–108; van Ittersum 2010; Straumann 2015, 208–18.

[23] LPB 137. As we will see below, in section 2.3, Grotius importantly qualified this claim in *De iure belli ac pacis*.

[24] III.iii.1, 630, citing *Digest* L.xvi.118, as well as XLIX.xv.19, 21, 24.

[25] III.iv.1, 641.

[26] III.iii.1–5. Grotius's discussion is strikingly similar to Balthazar Ayala's in *De Iure et Officiis Bellicis* (1581). Ayala also refers to formal procedures in Roman civil law in his discussion of war, including marriage, "competence to bring suit," and the age of attaining majority, to convey the peculiar sense of the Roman *bellum iustum* (I.ii.34, in Ayala and Westlake 1912, 22). For a detailed discussion of the Roman sources behind Grotius's presentation, see Haggenmacher 1983, 577–9.

[27] III.iii.11.

A second important reason for declaring war is to alert third parties to take measures and prepare for the foreseeable disruptive effects of war.[28]

This formally constitutive function aside, war declarations also typically state the substantive reasons why war is waged. Since states have an interest in being perceived as just—and their enemies unjust—they often publicize the reasons why they wage war, so that "the whole human race might judge of the justness of it."[29] War declarations appear in this way to preserve the just war requirement of just cause. However, even though public declarations may often include such reasons—and Grotius certainly hoped that sovereigns would follow the catalogue of *casus belli* that he so painstakingly articulated in book II of *De iure belli ac pacis*—they could also be purely formal speech acts without any content or substance. Furthermore, both sides in a solemn war could raise contradictory claims over disputed rights, and both would have valid legal standing, which is to say that both sides in a solemn war could simultaneously satisfy the formal conditions of *ius ad bellum*.[30]

Now, the now most unfamiliar and indeed shocking aspect of Grotius's doctrine of solemn war is his account of *ius in bello*, in particular the absence in any form of a principle of distinction in the conduct of war. As far as the law of nations is concerned, solemn wars take place literally between whole commonwealths and include a "promiscuous right of inflicting injury" which "permits the killing of enemies without distinction."[31] All subjects of the enemy state count as enemies, for when war is declared against a sovereign, it is declared against all its subjects.[32] Correspondingly, no combatant status exists in Grotius's presentation of solemn wars. Anyone who belongs to a belligerent state is permitted to kill members of the enemy state, not only those who take a "military oath" which formally designates them as coercive instruments of the state.[33] From this promiscuous right to kill a long set of permissions follow,

[28] III.i.5.

[29] III.ix.3, 704 II.xxvi.4, 593.

[30] III.iii.7. One of the formulas of war declaration provided by Grotius is drawn from Livy's account of the Roman fetials and goes as follows: "I bear witness that this people is unjust, and does not give satisfaction," which barely amounts to a statement of reasons for waging war (III.iii.7, 636). The contrast with just wars is clear. While the typical form of equality in just wars is the equal innocence of soldiers, in solemn wars there is equality in the rights and obligations that govern the condition of war.

[31] III.iv.8, 647, III.xx.43, 821.

[32] III.iv.6–9.

[33] III.xviii.1. Grotius argued that the obligation to take military oaths before fighting was part of Roman municipal law, not of the law of nations (III.xviii.1). He recognized that military discipline was vital for the effectiveness of force, as without discipline, "outposts might be abandoned or, with increased lawlessness, the army or a part of it might even become involved in ill-considered battles, a condition which ought absolutely to be avoided" (III.xviii.1, 788–9). But this, he thought, was a maxim of prudence, not an obligation in the law of nations. Indeed, Grotius's solemn wars amount legally to "total wars" in the modern sense, as Peter Pavel Remec points out (Remec 1960, 104–5).

including enslaving enemies; injuring or killing prisoners of war and those who surrender and depose arms; torturing enemies; and taking enemy property without restriction.[34]

It should be noted that, while predominantly permissive, the *ius in bello solenne* also contains some forms of restriction. One consists of restrictions derived from the obligation to keep promises made during war and includes in particular respect of truces, rights of safe-conduct, and returning prisoners in exchange for ransom.[35] Others derive from the proscription of certain means of war, including rape, the use of poisonous weapons, and "treasonous" assassins.[36] There are also restrictions associated to neutral states, which in virtue of a declaration of neutrality obtain certain immunities and incur in certain obligations vis-à-vis belligerent parties.[37] Among these restrictions are the prohibition to kill enemies in neutral territory and the protection of "innocent trade," that is, neutral ships with neutral cargo are immune to taking and neutral ships carrying enemy cargo could not be taken (but their cargo could be).[38]

Finally, if in just wars the central element of *ius post bellum* is the vindication of the right that supports the *iusta causa*, the central element in solemn wars is a negotiated peace treaty (*pacis pactione*) that formally concludes the condition of war.[39] It is assumed that belligerents understand that the disputed rights over which the solemn war was fought, as well as any claims derived from losses incurred during war, dissolve with the conclusion of war. There are only two ways to arrange a peace treaty, Grotius argued, either by restoring the *status quo ante bellum* or by letting "things remain as they are" at the conclusion of the war (*uti possidetis*). The latter is preferable because it is easier to implement and less likely to generate further conflicts.[40] For similar reasons, amnesties are presumed to always be part of peace treaties, as "the best reconciliations are those which do away with the anger and the remembrance of the injuries."[41]

[34] See respectively III.vii.1, III.iv.10–12, III.iv.18, III.vi.2.

[35] III.xxi.1.

[36] See respectively III.iv.19, III.iv.15, III.iv.18.

[37] III.xvii.1–3.

[38] See respectively III.iv.8, III.i.5. Grotius formulated these rules with the uncharacteristic caveats that there was little customs on record, and that the rules were unsettled by ongoing polemics between those who "champion the relentlessness of warfare" and those who defend "the freedom of commercial relations" (III.i.5, 602). Rights and obligations associated with neutral trade in European warfare remained unsettled until the mid- eighteenth century. Before that, the preponderance of belligerent powers over neutral commercial republics tended to inhibit all forms of trade with belligerents. Grotius provided one of the earliest formulations of the rules of neutral trade (Kulsrud 1936, 73–5, 216–18). I discuss neutrality further below and in section 4.3.

[39] III.xx.1–20. Grotius's account of peace treaties reflects emerging practice in early modern Europe, which among other things usually included amnesty provisions and tended to be agnostic about *iusta causa* (Lesaffer 2004).

[40] III.xx.11, III.xx.19.

[41] III.xx.17, 811.

Unless the treaty stipulates otherwise, the possession of movable goods and territory, as it stands at the conclusion of the war, becomes property and territorial rights upon signature of the treaty.[42] Similarly, by default belligerents are not liable for damages caused to private property. Owners whose private property is destroyed or taken during war have no remedy for their losses in the law of nations (but it is commendable if municipal law contemplates remedies).[43] The far-reaching practical effect of these provisions is to give legal sanction to the nearly complete license that governs property and territorial takings during solemn war, as "any one at all becomes owner, without limit or restriction, of what he has taken from the enemy."[44]

2.2 Natural law and the external law of nations

So how and in what sense could these morally appalling "legal effects" of solemn wars ever be permissible—the impunities, indiscriminate killings, theft and destruction, territorial takings, the enslavement of the vanquished? Grotius hints at the answer already in the Prolegomena of *De iure belli ac pacis*, where he announces that, in order to properly establish the rights of belligerents, he had to distinguish clearly between matters of natural law, law of nations, and municipal law. But in addition to this standard three-fold division, it was also necessary to distinguish within the law of nations, "between that which is truly and in every respect law (*ius*) and that which produces merely a kind of external effect simulating that primitive law."[45] It is this "external law of nations" that regulates solemn warfare, but its proper place within Grotius's legal world is somewhat elusive.

In his general jurisprudential remarks, Grotius distinguished between natural law and the law of nations on the basis of their sources. Natural law was supposed to reflect the conditions necessary for social life, and could be inferred rationally from the inherent "agreement or disagreement of anything with a rational and social nature."[46] He understood social life in a rather minimalist way, essentially as peaceful coexistence in the undisturbed enjoyment of one's subjective rights.[47] In virtue of a moral imperative to preserve oneself

[42] III.xx.11–12.
[43] III.xx.15.
[44] III.vi.2, 664; also III.xx.12, III.viii.4.
[45] Prolegomena §41, 24.
[46] I.i.12, 42.
[47] Haakonssen 1985, 240–2.

and live socially, what the law of nature prohibits or commands has "a quality of moral baseness or moral necessity" that not even God can change.[48] The law of nations, on the other hand, while oriented toward the advantage of "the great society of states," was established on the basis of "unbroken custom and the testimony of those who are skilled at it," including importantly the ancient historians.[49] So while natural law is the product of rational reflection on the necessary conditions of human social life, and as such universal and unchangeable, the law of nations is "volitional" and the contingent product of human will and practice.[50]

When discussing the relationship between these two bodies of law, Grotius at some points appears to align himself with Spanish scholasticism, for which the law of nations was both volitional and also a necessary complement to natural law. Since the function of the law of nations within the natural order is to complete and make more precise the law of nature, they cannot contradict each other. Grotius held similarly that human laws, and the law of nations in particular, "indisputably have it in their province to go further than nature in regard to many points, but never to go contrary to nature."[51] The law of nations could prohibit or command what the law of nature permits, but not mandate what it prohibits nor prohibit what it mandates.[52]

Elsewhere in *De iure belli ac pacis*, however, Grotius flatly contradicted these general statements in far-reaching ways, most extensively in the doctrine of solemn war. The external law of nations permits things forbidden in natural law (e.g. killing without just cause) and forbids things that are naturally prescribed (e.g. to exact reparations for injuries received.) And yet it is only because the external law of nations is valid law that solemn wars can be legally sanctioned. To further complicate things, when it came to establishing the contents of the external law of nations, Grotius not only selectively documented established customs and practices among nations, but also offered arguments presented as conditions of international sociability to establish the contents of the external law of nations. This led Jean Barbeyrac—Grotius's influential

[48] I.i.10, 38–9.

[49] Prolegomena §17, 15, I.i.14, 44.

[50] The distinction between natural law and law of nations becomes less clear cut as *De iure belli ac pacis* unfolds, however, as not all elements in the law of nature are inferred rationally but some may be established inductively, on the basis of what was historically believed to be part of the law of nature "among all nations, or among all those that are more advanced in civilization" (I.i.12, 42). The question of how this historical or *a posteriori* law of nature could be distinguished from the law of nations has perplexed students of Grotius, but it was not addressed by him (Tadashi 1993a, 41–43; Haakonssen 1985, 247–51).

[51] II.iii.6, 208.

[52] II.ii.5.

eighteenth-century commentator and French translator—to conclude that, properly understood, solemn wars were really creatures of natural law, not solely of the law of nations, as Grotius had claimed.[53]

The solution to this apparent contradiction lies in Grotius's novel distinction between external and internal justice, which underpins his construction of the external law of nations and hence of solemn war doctrine.[54] It is with this distinction in hand that Grotius could bring together into a single legal system the contrasting normative logics of just war and solemn war. This system of law has two separate tiers, which allow for the simultaneous evaluation of war from two conflicting legal standpoints. An action in war can be both valid from the standpoint of external justice and wrong as a matter of internal justice, and vice versa. Each standpoint addresses separate dimensions of practical action and reflection.

Indication of what precisely is at stake behind Grotius's distinction between internal and external justice has to be gleaned from multiple passages scattered in *De iure belli ac pacis*. In the Prolegomena, Grotius described the subject of book III, which is largely devoted to external justice, as "that which is done with impunity, or even that which among foreign peoples is defended as lawful," in contrast to "that which actually is free from fault."[55] The permissions presented in book III, he later clarified, created obligations "not to put any hindrance in the way of him to whom permission is given," but did not amount to full authorizations.[56] External permissions are "incomplete," as they grant a freedom from punishment and a right of non-interference but deviate "from the rule of right."[57] And yet, even though external permissions deviate from the rule of right—and even though failure to punish could well amount to the "destruction of the law"—Grotius argued that they have to be recognized and respected as legally valid among nations.[58]

What emerges from these and other passages is the thesis that, while internal justice speaks directly to the moral conscience of individual human beings, external justice regulates the use of enforcement powers by sovereign states, in

[53] See Barbeyrac's gloss to III.iv.4 in Grotius and Tuck 2005, 1275–6. Regarding Grotius's selection of sources, Remec shows that he chose illustrations mostly from ancient history and very selectively to support his theoretical priors (Remec 1960, 99–100). Straumann argues that Grotius's turn to Roman sources in *De iure praedae* was partly a strategic recourse to neutralize the force of precedent of the papal bulls, which gave jurisdiction to Spain and Portugal in their overseas expansions (Straumann 2015, 28–31, 42).

[54] On this crucial distinction, see further Haggenmacher 1983, 571–5; Tadashi 1993b, 294–304; Remec 1960, 96–100.

[55] Prolegomena §35, 22.

[56] I.i.9, 38.

[57] III.x.1, 716; also I.i.17, 49, III.xvi.1.

[58] I.ii.7, 67.

particular with regard to the material consequences of war. Recognizing something as an external right in the law of nations means that the right-holder can seek remedies in national courts for its infringement, and third parties have an obligation not to use force to oppose the exercise of the right. But even though claimable in court, external rights do not create "bonds of conscience" (*animo obligationem*); opposing them is unlawful and liable to punishment or restitution, but neither sinful nor wrong.[59] The adjudication of external rights is in this sense a narrowly legal affair, not concerned with the virtue of justice broadly understood, but only with what the law of nations recognizes as enforceable and claimable in court.[60]

In a radical departure from Spanish scholasticism, Grotius's distinction in effect decouples the international regulation of state force from the moral conscience of agents—he separates statecraft from soulcraft. If for Grotius external rights in the law of nations were binding in *foro externo* but not in *foro interno*, for the Spanish scholastics all *iura gentium* were binding in both fora. Originally the distinction between fora was meant to separate the judgment of manifest and punishable sins at public courts from the judgment of less visible sins; the latter had to be declared voluntarily and in the sacrament of confession, and penance not punishment was the proper response.[61] For the Spanish scholastics, as we saw in Chapter 1, *ius gentium* generated obligations in conscience that rulers were expected to take seriously and discuss with theologians in confession. Because the *arcana* of statecraft, and the dilemmas and difficulties proper of political rule, could be discussed and assessed together by rulers and confessors, the *ius gentium* could be brought directly to bear in the forum of conscience.

This option was of course not available to Grotius. He decoupled the two fora and began thinking systematically about the purely external workings of law enforcement among sovereign states, particularly when they faced the politically charged and destructive effects of war. The use of enforcement powers by states thus became in his work a relatively autonomous normative and regulatory sphere, with its own distinctive forms of validation and justification.

Grotius's construction, it may be noted, is also fundamentally different from that of Thomas Hobbes, who famously defended the opposite claim that the *ius gentium* was binding in *foro interno* but not in *foro externo*. Since the law of

[59] III.vii.6–7, 693–5.

[60] III.xx.25.

[61] On the theological sources of Grotius's distinction between the two fora, see Haggenmacher 1983, 581. As Goering notes, while the external forum proceeds "under the supervision of experienced judges, lawyers, and trained personnel," the penitential forum is "more informal and less concerned with procedural details" and can be entered only of one's own free will (Goering 2008, 380).

nations is identical with the law of nature, it always obliges in *foro interno*—its principles are binding in conscience "to a desire that they should take place"—but not in our external interactions with others.[62] Lacking proper external assurances of compliance by others, if we unilaterally abide by the principles of natural law, we would foolishly expose ourselves to preying instead of securing our own security and livelihood.[63] So if for Hobbes the law of nature, and indeed virtually every form of obligation, is externally on hold pending the institution of an assuring sovereign, for Grotius the external law of nations is different from, indeed inconsistent with natural law, and it is binding *in foro externo* notwithstanding its lack of centralized enforcement.

2.3 Why might can make right

To grasp the precise nature of Grotius's justification of the rules of the external law of nations in solemn wars, it is useful to revisit briefly Jean-Jacques Rousseau's outraged and incisive attack on Grotius at the beginning of *On the Social Contract*. The privileges of solemn war provide the paramount target for Rousseau's famous denunciation that in Grotius, "the most frequent mode of argument is always to establish right by fact."[64] External rights acquired in war are literally the outcome of a contest of force between belligerent powers; in solemn wars, facts create rights. For Rousseau, by contrast, giving legal sanction to unconscionable acts of war was not only immoral but also absurd, as it confuses the authority of the law with the sheer reality of power.[65] Grotius's external law of nations cannot be a genuine source of obligations because, as Rousseau famously wrote,

> once force makes right, the effect changes together with the cause; every force that overcomes the first, inherits its right. Once one can disobey with impunity, one can do so legitimately; and since the stronger is always right, one need only make sure to be the stronger . . . If one has to obey by force, one need not obey by duty, and if one is no longer forced to obey, one is no longer obliged to do so. Clearly, then, this word 'right' adds nothing to force; it means nothing at all here.[66]

[62] *Leviathan* I.xv.36–7 (Hobbes and Tuck 1991, 110); see also *Elements of Law* I.17.10.
[63] *Leviathan* I.xiv.5.
[64] SC I.ii, 42.
[65] SC I.iii.
[66] SC I.iii, 44.

While profound and powerful, this critique is not quite accurate or fair to Grotius. There is no question that for Grotius power can be the source of rights, but this need not dissolve the legality of solemn war regulations. On the contrary, Grotius insisted that the rule of might in solemn wars has only the duration of a legally declared "condition of war" and applies only to sovereign belligerent powers. Furthermore, the laws of solemn war regulate not only the relationship among enemies but also that of neutral states, whose rights and obligations foreign courts are compelled to protect. And while it is true that, the more frequent the practice of solemn wars, the more in flux and unsettled property and territorial rights would be, it is not the case that every change of power would be immediately reflected in a change of rights. Among states, resort to war is presumed to be exceptional enough to give sufficient stability and permanence to the rights settled as legal effects of war. In a sense, Grotius defended the concessions that law makes to power in solemn wars precisely in order to facilitate the restoration of a full condition of right.

Grotius's defence of solemn wars can be analyzed in three separate lines of argument. The first aims to justify specific provisions in the external law of nations that were evidently problematic and contrary to internal justice. These include the right to enslave captured enemies, the validity of peace treaties signed under threat, and the principle of *uti possidetis*, according to which actual possession at the conclusion of war becomes property and territorial rights. The second line of argument justifies the right of third parties to declare themselves neutral, that is, to be agnostic about the justice of a foreign war. The third line shows why only sovereign states could be entitled to the special privileges of solemn war. While separate and distinct, the three lines ultimately converge on a single general imperative: to limit the spread, duration, and lethality of war. If the defining aim of Grotius's (and the scholastics') theory of just war was to protect and vindicate subjective rights, the distinctive aim of the theory of solemn war is to manage and limit the destructiveness of inter-state wars.

Grotius's first line of argument in defense of the specific permissions of solemn war follows a logic of consequences and is grounded on the moral obligation to pursue the lesser evil. In all instances, the argument has the same form: if attempts were made to include the full rights of internal justice in the regulation of warfare, this would lead to a situation far inferior to the world of internal justice as an unintended consequence. In order to avoid that morally inferior situation, the degraded rights and rules of external justice must govern inter-state wars, and as such be recognized in the law of nations and state practice.[67]

[67] A complete moral argument based on the principle of lesser evil would also have to show that no superior alternative is available to the alleged lesser evil. Several Enlightenment thinkers, including Montesquieu, Rousseau, and Vattel, argued that there is a viable alternative to Grotius's solemn wars, i.e. the practice of war in which the privilege to kill enemies applies only during declared states of war and only against enemy soldiers. I discuss this more limiting alternative in Chapter 4.

Consider first the right to enslave enemies during war. Even though enslaving the innocent is "wrong in its intrinsic nature," argued Grotius, it has to be permitted as an incentive to "induce captors to spare captives."[68] Unquestionably the best moral world would be one without slaves, but if the practice of enslaving captives were forbidden, more people would die as a result of war. By contrast, if enslavement is permitted, "the captors, mollified by so many advantages, might willingly refrain from recourse to the utmost degree of severity, in accordance with which they could have slain the captives, either immediately or after a delay."[69] Since in solemn wars the right to kill enemies is indiscriminate, there is a choice for potential targets between sacrificing life or freedom. Grotius assumed that anyone would favor life and agree to become a slave (he also assumed, incidentally, that belligerents will not in fact be motivated by internal justice). Grotius defended in a similar way the right of victors to conquer territory and subject its inhabitants to patrimonial rule. "Life, to be sure," he wrote, "which affords the basis for all temporal and the occasion for eternal blessings, is of greater value than liberty. This holds true whether you consider each aspect in the case of an individual or of a whole people."[70]

The structure of this external right to enslave enemies is peculiar. On the one hand, slaves have no obligation in conscience to obey their master—they are not morally guilty of theft if they escape—but, on the other, if caught by public authorities, they may be forced to return to their owners.[71] Furthermore, slaves cannot permissibly use force against masters or public authorities to avoid capture.[72] The reason for this mismatch between internal rights and coercion is that without a grant of legal title, the incentive to spare life would dissolve. In this sense, the external right to enslave was established "not according to equity, but to avoid greater evil."[73]

The case of coerced peace treaties is analogous. Internal justice requires that all contracts be a genuine expression of will. If a promise is forced by the promisee through unjust threats, it cannot become a source of obligation.[74] This is reflected in civil law with a duress exemption that frees the unjustly coerced party from contractual obligation. However, if such exemption were recognized in the law of peace treaties, then the stronger party would continue fighting up

[68] III.vii.6, 694. A similar argument can in fact be found in the Spanish scholastics (Brett 2011, 93–4).
[69] III.vii.5, 692.
[70] II.xxiv.6, 573–4. Rousseau famously denied that life could be ranked above liberty; on the contrary, freedom is to be cherished above life (SC I.iv).
[71] III.vii.7.
[72] III.xiv.7.
[73] III.vii.6, 694.
[74] II.xi.7.

to the complete subjugation of its enemy. Since he knows that any agreement to bring war to an end would be voided *ex post* by the undeniable existence of the threat to continue war, he would have no reason or incentive to negotiate peace. "Unless this rule had been adopted," writes Grotius, "no limit nor termination could have been fixed for these wars which are extremely frequent. Yet it is to the interest of mankind that such bounds be set."[75] The structure of external rights derived from peace treaties is again peculiar. Even though they have full legal force, from the perspective of "an upright and honourable man," contracts made under duress should not be the source of profit.[76] As a matter of internal justice, the stronger party should forgo any excessive advantages obtained, but he cannot be commanded to surrender them in court.

Finally, Grotius's defence of *uti possidetis* goes deeper into the practical limitations of law enforcement among sovereign states. It is a matter of internal justice that property relations be governed by principles of corrective justice. In the case of war, only the just side should have a right to take enemy property, and only as much as necessary to right the wrong for which the war is fought. Innocent property taken as remedy should be compensated by the unjust state.[77] However, if this principle were part of the law of nations, all property rights and transactions would be conditional on establishing the justice of the war. But since no centralized court exists with jurisdiction to adjudicate the case, the parties to these transactions would have to do it themselves, which means they would have to take sides in the war. There are for Grotius strong prudential and epistemic reasons against so burdening transacting agents or their states, as we will see presently. The upshot of his argument is that, even though *uti possidetis* is fundamentally contrary to corrective justice, it must be accepted because "to controvert this principle would in truth be to make wars spring up from wars," that is, it would force countless third parties to take sides in disputes that escalated to war.[78] Instead of corrective justice, Grotius

[75] III.xix.11, 799. The law of nations does recognize a small set of "unjust fears" that could invalidate peace treaties, which include "a promise extorted from a captured ambassador," threat of rape, and "terrorizing of any other sort that involves violation of pledged faith" (III.xix.12, 799). These are all violations of the external law of nations.

[76] III.x.5, 720.

[77] III.xx.7–8.

[78] III.ix.4, 704. It is remarkable that Grotius would validate this suspension of corrective justice, given how central corrective justice is in his general justification of state authority, and how disinclined he was to allow expropriation of private goods by state authorities (on which see Straumann 2015, 196, 200–1). Hathaway and Shapiro suggestively read Grotius here as arguing that making all property transactions conditional on a determination of *ius ad bellum* would undermine the emerging global trade system, which the Dutch were leading at the time and Grotius was keen to defend (Hathaway and Shapiro 2017, 14–27). However, in these passages Grotius appears more troubled by the spread of conflict than the paralysis of markets. The contrast with Vattel, who did argue explicitly in terms of

introduced a nullification principle, in virtue of which nations are assumed to "have decided that the property of enemies should stand to enemies in the same relation as ownerless property (*res nullius*)," and as such be free for taking by belligerents while the state of war lasts.[79]

This imperative to avoid the spread of conflict is underwritten by a more general argument that also served to justify the right of states to declare themselves neutral vis-à-vis foreign wars. The argument was made concisely in an often-quoted passage of *De iure belli ac pacis*:

> To undertake to decide the justice of a war between two peoples had been dangerous for other peoples, who were on this account involved in a foreign war . . . Furthermore, even in a just war, from external indications it can hardly be adequately known what is the just limit of self-defence, of recovering what is one's own, or of inflicting punishments; in consequence, it has seemed altogether preferable to leave decisions in regard to such matters to the scruples of the belligerents rather than to have recourse to the judgment of others.[80]

The undertaking to which Grotius refers—"the just limit of self-defence, of recovering what is one's own, or of inflicting punishments"—is of course at the heart of the doctrine of *ius ad bellum* in just wars. Accurately establishing the *ad bellum* justice of war should be expected to be difficult, Grotius tells us here. Not only may "external indications" be insufficient, but also the law of nature, which directly governs just wars, can sometimes be as intricate as advanced mathematics. And just as the decisions of rulers are typically contested and subject to disagreement internally, similar if not more acute contestation may be expected in foreign affairs.[81] Adjudication being so demanding epistemically, it would be excessive to require third parties to adjudicate foreign wars.

protection of global trade, is illuminating (see below, section 4.3.) Grotius did consider the impact of solemn war permissions on property regimes and therefore global trade, for which he formulated some rudimentary rules for the protection of neutrals in trade (III.i.5). For more nuanced discussion of the complex ways in which Grotius's thought supported the emergence of global trade, see Koskenniemi 2013b and 2019.

79 III.vi.8, 670.

80 III.iv.4, 644, and see also III.ix.4, III.x.5.

81 I.iii.9. Like mathematics, Grotius wrote, the law of nature contains basic principles that should be evident to any intelligent being, but also complex theorems that only few are equipped to grasp (II.xx.63). Unlike in mathematics, however, "certainty is not to be found in moral questions" (II.xxiii.1, 557). It is not the case, then, as Hedley Bull argued in his classic account of the Grotian tradition, that "the distinction between just and unjust causes of war is one which Grotius takes to be apparent to all men, by virtue of their endowment with reason" (Bull 1990, 87). While a good deal of Grotius's discussion of just wars does assume some measure of epistemic accessibility (but cf. II.xxiii.1–13), the intricate and uncertain nature of applied *ius ad bellum* is a central premise of his theory of solemn war.

Not only is the task of adjudication epistemically overburdening, it also puts third parties in danger and can cause wars to spread. Even if third-party states could easily determine who is just and who unjust in a war, they have a right to declare their agnosticism when it is in their interest to be "on neither side in war".[82] Since one of the main reasons for establishing sovereign rule is to protect the rights of subjects, states cannot be required by law to risk crossing powerful aggressors for the sake of universal justice. In such cases, writes Grotius, "it was not safe for those who desired to preserve peace to intervene," and therefore they were "unable to do better than to accept the outcome [of an unjust war] as right."[83]

Now, turning to Grotius's third line of argument in defense of solemn wars, it is important to note that all the arguments and legal rights above were meant to apply exclusively to sovereign powers. Private actors do not have the right to enslave captives indiscriminately during a just war.[84] Only peace treaties among sovereigns exclude the duress exemption. Promises made to "pirates" and "brigands" "under the compulsion of an unjust fear," in particular threats to life, are null and void; in international practice, violations of faith pledged to pirates and brigands were routinely dismissed.[85] And since private wars are governed directly by natural law not *ius gentium*, the legal effects of solemn war do not apply to them.[86]

So why are the external laws governing solemn wars applicable only to sovereign states? Why would the general arguments presented in this section not be applicable to private individuals? What difference does sovereignty make? Before discussing Grotius's answer, it is important to observe that *De iure belli ac pacis* does not support Grotius's famous thesis in *De iure praedae*, according to which all existing public rights must ultimately come from and be transferred by individuals. Any close analogy that *De iure praedae* may have posited between individuals in the state of nature and states in international society breaks down in *De iure belli ac pacis* with the doctrine of solemn war.

[82] III.xvii.1–3, 783, see also III.i.5, III.iv.8, III.x.5. Grotius qualified this neutrality by exhorting neutrals to do nothing that would advance the just cause, but this exhortation should not be read as implying an external obligation. As far as the external law of nations goes, states are free to act as they see fit toward foreign wars.

[83] III.ix.4, 704. To be clear, Grotius is not saying that states should always be agnostic about the justice of war. On the contrary, *De iure belli ac pacis* famously praises humanitarian intervention to protect vulnerable states from aggression (II.xxv.1–8). His point is that each state should have the right to decide autonomously on foreign wars, particularly in the case of humanitarian intervention, and indeed should decide whether or not to make a judgment at all.

[84] III.xiv.1–3.

[85] III.xix.4–5, 795, II.xvii.19.

[86] III.vi.27.

Sovereign states have special privileges that individuals do not have in the state of nature.[87]

There are two related strands of argument in *De iure belli ac pacis* to justify the restriction of such privileges to sovereigns. One emphasizes the jural nature of the state—its inherent orientation toward justice—and the other the practical necessity of keeping the power of the sword exclusively in the hands of public magistrates.

Grotius's discussion of solemn war in book III of *De iure belli ac pacis* begins with a contrast between sovereign states and groups of pirates and brigands. The contrast is meant to show why a state should still be recognized as a state even if it commits wrongs, in particular the wrong of waging unjust war. The crucial difference, says Grotius, is that while pirates and brigands are "banded together for wrongdoing," members of the state, "even if at times they are not free from crime, nevertheless have been united for the enjoyment of rights, and they do render justice to foreigners."[88] A state remains a state for as long as it has tribunals and other agencies necessary to competently administer justice to both citizens and foreigners. When violence and wrongdoing become too extensive in a state, then it first "becomes full of faults, and finally ceases to be"—it becomes in effect a band of brigands.[89]

This orientation of states toward justice is reflected not only internally, in the exercise of jurisdiction by public magistrates and in the practices associated with civil law and corrective justice, but also externally in how states treat each other during and after war. International peace treaties take place within a "special community of legal obligation," Grotius wrote, in virtue of which states may expect their counterparts to keep promises made, an expectation that cannot be countenanced towards pirates or brigands.[90] Unlike pirates and brigands, states have by constitution a disposition to "render justice to each other," in particular during solemn war, as they may be expected to compel their subjects to keep the law of nations.[91] Private agents are not equally placed to deliver justice. As Grotius wrote in *De iure praedae*, courts are instituted

[87] In *De iure praedae* Grotius wrote that, "just as every right of the magistrate comes to him from the state, so has the same right come to the state from private individuals" (LPB 137). Contrast in this respect Tuck's reading of Grotius, according to which "the analogy between states and natural individuals" plays a crucial role in both works and tends to equalize morally states and individuals in the state of nature (Tuck 1999, 85, 95, 108).

[88] III.iii.2, 631.

[89] III.iii.2, 632.

[90] III.xix.2, 794.

[91] III.xxiii.10, 854. A similar argument emphasizing the trustworthiness of states, and on this basis their standing as legitimate enemies, can be found in Gentili (Schröder 2010).

precisely in order to avoid the pitfalls of private adjudication, in particular the excessive "love of self or hatred of another" that can lead to miscarriages of justice. Private wars are admissible only insofar as state courts are unavailable, but "as soon as judicial means can be employed," they must be. Likewise, in *De iure belli ac pacis* there is no legal mandate to recognize the effects of private war; their justice is open to adjudication in municipal courts.[92] States, in sum, are special in being communities oriented toward the provision of justice, and as such deserve special legal treatment.

The second strand of argument has to do with the monopoly of legitimate coercion and is closely connected to the broad functions that Grotius envisioned for the state. In the Prolegomena to *De iure belli ac pacis* he argued that when individuals associate in a state they are driven not only by natural inclination, as the Aristotelians had claimed, but also by an interest in securing their own.[93] The purpose of associating is that each individual obtain protection for his rights "through community of resource and effort."[94] "The state (*civitas*) is a complete association of free men, joined together for the enjoyment of rights and for their common interest."[95] Associations need to be able to use force to protect rights, just as individuals may need force to protect their own in the state of nature. But once political society is instituted, public magistrates come to have the privilege to use force, and private individuals must give up their natural rights to punish and exact reparations.[96]

It is of central importance for Grotius that once political society is instituted, only public magistrates, as authorized by the constitution, have enforcement powers. Allowing otherwise would fatally undermine "public tranquillity," lead to countless and potentially violent disputes, and ultimately turn the state into a "non-social horde."[97] From this general statement, Grotius famously drew the conclusion that laws and decisions lawfully rendered by the sovereign which are contrary to natural law are nonetheless binding, to be endured by subjects rather than resisted by force. As he wrote, "subjects cannot legally hinder by force the execution of a judgment even if it is unjust, or assert their rights by force against it."[98] This rule has all the more force when it comes to the decision to wage war, in which the subsistence of the state as a whole may be at stake, and which must consequently belong exclusively to the holder of

92 LPB 130–3, and similarly RWP I.iii.1.
93 Prolegomena §§16–17.
94 I.ii.1, 53.
95 I.i.14, 44.
96 I.iii.4.
97 I.iv.2, 139.
98 III.ii.5, 627, also I.iv.1.

supreme power.[99] If lesser public officials or private subjects could object to their superior's command and decide autonomously on matters of war, the state would fall apart.[100]

Already within the state, then, the administration of coercion can diverge from natural law. The reason why this divergence is admissible in municipal law can also account for the divergence found in the external law of nations. If the centralization of jurisdiction and the decision to wage war means domestically that subjects have an obligation to follow the sovereign's command, internationally it entails recognizing the legal effects of solemn war, which result ultimately from sovereign decisions. Opposition to external rights on grounds of internal justice (injustice of cause, lack of proportionality or necessity, etc.) constitutes a challenge to sovereign judgment. If permitted, it would throw into disarray a world order made of associated sovereign states, which Grotius was keen to defend. In this sense, the theory of solemn war spells out the implications of the monopoly of coercion in sovereign states for the legal regulation of war.[101]

2.4 *Temperamenta belli*

So which normative conception of war did Grotius ultimately favor? Was he a just war theorist at heart, or rather a defender of the neo-Roman doctrine of solemn war? There is a common interpretation according to which Grotius relegated internal justice and other moral virtues to the merely hortatory, which is morally praiseworthy but not enforceable and consequently not

[99] I.iii.4.

[100] I.iii.5, I.iii.8–9. A caveat is in order, however. As Straumann points out, Grotius did not rule out the possibility of constitutional arrangements that reserved in the people the right to punish rulers for constitutional breaches (Straumann 2015, 202–206). Grotius held a radically pluralist view of the constitutional arrangements of internal sovereignty, which could in principle include review powers of executive action directly in the people (Tuck 2015, 68–86). There are, however, powers of sovereignty that, in virtue of the defining functions of the state, could not be divided, in particular the power to wage war (Brett 2019, 17–18; Loughlin 2010, 73–76). Allowing the people to judge matters of state in parallel to their ruler, Grotius wrote, would "introduce such complete disorder" in the state that nobody had ever tried it. Internal division in matters of war breeds civil wars, which are worse than tyranny (I.iii.9, 111, I.iv.19).

[101] Revealing in this regard, the prohibition in the law of nations of poisonous weapons and "treasonous" assassins, which are permissible in natural law, was meant to protect the bearers of sovereignty in the state (III.iv.15, III.iv.18). As Grotius wrote, "agreement upon this matter arose from a consideration of the common advantage, in order that the dangers of war, which had begun to be frequent, might not be too widely extended. And it is easy to believe that this agreement originated with kings, whose lives are better defended by arms than those of other men, but are less safe from poison, unless they are protected by some respect for law and by fear of disgrace" (III.iv.25, 652). Protecting the life and immunity of heads of state is essential for the stability of the system.

properly speaking law.[102] He is really a solemn war theorist at heart, removing as he did all legal force from just war theory and confining it to the inner conscience of decision-makers. Alternatively, a more plausible reading would suggest that Grotius was neither a just war nor a solemn war theorist. For while he considered what various bodies of law and types of justice would permit or forbid in war, he never answered conclusively and univocally what *the* law is in concrete situations.[103] He was not fully committed to either the just war or the solemn war frameworks; neither internal nor external justice has priority, despite both generating inconsistent rights and obligations. For the same reason, Grotius can also be read as *both* just war theorist and solemn war theorist, since he was able to advocate forcefully for both legal regimes and to stress in the process their contrasting strengths and weaknesses.

The inconclusiveness of Grotius's legal pronouncements has been considered a failure of legal technique, but it may be seen rather as the reflection of a particular and now largely lost conception of legal science.[104] His task, as Grotius understood it, was not to produce a single and conclusive pronouncement of law, but rather to lay down the rich and complex legal landscape that governs voluntary actions in war, which must include heterogeneous sources. As we have seen, the rules of solemn war govern armed conflict among sovereign states, while the rules of just war govern the use of force both before the internal court of conscience and by individuals and private corporations outside the jurisdiction of constituted public powers. Only in the latter case are belligerents required and allowed to apply natural law directly.

Once we recognize the richness of this science of law, we can bring to the fore the significance of a recurring theme in *De iure belli ac pacis*, namely, Grotius's insistence that the place of the external *ius gentium* within his larger legal universe is marginal and morally degraded. In contrast to contemporary invocations of International Humanitarian Law, which often aim to legitimize military campaigns, for Grotius to say that a given action is permissible *ex iure gentium* amounted to very little as far as justification or legitimization go. For him the external law of nations barely constitutes a legal order,

[102] For a review of sources giving this interpretation, see Jouannet 1998, 176–83; Haggenmacher 1983, 574; Grewe 2000, 191–3.

[103] This is Hersh Lauterpacht's reading of Grotius. As he accurately wrote, "on the whole the various distinctions [between expletive and distributive justice, internal and external rights] are unhelpful for the purpose of assisting the student or the statesman in discovering what is the legal rule on the subject. There is no hierarchy of legal norms to assist the seeker after the correct rule of law. There is often little to guide us as to whether in case of conflict the law of nature (in its various and often contradictory meanings) is to prevail over the law of nations or conversely" (Lauterpacht 1946, 11).

[104] For valuable commentary on the breadth of Grotius's legal universe and his particular conception of legal science, see Haggenmacher 1983, 571–88; Brett 2019, 5–14; Koskenniemi 2019, 38–41.

narrowly directed as it is to the regulation of the always regrettable material consequences of war, and oriented as it is by the minimalist imperative of containing the spread, duration, and lethality of inter-state wars.

This minimalism must be read against the background of one of the central thesis in *De iure belli ac pacis*—Grotius's answer to Carneades—which is that the precepts of corrective justice (including respect for another's property and the fulfilment of promises) are necessary for social life, in particular for international society, and that respecting these precepts will ultimately contribute to one's own self-interest. The unfortunate fact that allowing states to enforce corrective justice directly in the law of nations is likely to be counterproductive does not diminish the force of this argument. Good political rule must take into account the importance of corrective justice for social life and long-term self-interest, especially in war contexts. The precepts of internal justice must be taken seriously by political rulers, among other reasons because it is in their interest to do so, even if they are unenforceable in the law of nations.

When it comes to truly important matters of virtuous and humane action, of good conscience and Christian salvation, the external law of nations is virtually irrelevant. Those who wage solemn yet unjust wars "cannot reach the Kingdom of Heaven" unless they repent and provide just compensation for the wrongs committed.[105] At the end of his presentation of the outrageous privileges of solemn wars, when he begins introducing his famous *temperamenta belli*, Grotius shifts to a theological register and cites approvingly Seneca's claim in *On Benefits* that innocence in the eyes of the letter of the law amounts to very little morally; more important is displaying a proper sense of honor, "devotion to gods, country, and kin, kindness, generosity, justice, and good faith."[106] These categories overflow the tripartite division of law that sets the stage in the Prolegomena to *De iure belli ac pacis*, but they constitute for Grotius the complete space of law.

In particular, the "rules of love" continue to apply in all wars, and they are broader than the "rules of law." They include precepts of internal justice, including a principle of distinction which gives immunity of those who "do not share the guilt of the war."[107] The purpose of introducing the *temperamenta belli* is precisely to bring a broader spectrum of practical evaluation to bear on the conduct and conclusion of war, and in this process to relativize and put

[105] III.x.3, 719.
[106] III.x.1, 717.
[107] III.xiii.4, 759.

in their proper context the obligatory force of the laws of solemn warfare.[108] Within this spectrum there is a place for *humanitas*, but not as an element of the external law of nations but rather as a basic "instinct" or "feeling" of sympathy toward fellow human beings, which should be cultivated and practiced during war and elsewhere in life.[109] It is therefore somewhat ironic that Grotius has come to be remembered as one of the "founders" of international law, given how little moral weight he gave to the external law of nations. And yet the impact and wide reception of the concept of solemn war by later publicists and promoters of the law of nations reveals just how powerfully the concept captured the emerging realities of the post-Westphalian world.

It has often been noted that Grotius was not an innovator or path-breaker, but rather an eclectic articulator of multiple legal concepts drawn from the manifold traditions available in his time. As we will see in the following chapters, Grotius's distinctive concepts of external law of nations and solemn war did prove to be path-breaking, as they provided the foundations for Enlightenment accounts of "regular war," which in turn provided the ideological basis for the international codifications of the laws of war at the end of the nineteenth century.

[108] III.x–xvi.

[109] III.xi.7, 733, III.xii.7, III.xiv.5. On the concept of humanity in Grotius, see further Haggenmacher 1983, 601–3; Tadashi 1993b, 302–4.

3

Regular War and Resort to Force in the Enlightenment

Christian Wolff and Emer de Vattel are arguably the most important and influential Enlightenment heirs to Grotius's ideas on solemn war and the external law of nations. Unlike Thomas Hobbes and Samuel Pufendorf, the two foremost theorists in the modern natural law tradition of the seventeenth century, Wolff and Vattel followed Grotius in conceiving of the law of nations as a distinct and autonomous legal sphere, separate from the law of nature and endowed with its own distinct forms of justification and enforcement mechanisms. Also like Grotius, they simultaneously defended principles of just war drawn from natural law and a neo-Roman conception of war understood as an institution of the positive or "voluntary" law of nations.[1]

But if for Grotius the "external law of nations" and the doctrine of solemn war were to be admitted largely as lesser evils, for the Enlightenment theorists the voluntary law of nations and "regular war" were constitutive elements of state sovereignty and of a pluralist conception of international society they were keen to defend. Their views on war and the law of nations were both more affirmative and more systematically developed than Grotius's. And while for Grotius sovereign states deserved to be granted the special privileges of solemn war because of their jural orientation and the wisdom of keeping the power of the sword exclusively in supreme magistrates, Wolff and Vattel affirmed and defended ideals of civil prudence and reason of state that went beyond Grotius. In a sense, for Wolff and Vattel the law of nations exists and operates as an enabler for the virtuous and necessary practices of reason of state, which have great value and can override a great deal of competing normative political considerations. Far from opposites, the law of nations and reason of state were for Wolff and Vattel mutually constitutive and reinforcing, as the following will show.

[1] Valuable general discussions of the political and legal thought of Wolff and Vattel include Jouannet 1998; Hurrell 1996; Pitts 2018; Whelan 1988; Haggenmacher 2011. An earlier and shorter version of this chapter was published as Kalmanovitz 2018.

The Laws of War in International Thought. Pablo Kalmanovitz, Oxford University Press (2020). © Pablo Kalmanovitz.
DOI: 10.1093/oso/9780198790259.001.0001.

Furthermore, while Wolff and Vattel did not share Hobbes and Pufendorf's skepticism about the existence and practical viability of a positive law of nations, they did take seriously the dangers created by state sovereignty and the "evil of separate sovereigns" in international society.[2] With Hobbes, they perceived sovereignty as both valuable and threatening, a source of both protection to subjects and threat to other states. Even though their project of regulating inter-state war in the law of nations was largely built on Grotius's ideas on solemn war, their attention to the peculiar conditions of insecurity in international society, and to the potential depth of discord among a plurality of sovereigns pursuing each its own reason of state, is informed by a conception of sovereignty they got not from Grotius but from Hobbes and Pufendorf.

This chapter examines how Wolff and Vattel sought to regulate resort to war by states in the law of nations, that is, how they articulated a doctrine of *ius ad bellum* in the theory of regular war. Against an influential interpretation, the chapter shows that they gave legal weight to both the status of sovereignty and the justice of the cause. Their views on just cause, however, were fundamentally different from those in scholastic just war. They understood the justice of the cause not in analogy to a legal trial but rather in the context of a specific international practice, which consisted in the publication by states of "war manifestoes" that contained their reasons for waging war. These reasons had to be framed in the language of the law of nations and show publicly that sovereigns took seriously the legal rights of other nations and the validity of the law of nations in general. So if for Grotius war declarations in solemn wars were essentially formal speech acts of sovereigns, for Wolff and Vattel they embodied a legal obligation to publicly justify war. In this practice of public justification, the law of nations became a vernacular of public diplomacy, which in Enlightenment fashion Wolff and Vattel thought could be an instrument of moderation and progress.[3]

Contemporary commentaries on the theory of regular war have been widely divergent. According to the influential reading of Carl Schmitt and Reinhardt Koselleck, Wolff and Vattel transformed earlier accounts of *ius ad bellum* by altogether excluding considerations of *iusta causa* from the law of nations, and

[2] To use F.H. Hinsley's expression (Hinsley 1963, 44). On Hobbes's contrasting theory of the law of nations, and on his (and Pufendorf's) influence on Vattel's concept of self-interest, see Christov 2015, 115–22, 241–5.

[3] Within the manifold "movements of Enlightenment" (Pocock 2001, 5–10), Wolff and Vattel had a distinctive faith in the civilizing force of public law and diplomacy. This faith contrasts with the denunciations of many French *philosophes*, who saw diplomacy and international law as a rather hopelessly vain and corrupt enterprise. For an overview of the latter position, see Ruddy 1968, and for the former Bélissa 2004.

putting virtually all emphasis on the formal status of sovereignty.[4] Only sovereign states can wage regular war, and their reasons for doing so are beyond juridical determination. This move they celebrated for its moderating and pacifying effects. By defending on general grounds a non-discriminatory concept of war, Wolff and Vattel would have helped bring into juridical doctrine the costly lessons of religious warfare in Europe. The Vattelian law of nations substituted prudence and reason of state for the righteousness and zealotry of religious war. War became more limited and civilized as a result, and Europe more stable and pacified under the *ius publicum europaeum*.

Following the same hermeneutical line, others have reached the opposite normative conclusion. Wolff and Vattel's disproportionate emphasis on formal status would have foreclosed the possibility of much needed legal critique of sovereign decisions. They in effect freed political sovereigns to undertake war at will, to appropriate as much territory as they could control, and in this way destroyed the very notion of territorial rights and international legality.[5] Wolff and Vattel's deference to sovereign will and reason of state dissolved the normative force of natural law and the law of nations. Vattel in particular belongs to a republican tradition in which liberty and war are tied together, the model of which is a post-Renaissance state engaged in unrestrained "international adventurism and exploitation."[6]

Yet others have opposed this interpretive line and present Wolff and Vattel as continuators of the just war tradition. Their frequent references to just cause and just war have to be taken seriously, for they themselves took seriously the challenge of making justice compatible with state liberty.[7] Vattel's elusive concept of "enemy of mankind" should be read as equivalent to the aggressor in just wars, and as such is proof that the *ius ad bellum* of regular wars can be seen as a continuation of scholastic just war doctrine. Supporting this reading are also late eighteenth century appropriations of Vattel, in which righteous callings for total war were made against enemies of mankind precisely in the ways that Schmitt associated with just wars.[8]

Given these polar readings, it is no wonder that some other commentators have found Wolff and Vattel to be simply inconsistent or incoherent, at best relativists for whom ultimately no definitive truth-value could be assigned to

[4] Schmitt 2003, 152–71; Koselleck 1988, 41–50.
[5] Vollenhoven 1919, 26–32; Brierly and Clapham 2012, 35–40; Hochstrasser 2000, 181–2.
[6] Tuck 1999, 195–6; see also Midgley 1975, 175–92; Holmes 1992, 201–8; Anghie 2011.
[7] Zurbuchen 2009; Johnson 1975, 240–55.
[8] Silvestrini 2010; Edelstein 2008.

claims of justice.[9] By contrast, this chapter and the next will present a fairly consistent and indeed powerful theory of regular war in Wolff and Vattel. I will show that they did not altogether exclude the criterion of just cause, nor did they dissolve international legality, nor is their theory a version of just war but rather a distinct account of the legality of international war.

Before proceeding, a few words on the relationship between Vattel and Wolff are in order. In the preface to *The Law of Nations* (1758), Vattel declared that his original plan was simply to make accessible Wolff's ideas, which had been written in Latin, in many volumes, and *more geometrico*. As he wrote, "these circumstances present obstacles which render it nearly useless to those very persons in whom the knowledge and taste of the true principles of the law of nations are most important and most desirable."[10] Vattel's success in this task seems to have surpassed even his own wildest expectations. *The Law of Nations* is *the* textbook of eighteenth-century international law, its influence extending well into the nineteenth century.[11] Part of its success may have to do with Vattel's good style and accessible French, which by mid-eighteenth century had become established as the language of diplomacy. It seems fair to say that without Vattel's reformulation of Wolff in French, Wolff's ideas would have remained obscure and with little impact on international affairs, but without Wolff's theory of law and international order, Vattel could not have written *The Law of Nations*. While Vattel's debt to Wolff is recognizable throughout the text, there are some important differences between the two, as Vattel himself noted and some commentators have emphasized. In what follows, however, I tend to focus on convergence rather than divergence, as I will be paying a great deal of attention to questions of international legal theory on which there is extensive overlap.

[9] Midgley 1975, 189–90; Jouannet 1998, 224–6, 247–8; Linklater 1982, 80–96; Hurrell 1996, 250–1; Koskenniemi 2005, 106–22.

[10] LN Preface, 12. Unless otherwise indicated, all citations of Vattel are from this book. I indicate book and paragraph numbers, and page numbers when quoting.

[11] According to Wilhelm Grewe, Vattel's was "the most widely read and disseminated book on international law in the eighteenth century," its doctrinal influence extending well into the nineteenth (Grewe 2000, 287). Much to his regret, Van Vollenhoven admits that the "second stage of the law of nations" (1770–1914) could well be named after Vattel (Vollenhoven 1919, 32). By 1863, the book had had twenty editions in French, and eighteen reprints in English in the United States; there were also six editions of *Le Droit des Gens* in Spanish between 1820 and 1836, and translations into German and Italian (Beaulac 2003, 288). In the United States, Vattel was "quoted by judicial tribunals, in speeches before legislative assemblies, and in the decrees and correspondence of executive officials. It was the manual of the student, the reference work of the statesman, and the text from which the political philosopher drew inspiration" (Fenwick 1913, 395; also Ruddy 1972).

3.1 State sovereignty in international society

Following Hobbes and Pufendorf, Wolff and Vattel conceived of nations as personified collectives or unified "moral persons" which, even though radically unequal in size, power, constitutional form, confessional type, and much else, were to be treated as independent legal equals in international society. "Just as the tallest man is no more a man than the dwarf," Wolff wrote, "so also a nation, however small, is no less a nation than the greatest nation."[12] Somewhat surprisingly, Vattel credits Hobbes for being "the first who gave a distinct though imperfect idea of the law of nations," which he did by postulating the fundamental principle according to which sovereign states exist as equals in a state of nature.[13] "As a consequence of that [natural] liberty and independence," Vattel explained, "it exclusively belongs to each nation to form her own judgment of what her conscience prescribes to her—of what she can or cannot do—of what it is proper or improper for her to do," including in particular the right of each nation-state to judge independently what her duty requires.[14] A defining feature of sovereign nations is the power to decide independently on the best conduct of their own affairs, which Vattel described as a "right of judgment." It includes the power to decide autonomously on constitutional form and internal legislation and policy, as well as on foreign policy and the use of force.[15]

This sovereign "right of judgment" is grounded on a far-reaching conception of state authority.[16] Formally, states are the product of a social contract. Civil society is the source of political obligation and comes into existence through a compact of individuals or families living in a state of nature. Once established, civil societies set the terms under which civil power is to be exercised. Political authority is transferred from civil society to rulers, who are appointed on the basis of that society's "fundamental laws" or constitution.[17]

But while formally states are created contractually, their value rests on the many functions they can perform. Political association in a state is a means to promote individual wellbeing and "perfection," along with the common good

[12] JG §16, 15, and equally if more famously Vattel in LN Preliminaries §18.

[13] Preliminaries §8.

[14] Preliminaries §16, 74.

[15] LN Preliminaries §16, 74. Similarly Wolff in JG §2; IDNG §§978, 981.

[16] Valuable discussions of Wolff's theory of the state include Haakonssen 2006, 259–60, 268–78; Jouannet 1998, 312–18; Hochstrasser 2000, 159–83; Hunter 2001, 265–8; Schneewind 1998, 431–44. On Vattel's theory, see Whelan 1988; Jouannet 1998, 322–40; Hunter 2010, 115–22.

[17] IDNG 1772 §§972–89; also Vattel LN I.1–37.

and collective self-preservation.[18] Vattel identified among the functions of the state:

> to procure for the citizens whatever they stand in need of, for the necessities, the conveniences, the accommodation of life, and, in general, whatever constitutes happiness—with the peaceful possession of property, a method of obtaining justice with security, and, finally a mutual defense against all external violence.[19]

To pursue these ends, states must in particular generate incentives for the industriousness of its population; maximize agricultural output and oversee a regime of private property; be responsible for minting and for preserving the value of national currency; build and maintain public roads; provide basic education that promotes civic virtues; and support the arts and sciences, among other tasks. The pursuit of these functions defines the universe of legitimate state action vis-à-vis its citizens.[20]

Centrally for present purposes, states must have coercive powers to protect and promote these public functions against both internal and external foes. Internally this need underwrites the public power to punish, and externally a "right to security" which authorizes states to use force when the "preservation, perfection, and happiness" of their members and civil society are threatened or undermined.[21]

The right to security does not protect any specific or well-defined set of state interest or public functions but is rather a second-order general right to use force when state rights or public functions are threatened or obstructed. It can cover a wide range of public actions and lead to conflict among self-perfecting states. For just as including happiness and perfection in the catalogue of state *teloi* could lead to extremely broad powers in sovereigns vis-à-vis their own subjects—Wolff can be read as a defender of Enlightened absolutism in Prussia—it could also lead to expansive foreign policies and consequently generate international conflicts.[22] Given the breadth and scope of the right to security, and its orientation toward the preservation and strengthening of the state,

[18] IDNG 1772, §§29, 972–89; LN I.14–16. The Leibnizian concept of "perfection" denotes here the extent to which the state has achieved the constituting goals of its underlying civil society. It is not to be confused with the Aristotelian concept of perfection as realization of the commonwealth's natural final cause.

[19] I.15, 86.

[20] LN I.72–176; IDNG 1772, §980.

[21] LN II.49, 288; JG §254.

[22] On Wolff as defender of Enlightened absolutism in Prussia, see Haakonssen 2006, 260; Hunter 2001, 267–8, and on expansive foreign policies Tuck 1999, 195–6.

commentators have rightly placed Wolff and Vattel in the tradition of reason of state. Their conception of reason of state is more legalistic and perhaps restraining than Renaissance accounts, but the scope of the right to security, and hence of admissible state action, is very broad indeed.[23]

In contrast to the line followed by Wolff and Vattel, worries about the growing power of sovereign states in eighteenth-century Europe, and the hope of uprooting the evil of separate sovereignties, motivated the famous proposals of Sully and Saint-Pierre to federalize and bring "perpetual peace" to Europe. Rousseau described with perfect clarity the perceived danger in his summary of Saint-Pierre:

> No man can have thought long upon the means of bringing any government to perfection without realizing a host of difficulties and obstacles which flow less from its inherent nature than from its relation to its neighbors. The result of this is that the care which ought to be given to its internal welfare has to be largely spent upon its outward security; and we are compelled to think more of providing for its defense against others than of making it as good as may be in itself . . . [E]ach one of us being in the civil state as regards our fellow citizens, but in the state of nature as regards the rest of the world, we have taken all kinds of precautions against private wars only to kindle national wars a thousand times more terrible.[24]

Saint-Pierre's proposed remedy, which Rousseau of course found hopeless, was to create international institutions to which states would defer in matters of armed force. Just as states are needed to protect and coordinate individual perfection, so supra-national institutions are needed for states to attain their perfection. Relative to states, international institutions would fulfill some of the functions that states fulfilled vis-à-vis individuals.

Vattel rejected this approach, again following Hobbes: "it is easy to perceive that the civic association is very far from being equally necessary between nations, as it was between individuals." Once a large number of people associate under a common ruler, they can "supply most of their wants" together, and when it comes to regulating their interaction with other political associations, a relatively thin legal system could suffice.[25]

[23] Armitage 2012, 154–71; Devetak 2011. For the broader historical background of invocations of reason of state in this context, see Foucault 1981, 240–54; Malcolm 2007, 92–123.

[24] Rousseau 1991 [1761], 54.

[25] LN Preface, 15; II.3.

In so arguing, Vattel joined the bulk of eighteenth-century European intelligentsia in finding proposals such as Saint-Pierre's hopelessly "chimerical," requiring as it did a substantial number of precisely those sovereigns whose evils were denounced to become enlisted in the project.[26] In some cases, implementation could conceivably proceed by sheer force, if sufficient force could be brought to the task, but then it would be "impossible to carry into execution without injustice and violence."[27] Not only were international institutions not as necessary for states as states were for individuals, but they could be co-opted by powerful states for their own agendas and forced upon smaller states. The hegemonic threats of Prussia, in particular against Vattel's own Neuchatel, and the history of Spanish and French monarchical encroachments on the affairs of small states, indicated that the threat of "universal monarchy" could not be effectively contained with perpetual peace proposals.[28]

Vattel and Rousseau coincided in this respect, but Rousseau did not endorse the alternative offered by Vattel, that is, an international society ordered on the basis of the balance of power, whereby defensive and trade alliances, and in the limit armed force, were mobilized "to oppose the more powerful potentate, and to prevent him from giving law to his neighbors."[29] The balance mechanism could help to avoid the political encroachment, oppression, and subjugation—in the extreme, "servitude and enslavement"—that would result from the "injustice, rapacity, pride, ambition, or an imperious thirst of rule (*un désir impérieux de faire la loi*)" of raising hegemons.[30] Falling prey to a ruthless conqueror, or being at the discretion of a foreign ruler with no stake or interest in one's good or the public good of one's community, is a clear moral and political bad. To avoid it, nations, particularly small ones, must have the legal power to judge and decide where to seek security and protection.[31]

[26] The term "chimerical" is used by Vattel in Vattel 1765, 73. On the reception of the proposals, see Belissa 1998, 42–7; Hinsley 1963, 45. Wolff did not reject them explicitly, but his society of states—or "supreme state" (*civitas maxima*)—is incompatible with perpetual peace projects, as it lacks by definition centralized adjudicative or coercive powers (JG §§9–22). Wolff made clear that the concept of *civitas maxima* was a juridical fiction, not meant to refer to a global state nor as a basis for the creation of international organizations (JG §21) (for discussion see Onuf 1994). Contrast Leibniz's qualified endorsement of Saint-Pierre's project in Leibniz and Riley 1988, 176–84.

[27] As Vattel said of Sully's project (III.48, 497).

[28] LN III.44. Rousseau perceptively noted that perpetual peace projects could easily become hegemonic instruments in his "Judgement of Saint-Pierre's Project" (Rousseau 1991 [1761], 98–9). On the threat of universal monarchy, see further Whatmore 2010, 115–22; Christov 2013, 181–4; Malettke 1998; and cf. Hinsley 1963, 35–6.

[29] III.48, 497. See Wolff JG §§642–52 for a somewhat contrasting position.

[30] LN III.44, 492.

[31] LN III.49–50. By the mid-eighteenth century, the threat of universal monarchy was no longer imminent, and attention turned to the routine management of the balance of power (Malettke 1998, 57; Hinsley 1963, 177). Reflecting this state of affairs, Montesquieu argued in *Réflexions sur la Monarchie Universelle en Europe* that, after Louis XIV's failed attempt, it was clear that no single power could attain

Power balancing and the national rights of security and judgment give Vattelian international society its distinctive character. While any form of political obligation—national or international—must be oriented toward individual wellbeing and "perfection," there is a division of labor in international society. States are in charge of *directly* promoting individual wellbeing and perfection, while the law of nations protects the integrity and independence of states.[32] If the legally constituted society of states runs as it should, each state will be allowed to advance its self-regarding duties, notably through international commerce and alliances, and this will ultimately increase the prosperity and wellbeing of all states and their members. Moral progress is thus attained at two levels of political and legal action. Progress occurs directly within states, but the law of nations promotes it indirectly by creating the conditions under which sovereign states can thrive, and even help each other thrive. There is little room in this account of the law of nations for the direct international promotion of individual wellbeing, in particular no international protection of individual rights.[33]

As a reflection of this two-tier construction, states have two types of obligation. First, they must protect the safety and promote the wellbeing of their own members. To do so, they have a right to decide what safety and perfection require, and other states must abstain from judging on the adequacy of their policy choices. But, secondly, states have duties vis-à-vis other states, which can limit their self-regarding pursuit of security and perfection. As Vattel wrote, "in virtue of the natural liberty of nations, each one has a right to make her own judgment the sole guide of her conduct with respect to her duties *in every thing that is not determined by the perfect rights of another*."[34] "Perfect sovereign rights," in particular the right to security, thus mark the limits of national liberty. The distinctive aim of the doctrine of *ius ad bellum* in regular war is precisely to regulate the pursuit of perfect rights by a plurality of agents in

supremacy in Europe (Montesquieu and Porret 2000 [1734]). Rousseau similarly argued that the distribution of power in Europe was such that all states would remain in constant but simmering conflict, no single one able to conquer the rest and pacify Europe (Rousseau 1991 [1761]).

[32] This is stated explicitly by Wolff and Vattel, see respectively JG §§8–9 and IDNG §§972, 980; LN Preliminaries §§6, 12, I.1, II.218.

[33] Wolff and Vattel argued that sovereigns have the right to refuse to fulfill other-regarding duties, in particular the provision of "offices of humanity" to peoples in need. While it may be wrong to fail to discharge these duties when feasible, they are not enforceable (JG §166–70; LN II.8–9). The primacy of national self-regarding duties leads Linklater to describe (not inaccurately) and criticize Vattel's views as a form of "state libertarianism," inherently incapable of institutionalizing human rights and cosmopolitan values (Linklater 1982, 80–96). On the Leibnizian metaphysical roots of Wolff and Vattel's national egoism, see Jouannet 1998, 213–16; and cf. Hochstrasser 2000, 161–3; Christov 2015, 241–5..

[34] II.335, 456, emphasis added. Likewise Wolff in JG §888.

international society. As we will see in the next section, only violations of perfect rights could be invoked to justify publicly resort to force.

3.2 Voluntary law of nations and belligerent equality

Arguably Christian Wolff's most important contribution to the Grotian tradition of solemn war is the concept of "voluntary law of nations," which results from a fundamental theoretical re-articulation of Grotius's concept of external law of nations. Like Grotius, Wolff distinguished between the internal or "necessary" law of nations—natural law applied to international affairs—and the external or "voluntary" law of nations by stipulating that, while both have normative force, only the latter could be invoked to justify the use of force.[35] Also like Grotius, Wolff's motivation for drawing this distinction was to adjust the norms and principles of natural law to the realities of power in international society, in particular to the growing assertiveness of powerful monarchies and the absence of centralized adjudication and law enforcement. Unlike Grotius, however, Wolff understood the voluntary law of nations to be about much more than the suspension of natural law justified by the moral imperative to pursue the lesser evil.

Contrary to what the term might suggest, the voluntary law of nations is not based on the consent of states but rather on the presumption that states agree to belong in a society of *de iure* equal and independent states. While paying formal tribute to the legitimating role of consent, Wolff and Vattel in fact established the principles of the voluntary law a priori. These principles constitute the normative core without which a legally regulated society of equal and independent sovereign states could not exist.[36] States are not free to withhold their consent to this society, because doing so would amount to not recognizing the reality of themselves and other states, which would be absurd.[37] The voluntary law is therefore again in a sense a hybrid of positive and natural law. It is positive in deriving the validity of its norms from consent, albeit only hypothetical, and it has moral value in embodying the conditions of existence of a plurality

[35] JG Preface, 6–7, §§4, 20, 22, 26. See similarly Vattel LN Preface, 7–8, Preliminaries §§7–9.

[36] JG Preface, 6–7; LN Preface, 16. On the voluntary law of nations as a set transcendental conditions of existence of international society, see Perreau-Saussine 2011. For further commentary on the voluntary law, to which my discussion is indebted, see Jouannet 1998, 221–30; Remec 1960, 141–64; Koskenniemi 2005, 106–24; Hurrell 1996.

[37] JG §12; LN III.192.

of legally equal sovereigns, in coordinating their excercise of sovereignty, and in contributing to moderate the evil of separate sovereignties.

As Wolff and Vattel were keen to emphasize, however, the fact that the voluntary law has moral value does not mean that it can be equated with natural law. The voluntary law contains a number of concessions to the political realities of international society, which force its displacement away from both interpersonal and international natural law. And yet, somewhat paradoxically, the voluntary law has to be distinguished from natural law, and in some instances override it, *in virtue of natural law itself*. This interpretive conundrum lies at the heart of the theory of regular war, and its solution reveals the sense in which it can be read both as a moral theory and the source of a positive legal doctrine.

In some passages, Wolff and Vattel did justify the voluntary law as a lesser evil, very much in the spirit of Grotius.[38] If war were understood in strict line with natural law, that is, as a form of adjudication and vindication for injuries received, more violations of right would occur than if war is waged under the apparently more permissive rules of the voluntary law of nations. This is because understanding war as a form of law enforcement would incline belligerents to treat their enemies as delinquents, who by doing wrong have forgone virtually all rights and immunities. But since both sides will predictably claim justice for their own cause, the likely result will be both sides treating each other as criminals. Violence will escalate out of all bounds and more rights will be violated as a result than if belligerents recognized each other as legitimate and equals before the laws of war.[39] In order to avoid the escalation of violence, states are required to treat each other as belligerent equals—as enemies not "private foes"—even if they are wrong about justice.[40] This, Wolff readily admits, is a big concession to make for the sake of avoiding limitless violence. One side's mere opinion about justice may legally equalize the parties at war, but surely a belligerent's bad faith or poorly considered opinion that war is justified counts for nothing as far as justice is concerned.[41]

In addition to this consequentialist argument, Wolff and Vattel provided a less familiar but theoretically deeper defense of the legal equality of belligerent states. This defense is rooted not on a contingent estimation of consequences, but rather on the value of sovereign judgment and the division of moral labor in international society. One way to see how deference to sovereign judgment can provide the basis for belligerent equality is by unpacking the assumption

[38] E.g. JG Preface, 6, §892; LN III.192.

[39] JG §888–892; LN III.188, III.192.

[40] The quote comes from Wolff, JG §722, 373; similarly Vattel in LN III.69.

[41] JG §§823, 891.

that both sides at war will claim justice for their own cause. Three layers of argument can be distinguished in Wolff and Vattel, each revealing one important dimension of the voluntary of law of nations.

First, justice in war could be claimed in good or bad faith. The following from Wolff emphasizes the latter:

> If good faith were as sacred to nations as it ought to be, and if it were not for the fact that they prefer to be ruled by their impulses rather than by their reason, or if their honor, which they ought to cherish, restrained them from being compelled only unwillingly to agree to that to which they did not wish to agree, their controversies could be settled as the law of nature prescribes, nor would there be need of settling them by force of arms. And then there would be no voluntary law of nations, for which only the perverse customs of nations makes a place, and which a nation is bound to use even against its will and its more enlightened judgment.[42]

The voluntary law of nations appears here as an adjustment of natural law to the impulsiveness and immorality of rulers, and to the perverse practices and customs of international politics. The voluntary law embodies the best "caring for the happiness of nations as far as is possible in their weakness, or obstinacy and wickedness, that are to be endured like tares incapable of being uprooted."[43] While natural law contains precepts for living well, the voluntary law of nations applies a realist filter to base motives and moral failure, and seeks to moderate the bad effects of moral weakness, mischief, and impulsiveness. In particular, equalizing belligerents before the law of nations forecloses the possibility of one side co-opting in bad faith the principles of just war when accusing its enemy of aggression. Claiming the high moral ground can be made into a problematic weapon of war, which equalization before the voluntary law of nations can help to mitigate.

Conflicting claims of justice can also be genuine and made in good faith. Genuine disagreements about *ius ad bellum* can be subjective or objective. Subjective disagreements are caused by the fallible cognitive abilities of the parties in conflict. For all his rationalism, Wolff took seriously the epistemic limitations of human judgment, and strongly cautioned against expecting too much from reason in politics. A philosopher should know that the "theory of affairs" is uncertain and far from perfect, and that "it is not always in our

[42] JG §574, 294; also §632.
[43] JG §887, 454; similarly Vattel in LN III.189.

power, however diligent we may be, to know each and every circumstance that concerns the case at hand." While an exact science of probability could provide some help, this is limited because "many impediments present themselves which cannot be foreseen and which often come to our knowledge only after the business is over, sometimes escaping all notice."[44]

One remedy for such cognitive limitations is to accept as legally valid only transparent action-guiding rules, even if it is at the cost of diverging from the more accurate but cognitively demanding standards of natural law. As Vattel wrote, "as to the external effects of the law among men, we must necessarily have recourse to rules that shall be more certain and easy in the application, and this for the very safety and advantage of the great society of mankind."[45] The voluntary law of nations appears here as a pragmatic, rough and ready adaptation of natural law to the epistemic rather than moral shortcomings of sovereign decision-makers and their designated agents.

Objective disagreements, on the other hand, could result not from the insufficient cognitive capacities of decision-makers but from real uncertainty about facts, laws, and risks. While subjective uncertainty and moral vice may be to some extent manageable, objective uncertainty cuts deep into the fabric of natural law and points to an altogether different function of the voluntary law. Here the voluntary law is not an adjustment of natural law to the moral and epistemic shortcomings of decision-makers, but rather a reflection of the inherent limits of pursuing the right to security in the post-Utrecht European world.

Wolff and Vattel recognized that there could be "doubtful disputes" in which even perfectly competent decision-makers acting in good faith would face uncertainty. According to Wolff's definition, in doubtful cases disputants bring equally plausible arguments to support their case.[46] Doubts could arise from fact, law, or principle, as when it was unknown who first occupied a disputed territory, or what the exact implications of a treaty were, or which is the true religion.[47] Crucially for present purposes, the uncertainty clouding these disputes could be such that resort to force was permissible without previously attempting negotiation or arbitration. As Wolff put it,

[44] This warning appears in Wolff's 1730 lecture "On the Philosopher King and the Ruling Philosopher," where he made a case for enlightened monarchy (Wolff 1992 [1730], 203–5). Wolff had less hopes than his mentor Leibniz with regard to the use of probability calculations and formal logic in public affairs (on which see Capozzi and Roncaglia 2009, 126–8).

[45] III.189, 590; similarly Wolff in JG §892.

[46] JG §421; compare Vattel in LN III.38.

[47] See respectively JG §§106, 420, 261.

> By the voluntary law of nations arms are not unjustly taken which are taken up in a doubtful case for the purpose of obtaining a settlement, even if a conference or arbitration has not been attempted... In disputed matters of great importance among nations, since it is scarcely to be hoped that the controversy can be settled by a conference and arbitration accepted, on account of fear of the zeal of the parties, and since the acceptance of a conference may not be above suspicion, when it can be easily foreseen that a conference or arbitration is not going to be accepted, or, if it should be offered, that there is no other outcome to be expected than delay harmful to the one offering, arms may lawfully be taken up without attempting a conference or arbitration.[48]

Uncertainty regarding both the material dispute and the trustworthiness of the other side leads to an objectively uncertain situation. The more important the matter, the less a responsible ruler could afford to trust the other side, for his betrayal would be catastrophic and natural law commands rulers to be prudent and circumspect.[49] In these cases, vulnerability, the absence of sufficient assurances, and the distinct responsibilities of political rule make the voluntary law of nations not a second-best law but rather the only pertinent normative frame of reference. In virtue of the voluntary law, the natural law imperative to solve disputes amicably is displaced by the imperatives of good statecraft and political prudence.[50]

Neither Wolff nor Vattel speculated about the frequency of conflicts of this type, but it could well be high, as moral vice, subjective cognitive failure, and objective uncertainty could feed into each other. The presumption of untrustworthiness is supported by the belief that moral vice is rampant and that rulers often fail to adequately understand their own states' true interests and how best to promote them. The type of judgment that is called for in such circumstances may be called *political judgment*, that is, a form of practical judgment made in situations that compel action but are pervaded by epistemic and moral uncertainty. Wolff argued that no science of probability could dispel the uncertainty under which rulers must make such political decisions, "under pressure to act" and without "determinate enough or entirely evident" ideas.[51]

[48] JG §574, 293; equally Vattel in LN II.335.

[49] JG §573.

[50] JG §§621, 628, 740.

[51] Wolff 1992 [1730], 200. On political judgment, see Geuss 2010, 1–16. I am grateful to Bryan Garsten for pointing me to the relevance of the concept of political judgment in this context. Ian Hunter has suggestively characterized this form of judgment in Vattel as "diplomatic casuistry," which takes place in light of both the law of nations and state interests (Hunter 2010). While the concept of casuistry does capture the necessary context-dependence of such judgments, it misses the pressing imperative to act, which Wolff emphasized. The image of a casuist painstaking and contextually rich examination

Political judgments are inherently subject to dispute and contestation, both inside and outside the state. By recognizing the simultaneous validity of conflicting sovereign judgments, the voluntary law in effect creates a space of legal neutrality for such contestation to take place. The law recognizes the validity of plausible but conflicting sovereign claims, and instead of having to pronounce on who is right and wrong, it defines procedures that lead to settling their dispute.

This deference to sovereign contestation sits uneasily with universal rationalist accounts of law and politics, in particular Thomistic accounts of objective justice. Wolff deceivingly states at the outset of his *Jus Gentium* that the legislator of the global *civitas maxima* is right reason itself, which can be established "following the leadership of nature."[52] And yet the principle of equal sovereignty, and deference to sovereign political judgment, fracture this universal and unifying reason. The principle of equal sovereignty implies that one state's judgment about the legitimacy of force cannot simply override another state's conflicting judgment, even if it reflects truth and right reason itself. This is not because all political judgments are equally valid, as a relativist might claim, nor solely in virtue of a purely formal jurisdictional argument, as a legal positivist could argue, but rather because truths are usually not transparently available in international politics.[53]

One important implication of the uncertainty that clouds international politics is that wars can be just on both sides not only subjectively—when one side cannot possibly know that his claim is in fact unjust, as the Spanish scholastics had argued—but objectively. In fact, the whole scholastic distinction between subjective and objective conditions of justice appears to lose ground in the Enlightenment theory of regular war. Subjective judgments, and the expectations they can generate, create objective conditions.

In principle, regular wars are justified only when the perfect rights of states are violated. But perfect rights have overlapping areas and fuzzy boundaries which states are left to determine autonomously. Two grounds for going to war may be distinguished. The first is familiar from the scholastic doctrine of just war and rare in history: war in response to actions that manifestly and unquestionably violate the perfect claim rights of states. The second is distinctive of regular war theory and arises from doubtful cases. Of all perfect rights, by

does not quite capture the potentially agonizing uncertainty and pressure to act that sovereign rulers can face.

[52] JG §21, 17.
[53] As Vattel notes, see LN Preliminaries §21.

far the most encompassing is the right to security, which allows states to use force against those who obstruct their "preservation, perfection, and happiness." Since such obstructions are proscribed in the law of nations, security is nominally a claim right, its correlate being an obligation of non-interference. However, because nations may be expected to clash when pursuing their preservation and perfection, they can lawfully undermine each other's rights to security. In reality, the right to security is rather a liberty right, which authorizes states to pursue their security according to their own lights. When such pursuits escalate to war, wrote Vattel, "it is equally possible that either of the parties may have right on his side." It could be said, more strongly, that both sides may be justified in using force.[54]

Consider the following case from Vattel:

> If a weak state attempts, without necessity, to erect a fortress, which she is incapable of defending, in a place where it might become very dangerous to her neighbor if ever it should fall into the hands of a powerful enemy, that neighbor may oppose the construction of the fortress; and if he does not find it convenient to pay the lesser state a compensation for complying with his desire, he may force her compliance, by threatening to block up the roads and avenues of communication, to prohibit all intercourse between the two nations, to build fortresses, or to keep an army on the frontier, to consider that little state in a suspicious light, &c."[55]

The tenor of Vattel's description is objective—there is no need to build a fortress, the weak state is in fact incapable of defending it—but suppose, more plausibly and in line with Vattelian premises, that these facts were contested.[56] The weak state plans to build a fortress based on its own estimate of its security requirements and capacities. The strong state cannot unilaterally overrule the small state's judgment, for a situation is certainly conceivable in which building the fortress, and even recruiting allies to counter the strong state's opposition, would be a legitimate pursuit of security against a strong neighbor. It may be the case that a powerful enemy of the strong state would gain significant advantage if it successfully occupied the weak state and took the fortress. But whether this is a decisive reason for the weak state to give up the projected

[54] III.68, 508.
[55] II.180, 354.
[56] See e.g. III.50. In a similar case Wolff favors the weak state, see JG §641.

fortress would depend on a variety of circumstances, including the observable and likely policies of this powerful enemy and its relationship to the weak state.

For present purposes, the relevant point is that, given the structure of the situation—its geographical, political, and military features—the parties involved may be unable to simultaneously enjoy acceptable levels of security. Each party can make a strong case for and against fortification so that, if the dispute escalates to war, neither could be described as aggressor. Since in such conflicts, "it is equally possible that either of the parties may have right on his side," each may permissibly use force. Their justice, in Wolff's words, "remains in suspense" for as long as a peace treaty does not restore a rightful condition between the parties.[57]

Other cases of bilateral justice can be constructed from premises of regular war theory. One of Vattel's important breaks with Grotius and the scholastic tradition was to defend the use of preventive force.[58] If there are good grounds to expect that a state's growth will lead to oppression and enslavement—and Vattel's assumption was that such grounds typically exist—it would be unreasonable to ask smaller nations to abstain from force until that threat was imminent or actualized. The proper response to such threats must be based on the assessment of the growing power's motives, along with estimations of the "compound ratio" of probability of attack and harmfulness.[59]

Vattel did not quite spell out the full implications of this doctrine, but one corollary is that two growing powers could pose threats to each other serious enough to make it permissible for both to use preventive force.[60] For Rousseau this was in fact the paradigmatic case of war. The security and preservation of a state, he wrote, "demand that it make itself more powerful than all its neighbors," but by striving to become relatively more powerful, states become threats to each other and are ultimately made less secure. Under such paradoxical conditions, the question of which side has justice is really out of place. If injustice had to be attributed to anyone, it would have to be to the

[57] JG §634, 325.

[58] III.42–50. In this important respect, Vattel contradicted Wolff. Wolff worried that making preventive wars permissible would altogether substitute prudence for right and ultimately dissolve international justice (JG §646). As he laconically wrote, "the weakness of one nation can set no limits to the power of another" (JG §649, 333). He granted nonetheless that the "slightest wrong" from a growing threatening power could be enough to warrant large-scale defensive force (JG §§650–1).

[59] III.44, 493.

[60] The way England and France faced each other in the Seven Years War (1754–1763) is a case in point, which Vattel knew well. The war originated in disputes between France and Britain as their colonies in North America were expanding. The confrontation had a remarkable symmetry, as both powers were increasingly dependent on the production and trade with the West Indies, and each would be seriously undermined if the other managed to take full control of North American territories (Baugh 2011).

international system as a whole for being so inherently and irredeemably destructive.[61]

3.3 War declarations and manifestoes

So how is this not a complete surrender of international legality and embrace of crude power politics and reason of state? Vattel recognized that the legal permission to wage regular war could be abused by nations that only "pretend that it would be dangerous for them to attempt pacific measures," and which barely "give a color of justice to their precipitation in having recourse to arms." He lamented that, in practice, opportunism and hypocrisy often substitute for political prudence within the bounds of the law of nations, and that rulers got away with whatever they may.[62]

However, the fact that political judgment is inherently contestable, and that some wars could be justified by both sides, does not mean that all uses of force could be plausibly framed in the language of perfect rights. The right of security is broad, but it does set boundaries on the legitimate use of force. We will see in this section that an essential element for the determination of these boundaries in the doctrine of regular war is the duty to publicly state the reasons for waging war, which the voluntary law of nations mandates. The practice of offering reasons, which could even become a public exchange of reasons in the form of "war manifestoes" and "counter-manifestoes," was articulated in the legal discourse of public diplomacy, which is neither a purely formal language nor empty of substantive moral content.[63] Wolff and Vattel understood well that, in the absence of centralized adjudication in the law of nations, *sui generis* procedures were required to establish the boundaries of perfect rights. Instead of the just war conception of war as adjudication and vindication of rights, they defended the legal duty to publicly state the reasons for waging war in the practice of war declarations. This duty appears in the voluntary law as an imperative to issue manifestoes which formally constitute a state of war, and in which the reasons for waging war have to be stated. Fighters in undeclared wars could be treated as "robbers" not enemies.[64]

[61] Rousseau's argument and quote come from his fragments on "The State of War" (Rousseau 1997 [1755], 169).

[62] II.335, 456; also Wolff in JG §618.

[63] On manifestoes and counter-manifestoes see Wolff JG §§740–2. My reading here may be contrasted with the purely formal and procedural interpretations of Haggenmacher 1992, 435–6; Schmitt 2003, 164–8.

[64] JG §§710, 740–2; LN III.64–5, III.68.

With these postulates, Wolff and Vattel brought into the theory of regular war a practice that was common in seventeenth- and eighteenth-century European diplomacy.[65] Their account of war manifestoes follows the neo-Roman tradition of Gentili and Grotius, but is richer theoretically than its predecessors. As in neo-Roman accounts, Wolff and Vattel held that war declarations followed the form of *rerum repetitio* and could function as ultimatums—restore the right or else face war—and as such constituted a form of fair warning and last attempt to avoid war.[66] Vattel also mentioned the role of war declarations in marking clearly the transition from peacetime to war. After a formal declaration, the rules of regular warfare come into effect, and a precise period could be identified for the *post bellum* recovery of property and territory in virtue of prize law and postliminium.[67]

Wolff and Vattel adapted this neo-Roman doctrine to the actual practice of war declarations in Europe. To reflect the fact that most wars in European practice were actually declared not prior but after hostilities began, they held that war could also be publicly justified during its course.[68] The gray areas of violence before formal declarations could be subsumed under the ambiguous legal concept of "reprisals," which denoted a provisional state of affairs.[69] Wolff distinguished between "pure declarations" and war "manifestoes" or "publications." The former constituted a formal state of war, and had to be issued at the outset of war, but the latter could be given after hostilities began and must include the substantive reasons for waging war. In practice, the latter were more important than the former.[70]

[65] On the history of war publications, see e.g. Baumgartner 2011; Neff 2005, 103–11; Piirimäe 2010a; Hathaway and Shapiro 2017, 31–55.

[66] JG §710–11; LN III.60.

[67] III.56; III.64.

[68] As the British legal historian Robert Plumer Ward concluded in an 1805 overview of the outbreak of European wars in the seventeenth and eighteenth centuries, "if all the declarations that have been published in Europe were to be critically examined; by far the greater part of them would be found to contain reasons for hostilities already begun, not notice of impending war" (Plumer Ward 1805, 4). Also Bynkershoek commented on this aspect of the practice (Bynkershoek and Frank 1930 [1737], 18–25). The third Hague Convention of 1907 returns to the neo-Roman conception when it states in art. 1 that, "The contracting Powers recognize that hostilities between themselves must not commence without previous and explicit warning, in the form either of a reasoned declaration of war, or of an ultimatum with conditional declaration of war."

[69] JG §715; LN II.354.

[70] JG §§708, 740. According to the influential late-eighteenth century publicist Georg Friedrich von Martens, by the end of the eighteenth century the duty to solemnly declare war at the outset had been superseded, but that of publishing war manifestoes explaining the motives for war was still mandatory. As he wrote in his *Précis* of the law of nations, "nowadays, nations content themselves with publishing a declaration of war through their own dominions, and explaining their motives to other powers in writing. Publishing of war in this manner is looked upon as so essential, that nations have often demanded a restitution of every thing taken from them by the enemy before such publication. Sometimes, however, nations get rid of such demands by insisting, that the war has been tacitly declared" (Martens and Cobbett 1795, 275).

War manifestoes must present for everyone to see—foreign rulers and own citizens—the relevant facts and identify the perfect right, the violation of which is the reason for using force. "Since no one wishes to seem to wage war unjustly," Wolff argued, "in manifestos not only is there indicated the fact that war has been undertaken with this or that nation, but also for what reason it has been undertaken."[71] In particular, manifestoes must display due recognition to the constitutive principles of the law of nations: the equal sovereignty of states and their immunity to attack except in plausible pursuit of perfect rights.[72] In contrast to Grotius, then, for Wolff and Vattel the most important aspect of war manifestoes is not to formally constitute a state of war, but rather to justify publicly resort to force.[73]

Wolff theorized the practice of publishing war manifestoes and distinguished three types of reason that could be offered: justifying, probable, and quasi-justifying reasons (or "mere pretexts" in Vattel). Justifying reasons are valid and fully justify war; probable reasons make a plausible case for war; and pretexts could be found to be spurious upon examination.[74] In addition to these, Wolff distinguished the class of "persuasive reasons" or reasons of state, which belong to utility or advantage, not the law of nations, and as such need not be included in war publications.[75]

The arguments in the previous sections can be recast in this language. Because the justice of international disputes is usually not transparent, states will often have only probable reasons for war, and one side's having probable reasons does not exclude its enemy's having them as well. In cases where the justice of a dispute is manifest, only one side can give justifying reasons and the other at most pretexts. For Wolff and Vattel, a war is fully justified when it has both probable or justifying reasons and persuasive reasons that are "equitable" or protective of the belligerent nation's public good.[76] "Both the justifying and the persuasive reasons are to be considered, before war should be declared," wrote Wolff. "The former reasons belong to the law of nature and nations, that latter are matters of statecraft and politics (*prudentiam civilem*); the former make you act justly, but the latter make you act wisely (*prudenter*)." Legalism and reason of state appear here not as negations of each other, but rather as two complementary orders of consideration.[77]

[71] JG §740, 380, also §737.

[72] JG §§706, 742–4; likewise Vattel in LN III.25–26.

[73] JG §§706, 740, 742; LN III.25–6. Contrast Grotius in RWP II.xxvi.4.

[74] JG §§621–8, 740; LN III.25–33.

[75] In fact, persuasive reasons should usually be kept secret because they belong to the *arcana imperii* of good statecraft (JG §§621, 740; LN III.187).

[76] JG §628; LN III.32–3.

[77] JG §621, 316, also §254.

It was Wolff and Vattel's conviction that the obligation to publicly justify war could allow the law of nations to limit the pursuit of state interests through war. A condition for this conviction to be realized in practice is that states be able to detect and react to mere pretexts.[78] The overall tenor of Wolff's discussion is that there will be agreement on the type of reason offered, which is to say that there is no second-level uncertainty regarding the typology of reasons. Pretexts can be identified transparently upon examination, as the doubtfulness of a dispute is not itself disputable.[79]

Vattel, on the other hand, was somewhat equivocal on this crucial matter. He appears sometimes to hold that any state's claim could be taken as a probable reason, as when he wrote that "there [always] exists a possibility that she [a nation] may perhaps have justice on her side (*il se pourroit faire qu'elle eût droit*)" or that it is "nearly impossible" that a war would admit of no plausible justification.[80] Elsewhere, however, he distinguished clearly between mere pretexts and genuine reasons. Only thus could he suggest, somewhat perplexingly, that a hypocrite, who offers mere pretexts in war manifestoes, deserves some praise rather than all-out condemnation, for he "does not openly trample on what is most sacred in human society: he tacitly acknowledges that a flagrant injustice merits the indignation of mankind."[81] Wolff, by contrast, held clearly that those who gave mere pretexts had no care for justice: they in effect dissolved the law of nations into "the might of nature, so that as much is permitted as it is within one's power." Rather than praise, those who dared "wrongfully to harass any other nation at will" should be considered disturbers of international public security.[82]

Against such actors, decisive collective counteraction is required, because those who undermine legality constitute a threat to everyone; it is legally

[78] JG §618; LN II.309.

[79] JG §§624–5. Wolff can be read as claiming here that the distinction between justiciable and non-justiciable disputes can be settled by law. On this crucial aspect of Wolff and Vattel's account of *ius ad bellum*, contrast Koskenniemi 2005, 111–12.

[80] Preliminaries §21, 76, III.187, 588.

[81] III.32, 486–7. James Whitman has defended this Vattelian position, which he calls the eighteenth-century "doctrine of pretexts," by arguing that feeling compelled to offer a pretext shows regard for legal form, and hence a minimum degree of civilization (Whitman 2012, 127–32). By paying homage to virtue, the hypocrite would affirm, if only weakly, the norm he violates. Bad faith, however, would hardly seem to be proper regard for law. Alternatively, it could be said, following Jon Elster, that clothing one's self-interest in the garb of justice makes strategic sense only if one believes that at least some relevant agents do genuinely care about justice. Hypocrisy may be taken to be oblique proof of the compelling force of the law of nations. A proper defense of Vattel would have to establish that hypocrisy has what Elster has called "civilizing force." Rulers would have to feel compelled to moderate their foreign policies when presenting them as pursuant of a perfect right, and their future policies would have to be constrained by consistency with earlier claims (Elster 1999, 372–80, 401–2). For some early modern historical illustrations of moderation but not consistency, see Piirimäe 2010a, 135–7.

[82] JG §625, 318, §652, 336.

permissible and in everyone's interest that they be stopped.[83] Vattel recognized that giving mere pretexts, or not offering any justification at all, showed a tendency to undermine the foundations of international society. In his words,

> If there were a people who made open profession of trampling justice under foot —who despised and violated the rights of others whenever they found an opportunity— the interest of human society would authorize all the other nations to form a confederacy in order to humble and chastise the delinquents . . . In particular cases, where there is room for the smallest doubt, it ought to be supposed that each of the parties may have some right: and the injustice of the party that has committed the injury may proceed from error, and not from a general contempt of justice. But if, by her constant maxims, and by the whole tenor of her conduct, a nation evidently proves herself to be actuated by that mischievous disposition —if she regards no right as sacred— the safety of the human race requires that she should be repressed.[84]

Such "enemies of mankind," "public enemies" of international society, "disturbers of the common security of nations" threatened international society as a whole. Vattel cites as cases German tribes and barbarians in Roman times, "Turks and other tartars," and those monarchs "who make war from inclination purely" in contemporary Europe. The agents of such threats could be treated as "savage beasts," relative to whom the protections of regular *ius in bello* could even be suspended.[85]

There is a sense, then, in which the theory of regular war has room for something apparently analogous to aggression, but the analogy is misleading. First, because while every just war has an aggressor and a victim of aggression, in the practice of regular warfare "enemies of mankind" should be rare. As long as the prospect of concerted action dissuades warmongers as it should, wars will be fought only on the basis of justifying or probable reasons. Secondly, the status of enemy of mankind cannot be given on the basis of unilateral acts

[83] The role of collective security alongside the balance of power in Vattel's theory of war is highlighted by Rech 2013, 131–49. The Dano-Swedish War (1658–60) is a historical illustration of how "the failure to demonstrate the justice of one's cause could very well have adverse political consequences" (Piirimäe 2010b, 76). Sweden's attack on Denmark without any public manifesto, and in breach of the peace of Roskilde, was received with consternation across European courts. Sweden sought the military support of Britain but this was denied, "as the English were not happy to appear to be supporting the manifestly unjust side." The British did make some diplomatic efforts to prevent the Dutch from fighting with the Danes, but these were undermined by the lack of a Swedish manifesto. The Swedish king was not treated as a criminal for failing to justify the war, but the political consequences of his failure to publicize the war were not negligible (Piirimäe 2010b, 75–9, 2010a, 135–9).

[84] II.70, 297; see further III.49 and cf. III.32.

[85] II.222, II.56, III.34; also Wolff in JG §§626–7, 652.

of adjudication but must rather be based on something close to consensus. Multilateralism can operate as a filter against spurious disqualifications of one's enemies.[86]

Even if pretexts can be detected, whether this would motivate a fitting response is an altogether different matter. The duty to publicly offer valid reasons for war could effectively check sovereign policies only to the extent that there is widespread belief that abuse of war-making powers will elicit adverse reactions, and ideally that concerted military action will follow. Wolff and Vattel stood by the Grotian logic that rulers have a long-term interest in having a reputation for legal compliance, which could have disciplining effects.[87] But opposing powerful "enemies of mankind" could be very costly, as the historical record in Europe clearly shows.

Consider the case of king Louis XIV of France, a strong candidate for the title of enemy of mankind among European rulers if there is one, and against whom Vattel justified the use of preventive force to contain the threat of universal monarchy in Europe.[88] The following is the full text of Louis XIV's war declaration at the outset of the 1672 Dutch War:

> The ill opinion which his Majesty hath for some time past entertained of the Conduct of the States General, having proceeded so far that his Majesty without the diminution of his Glory cannot any longer dissemble the Indignation wrought in him for their acting so little conformably to the great Obligations, which his Majesty and the Kings his Predecessors have so bountifully heaped upon them; his Majesty hath declared, as he does now declare, that he hath determined and resolved to make War against the said States-General of the United Provinces, both by Sea and Land.[89]

Instead of a proper publication, the French king delivered a statement of his intention to attack the United Provinces. The reaction at the time was far from universal condemnation. Prior to the war, Louis had laid down the political ground for the war by enlisting key players with the promise of spoils of war and other forms of support, including England, Sweden, Cologne, and Münster. Their backing lasted only for the first two years of the war, until Louis's

[86] For a contrasting interpretation of this aspect of Vattel, see Silvestrini 2010.
[87] See e.g. JG §376; LN III.64.
[88] III.44.
[89] Quoted in Neff 2005, 107. As Plumer Ward remarks, the war was formally declared but it had "neither complaint, nor demand, for no injury was stated" (Plumer Ward 1805, 17).

boundless ambition motivated Spain and Austria to intervene, but the Peace of Nijmegen nonetheless gave Louis net territorial gains at the end of the war.[90]

Another clear candidate for the title of enemy of mankind is Frederick the Great, whom Vattel did label such in his diplomatic correspondence but not in *The Law of Nations*. In 1740, Frederick invaded Silesia—then under Austrian rule—without a declaration, and later issued a pretext that was, according to Frederick himself, the "work of a charlatan," after having reneged on his father's promise to recognize the Austrian empress.[91] The invasion was widely condemned at the time, and Austria complained about it "in every court of Europe, as ungenerous and unjust, contrary to the laws of the empire, and of good faith," but to no avail.[92] England sent a few troops to support Austria, but Russia did not spare any because at the time it was at war with Sweden. France, Spain, and Bavaria sided with Frederick in what eventually became the War of Austrian Succession (1740–48) at the end of which Silesia was annexed by Frederick and formally recognized as part of Prussia.

On the invasion of Silesia, Vattel was conspicuously agnostic in *The Law of Nations*. He wrote that Frederick "might have wise and just reasons for acting thus: and this is sufficient at the tribunal of the voluntary law of nations."[93] It was Frederick's invasion of Saxony and Bohemia in 1756 that moved Vattel to label him "enemy of mankind" in his correspondence, and to call foreign powers to coordinate and contain the growing threat.[94] This is somewhat odd, as Frederick did issue a plausible war declaration in 1756 alleging the justifiability of preventive force against the triple alliance of Austria, Russia, and France, and complaining for Saxony's injurious refusal of free transit into Bohemian territory. In his letter, Vattel dismissed these reasons as mere

[90] Black 1999, 41–8; Sonnino 1976.

[91] The admission is made in Frederick's diary, which includes also Frederick's "persuasive reasons" (cited approvingly by Carlyle): "Silesian War lies handy to us, and is the only kind of Offensive War that does; Country bordering on our frontier, and with the Oder running through it as a sure high-road for everything . . . Add to these reasons, an Army ready for acting; Funds, Supplies all found—and perhaps the desire of making oneself a name" (Carlyle 1864, 118).

[92] The quote comes from Plumer Ward 1805, 32. On this case, see further Holsti 1991, 92–3; Bély 1992, 490–4; Baumgartner 2011, 133–4.

[93] II.335, 457. In defense of Vattel's reading of the case, Whitman has argued that the invasion of Silesia was not a clear case of rapacity, contrary to standard present-day assessments. He presents a wealth of evidence that shows how lawyers at the time could obfuscate the issue enough to produce considerable debate among experts (Whitman 2012, 119–25). If this case was debatable among jurists, it seems every case can be.

[94] Seeking to mobilize oppostion to Frederick, Vattel wrote to the Conseil of Berne in 1757 as follows: "Il est certainement de l'intérêt et du salut commun des Nations, de réprimer celui qui foule aux pieds des règles, qui font l'unique fondement de leur repos, et sans lesquelles tout deviendront la proie du plus fort et du plus audacieux" (Béguelin 1929, 172–3). On Vattel's attempts to mobilize public opinion against Frederick in the late 1750s, see further Rech 2013, 144–9.

pretexts, even though both preventive force and the right of innocent passage were included in *The Law of Nations*.[95]

3.4 Belligerent status

There is no question that, in a world of self-regarding states with limited resources, collective security is a tall normative order. It is nonetheless an order that Wolff and Vattel defended over several conceivable alternatives, including criminal deterrence through punitive wars. Their embrace of international pluralism led them to produce a fallible and seemingly more permissive doctrine of *ius ad bellum* than that of just war theory. Instead of pressing for raising the bar of valid reasons for waging war, their account of *ius ad bellum* stressed the obstacles to the accurate adjudication of demanding standards, in particular the likelihood of appeals to *iusta causa* in bad faith, the insufficient epistemic capacities of decision-makers, and the existence of objective uncertainty and structural insecurity.

Their hope, however, was that, by carving a legal space for legitimate claim-making from a plurality of sovereign nations, they could avoid or at least mitigate unilateral, self-righteous, and exclusive appropriations of international legal discourse. In particular, they rejected the inherently asymmetrical logic of just war language, which could assist hegemonic agendas by its tendency to disqualify claims and interests of less powerful actors. In virtue of their raw power, hegemonic states could successfully block the operation of collective security, but the law of nations, as the Enlightenment jurists conceived of it, is not well suited to assist in this blockage. On the contrary, the theory of regular war prioritizes the political and juridical inclusion of all sovereign entities, as it abandons the aspiration of making war an institution of law enforcement and punishment against delinquent agents.

The most limiting and moderating practical effects of the theory of regular war come not from its doctrine of *ius ad bellum* but rather from the doctrines of *ius in bello* and *ius post bellum*, which will be discussed in the next chapter. Before that, I would like to conclude this chapter by examining briefly the question of *who* could have standing—which collective agents—to declare and wage regular war according to Vattel. I focus on him exclusively because his views on civil warfare are more developed and republican than Wolff's and show more clearly the emancipatory potential of the theory of regular war.

[95] Baumgartner 2011, 139–40.

Vattel defined civil wars in contrast to lesser forms of opposition to state authority, which include "popular commotions," "seditions," and "insurrections."[96] Civil wars are of such magnitude that they "break the bands of society and government" and "produce in the nation two independent parties, who consider each other as enemies, and acknowledge no common judge."[97] Upon such fracture, the parties to a civil war must be seen as two separate bodies, and their war treated on a par with inter-state wars because the same epistemic hurdles to establishing justice, and the imperatives of limitation and transition to peace, apply to them. In Vattel's view, the sheer capacity to oppose the sovereign, to effectively challenge its rule and territorial control by force, is sufficient for earning belligerent status and, if successful, for sovereign political standing.

Vattel's concept of nationhood displays a similar deference to facts. A nation exists in international society—"it makes an immediate figure in this grand society"—when an historical practice of collective self-rule can be detected.[98] Practices of self-rule coalesce in a constitution, the concrete form of which is the result of historical struggles that may include war.[99] And while nations may come together in federations for the sake of protection and mutual advantage, the units in these federations should still be recognized as independent nations, and in principle—unless the federal agreement says otherwise—be endowed with the right to use force.[100] Whether unified by common religion or ancestry, or by sheer attachment to territory, each nation has a distinctive collective identity.[101] It has a duty to know itself, in particular where it stands on its way to "perfection" and what suits best its particular character. Failure of self-knowledge leads to "improper measures," notably aping the policies and constitution of foreign nations "reputed wise and skilful."[102] The ruler and members of a nation are best placed to know and realize the full potential of their national character because, as long as foreigners can exit to better destinies, they cannot be trusted with legislation or policy.[103]

[96] Vattel's account of civil wars appears in III.287–96. For discussion of its historical significance, see Armitage 2017, 128–34.

[97] III.293, 645.

[98] I.4, 68.

[99] An example drawn from Swiss history is presented in IV.6. Vattel supported a version of what James Tully has called "ancient constitutionalism," although Tully himself counts Vattel as a "modern constitutionalist." Vattel treated long-standing custom as an "authoritative expression of the agreement of the people," and as such the source of binding constitutional law. It would run against his conception of nationhood to claim that customary law expressed only archaic or pre-modern forms of attachment to unreflective ways of being, as a modern constitutionalist would argue (Tully 1995, 88–9, cf. 79, 126–7).

[100] I.6, I.10, III.50.

[101] I.13, 85. For a useful overview of ideas of nationhood during Vattel's time, see Benner 2013, 36–41.

[102] I.25, 91.

[103] I.31.

For present purposes, it is highly significant that certain *facts* about political life—the existence of practices of self-rule, the capacity to challenge established sovereigns effectively—can be determinative of forms of standing that carry distinct rights and obligations in the law of nations. Through political struggle, in particular armed struggle, political rights in the law of nations could be *earned*, in particular the privileges of belligerence. Partly due to Vattel's influence, a "principle of defactoism" became standard in the law of nations until the end of the nineteenth century, according to which peoples that had declared independence and successfully maintained their independence were *eo ipso* treated as having sovereign standing.[104] This remarkable political and legal fluidity of the Vattelian world is now largely lost. The privilege of belligerence belongs now only in the already established and exclusive club of sovereign nations, membership to which is now jealously kept by current members.

[104] Alexandrowicz 1958.

4
Enlightenment Ideals of Limited Warfare

We saw in the previous chapter how Christian Wolff and Emer de Vattel formulated an account of *ius ad bellum* in regular wars that was deferent to the excercise of sovereign political judgment and reason of state. In virtue of their broad conceptions of the sovereign rights to security and independent judgment, states were legally authorized to resort to force in a wide range of cases. Reflecting a correspondingly pluralist conception of international society, their doctrine of *ius ad bellum* in regular wars is more permissive than that of just wars. As long as belligerents have sovereign status and offer plausible reasons for war in their public manifestoes, they are taken to be fighting lawfully. The case of outlaw states waging war with no colorable public reason is presumed to be rare and calls for exceptional measures.

This chapter turns to examine how the Enlightenment theorists' deference to reason of state plays out in the doctrines of *ius in bello* and *ius post bellum* in regular wars. Reason of state again plays a crucial role, but now in different forms depending on the strategic logic of specific areas in the practice of hostilities. Generally speaking, if in the case of resort to force reason of state stands as an eminently permissive principle, at least relative to the stricter *ius ad bellum* of just wars, when it comes to the conduct of hostilities and conclusion of war, the limiting dimension of reason of state—the restrictions derived from "civil prudence"—stand out. I will argue in this chapter that for the Enlightenment theorists the law of nations provided a vocabulary to articulate maxims of sound policy in the administration of a regular war's destructiveness. These maxims, in turn, reflect a proper understanding of an economy of violence that all states should follow during war and in the transition to peace. It is a maxim of enlightened rule that regular wars be limited and their destructiveness kept within certain conventional limits.

Things, however, are complicated by the fact that, at the center of the doctrine of *ius in bello* in regular wars, there is a tension between two competing state interests. On the one hand, all states may be assumed to have an interest in limiting the destructiveness of their clash of forces. In virtue of this general interest, states are taken to agree on certain general legal limitations applicable to the conduct of war. The Enlightenment publicist G. F. von Martens

The Laws of War in International Thought. Pablo Kalmanovitz, Oxford University Press (2020). © Pablo Kalmanovitz.
DOI: 10.1093/oso/9780198790259.001.0001.

captured this particular orientation of the law of nations when he wrote that the "civilized powers of Europe" had, after slow and painful experience, come to understand that it was in everyone's best interest to avoid unnecessary violence and to diminish the "scourge of war" by observing legal limitations on the means of warfare.[1] On the other hand, however, states are also known to have short-term interests in using all available means to overcome their enemy, in particular illegal means if they provide tactical advantages. The law of nations must mediate this core tension between short-sighted and crude reason of state and long-term enlightened interest in the practice of warfare. As will be seen in what follows, this corresponds to Wolff and Vattel's self-understanding: one of their tasks was to show rulers and military officers that their best interest required legal compliance in the conduct of hostilities and at the end of war.

Unlawful means may confer short-term advantages, Martens cautioned, but they eventually backfire against the deploying nation and ultimately impede the progress of civilized Europe. Montesquieu's famous governing principle of the law of nations may be the most compact and general summary of this fundamental tension: "the various nations should do to one another in times of peace the most good possible, and in times of war the least ill possible, without harming their true interests."[2] Doing the least possible evil during war, while upholding each state's interest, is arguably the defining challenge of *ius in bello* in regular wars.

To use contemporary language, one of my aims in this chapter is to show that the normative logic of the Enlightenment accounts of *ius in bello* and *ius post bellum* can be described as a form of rule-consequentialism with a realist constraint. While in general the rules of regular war aim to limit the destructive consequences of war, only those norms that could be upheld in self-enforcing equilibria can be part of the laws of war. The rules of regular war reflect the possibility of limiting equilibria among rational belligerents, but these equilibria are always fragile and unstable.[3]

[1] Martens 1801, 398–9, 405–6. On the importance of G.F. von Martens for the Enlightenment project of international law, see Koskenniemi 2008. Koskenniemi underscores how with Martens the law of nations became closely associated with a largely German science of politics and diplomatic practice, which had already internalized the legal theory coming from Vattel and the modern natural law tradition. However, the "turn to policy" in the law of nations, in particular the sound administration of a state's coercive apparatus, is already visible in Wolff and Vattel, as this chapter will show.

[2] Montesquieu et al. 1989 [1748], I.3, 7.

[3] In his study of the Napoleonic wars, David Bell holds that in the Old Regime "monarchs and generals did not practice the new style of warfare because of conscious calculations," but rather "because it came naturally to them as aristocrats: to fight, to fight bravely and gloriously but also with restraint, with self-control and honor" (Bell 2007, 50). This does not quite correspond to the views of Wolff and Vattel, who frequently refer to instrumental calculations in the conduct of regular wars. Vattel sometimes explicitly echoes the strategic thinking of eighteenth- and seventeenth-centuries generals and monarchs

The chapter proceeds by looking at various areas in the practice of regular warfare and identifying the strategic logic behind the laws proposed by the Enlightenment theorists. These areas include the definition of belligerent privileges; the immunity of noncombatants during sieges and requisitions; the immunity of neutrals; the use of reprisals for law enforcement; and the conclusion of war in peace treaties. My discussion highlights how, in all these areas, limiting equilibria are practically possible but always precarious. They depend, first and foremost, on political and military leaders having a sound understanding of, and adhering to, long-term state interests, which often they did not.

Before proceeding, it is important to note that humanitarian concerns play a very limited role in the doctrine of *ius in bello* in regular wars. Vattel did underscore and celebrate the humanitarian dividends of regular war limitations, but his emphasis is consistently on keeping the destructiveness of war within the limits of prudence and "sound policy," in particular avoiding or limiting its spillage into social and economic life. What Vattel called "offices of humanity" are non-enforceable obligations to give mutual aid to others in need; they are not part of the law of nations but of natural law, and include providing assistance or relief in cases of famine and natural catastrophes, in addition to military attacks.[4] Superfluous injury is cruel and inhumane but also, and centrally for Vattel, irrational and wasteful. In fact, Vattel thought there was a providential practical convergence between sound policy and "humanity," so that pursuing the former would always lead to protecting the latter.[5] Correspondingly, as we will see, his presentation of the rules of regular warfare appeal more to interest and policy than humane sentiment. This is not to deny, of course, that Vattel valued the relief of suffering and mitigation of horror that could result from observing the laws of war. There is, however, nothing in *The Law of Nations* to match the tenor of Grotius' *temperamenta belli*, which include humanitarian exhortations to abstain from causing suffering in war, and nothing comparable to the late nineteenth century emotive appeals for the incorporation of humanitarian principles in the law of nations.

(Bell himself recognizes their importance in the context of the immunities of prisoners of war, see Bell 2007, 143–4).

[4] LN II.1–10. Vattel's celebration of the humane effects of the laws of regular war can be found in e.g. III.145, III.147, III.150.

As in the previous chapter, unless otherwise indicated all citations to Vattel come from *The Law of Nations*. I indicate book and paragraph numbers, and page numbers when quoting.

[5] As he wrote, "it fortunately happens that, in this particular [the rights and duties of conquest] as in everything else, sound policy and humanity are in perfect accord" (III.201, 600). For some illustrations of convergence, see III.158.

4.1 Critique of *ius in bello* in just wars

We saw in Chapter 1 that scholastic accounts of just war derive the constraints and permissions of *ius in bello* from principles of corrective justice and natural law. War is justified only as a form of vindication for a violated right, and consequently belligerents have contrasting legal standings: one is in the right and his use of force justified, while the other is an injurer and as such under his victim's jurisdiction and enforcement power. The doctrine of *ius in bello* in just wars establishes the terms under which the vindication of rights can permissibly take place during and through war. In principle only those who directly contribute to the wrong that justifies the war can be targeted, either because they are personally guilty for the wrong or because they contribute to sustain a wrongful state of affairs. Only military actions necessary to vindicate the right are permissible, and any action necessary is justified. Actions that go beyond what is necessary for vindication are unlawful and sinful.

Wolff and Vattel rejected this account of *ius in bello* in just wars, objecting in particular to the unequal standing of belligerents and to the use of individual guilt as a criterion for targeting and punishment. Their first objection was drawn formally as a logical implication of the principle of sovereign equality. As Wolff reasoned, no sovereign could pretend to have the authority to stand as judge of another because all states must be regarded as legal equals, even if from the standpoint of natural law and before the eyes of God, at most one side can be truly just in war. This is the very problem of partiality that the Spanish scholastics recognized but dismissed. For Wolff the problem was serious enough to merit a fundamental revision of the scholastic account of *ius in bello*, even though he shared their view that from the standpoint of natural law and before God at most one side could be just (§888). As he wrote,

> it would be absurd for an enemy to be appointed judge in his own case, who, since he would not confess that his cause of war is unjust, would declare all force used against him illegal. The question as to the abuse of law in war would always be in dispute between belligerents; therefore the decision cannot be entrusted to that one of the contesting parties who complains of the abuse. This would be the same as if anyone should wish to claim for the plaintiff the decision of a case in court, a thing which any one recognizes is absurd.[6]

[6] JG §783, 404–5.

Additionally, Wolff and Vattel offered prudential reasons against giving asymmetrical status to sovereigns at war. For Wolff, strict adherence to the imperatives of natural law and corrective justice during hostilities would multiply the occasions for dispute and conflict, without providing any viable means of resolution. If punishment were allowed and a just belligerent became excessively punitive, then legal remedies would have to be made available to the other side. Likewise, if the just side used force disproportionately, the unjust side should be allowed to use counterforce. This, however, would only create countless disputes over *in bello* rights and duties:

> the rights of belligerents are so involved with their underlying causes, that they cannot be untangled by anyone, even if an arbiter should especially be appointed, much less without a judge or arbiter, such as nations free by nature are not bound to recognize. Since a natural obligation cannot be extended beyond what is possible, necessity itself demands that as regards the results arising from warlike acts the war should be considered as just on the part of each belligerent.[7]

The attempt to directly apply natural law and corrective justice during hostilities would undermine the moral imperative of "ending difficulties between nations and terminating suits."[8] The laws of war should facilitate, not obstruct, the termination of war, and to do so, they must help reduce, not multiply, the occasions for dispute during war.

Vattel added to this line of argument that giving asymmetrical legal standing to belligerents would not only multiply the occasions for conflict, but also unleash an escalation in the violence in such disputes:

> each party asserting that they have justice on their own side, will arrogate to themselves all the rights of war, and maintain that their enemy has none, that his hostilities are so many acts of robbery, so many infractions of the law of nations, in the punishment of which all states should unite . . . the quarrel will become more bloody, more calamitous in its effects, and also more difficult to terminate.[9]

[7] JG §892, 457.
[8] JG §887, 454.
[9] III.188, 589.

In the absence of a higher authority that could settle disputes and enforce its determinations, it would be reckless to make belligerent rights conditional on the justice of resort. Unless war is "accounted just on both sides," he wrote, it would be impossible to "introduce any order, any regularity, into so violent an operation as that of arms."[10] Effective regulation requires that enemies at war recognize each other as equally entitled and accountable before the law of nations.

For all these reasons, the aspiration to directly apply natural law and corrective justice to the regulation of hostilities must be given up. A more feasible and compelling aspiration is to limit the antagonism of war and facilitate its termination.[11] Along these lines, Wolff and Vattel claimed that the doctrine of *ius in bello* in regular wars could be seen as the bilateral application of the *ius in bello* of just wars. This is misleading, however, because they both rejected the use of punishment for *ad bellum* wrongs.[12] Among nations disputing their rights in war, wrote Wolff, "there is no place for penalties . . . such as are inflicted in a state by the sovereign upon those committing a crime" (an important exception is the violation of the laws of war, on which more below in section 4.4).[13] Belligerent states cannot claim that their enemy "deserves punishment for the killing of our citizens and the wasting of our property," nor can they treat lawful enemies as murderers or robbers, even when they objectively lack a just cause.[14]

The doctrine of *ius in bello* in regular wars can be described as a bilateral application of the rules of just war only in the sense that it usually operates under the assumption that each side in war is legitimately pursuing its own rights. In practice, the rights and obligations that belong properly to a condition of war do not depend on the justice of the cause but only on "the legality of the means themselves, that is, on every thing requisite to constitute a regular war."[15] As long as one's enemy has sovereign status and complies with the rules of regular warfare, there is no basis for complaint or punishment against its agents.

[10] LN III.190, 591.

[11] Wolff in JG §892. An associated and more famous principle appears as the sixth preliminary article in Kant's *Perpetual Peace*, according to which "no state at war with another shall permit such acts of hostility as would make mutual confidence impossible during a future time of peace" (Kant and Reiss 1970, 96). Kant had in mind the use of "dishonorable stratagems," such as the use of poison, covert assassins, and instigation of treason, which were also deemed unlawful by regular war theorists.

[12] JG §890; LN III.191.

[13] JG §789, 408, also §§814, 823.

[14] JG §804, 416. It was by no means rare to kill prisoners of war in the fifteenth and sixteenth centuries on charges of treason, rebellion, or *lèse-majesté*, i.e., for violations of *ius ad bellum* (Contamine 2000, 167–8). Still as late as 1680, the Grotian publicist Johann Wolfgang Textor held that the "authors or instigators of the [unjust] war" could and should be punished, "so that at times some greater protection might be afforded to public peace" (Textor and Bate 1916 [1680], 188). This rationale had all but disappeared by the mid-eighteenth century.

[15] Vattel in LN III.190, 591

4.2 Regulars, irregulars, barbarians

Arguably the most important principle for realizing ideals of limitation in regular war is to allow the use of military force only to designated combatants and to restrict its use only against designated persons and objects, as narrowly and clearly defined as feasible. Historically, the limit case of this form of "convention" is single combat, in which two designated combatants fight each other under mutually agreed conditions, and whoever wins gets to decide the stakes.[16] To the same class belongs the convention in virtue of which only regular forces get to engage in hostilities—armed forces which are created, trained, and maintained under the direct command of a sovereign ruler—and can permissibly use force only against a limited set of targets. Rousseau's famous passage in *On the Social Contract*, where he circumscribed enmity in war to those who bear arms, belongs to a similar limiting project.[17]

In *De iure belli ac pacis* Grotius discussed and rejected the practice of single combat in ancient Greece and medieval warfare. While this could be a valuable way to avoid afflicting "whole peoples with very serious evils," he argued, it was inconsistent with fundamental principles of just war.[18] To decide disputes through single combat could not quite match the seriousness of just warfare. Furthermore, it would be wrong for combatants to risk their lives in what was essentially a game, all the more so "if the issue at stake, such as the safety of many innocent persons, is worthy of war." In such cases, he argued, "we must strive with all strength to win it" rather than agree to the haphazard procedure of single combat.[19] On the other hand, Grotius's account of solemn war contains virtually no legal restrictions on the use of force, as we saw in Chapter 2. As far as the external law of nations is concerned, in solemn wars any subject of a belligerent state can use force against any enemy subject.

By contrast, Wolff and Vattel condemned the permissiveness of solemn wars and defended limiting principles.[20] In an eloquent statement of the limited war ideal, Vattel wrote in *The Law of Nations* that,

[16] The use of the term "convention" here comes from Mavrodes 1975 and more famously Walzer 1977, 44–7. Mavrodes offers a philosophical defense of something very close to the ideal of limitation in regular wars. For a recent philosophical defense of these "deadly serious conventions," see Waldron 2010.

[17] As Rousseau wrote in *On the Social Contract*, "since the aim of the war is the destruction of the enemy state, one has the right over its defenders as long as they bear arms; but as soon as they lay down their arms and surrender, they cease to be enemies or the enemy's instruments, and become simply men once more, and one no longer has a right over their lives" (SC I.iv, 47).

[18] RWP II.xxiii.10, 563.

[19] RWP III.xx.43, 821.

[20] JG §792; LN III.140.

> should two nations encounter each other with the collective weight of their whole force, the war would become much more bloody and destructive, and could hardly be terminated otherwise than by the utter extinction of one of the parties . . . It is therefore with good reason that the contrary practice has grown into a custom with the nations of Europe —at least with those that keep up regular standing armies or bodies of militia. The troops alone carry on the war, while the rest of the nation remain in peace. And the necessity of a special order to act is so thoroughly established, that, even after a declaration of war between two nations, if the peasants of themselves commit any hostilities, the enemy shews them no mercy, but hangs them up as he would so many robbers or banditti.[21]

The form of limited war which Vattel advocates is not single combat but rather the use of regular troops or well-disciplined militia, which can act as reliable instruments of sovereign rulers. They can be deployed according to the limited directives of reason of state and sound state policy, and within the channels defined by the law of nations.[22] Vattel repeatedly exhorted rulers to train and discipline their forces. Soldiers and designated auxiliaries are "instruments which [the sovereign] employs in asserting his right," and only when effectively under sovereign control could they wage limited wars.[23] As Wolff pointed out, while in actual practice "warlike operations (*operationes vero bellicae*) are not restricted to warlike force (*vim bellica*), for force is not used against the enemy in all cases," the rules of regular war nonetheless aspire to restrict as much as feasible warlike operations to warlike forces.[24]

The Enlightenment approach to the project of limited war begins with the principle established by Grotius in his theory of solemn war (see above, section 2.3): only sovereign states can have belligerent privileges. Wolff held that

[21] III.226, 613.

[22] For an illuminating contemporary discussion of the "channeling" function of the laws of war, see Berman 2004. As Berman points out, the laws of war cannot deal solely with the limitation violence, but must also construct and channel its use "into certain forms of activity engaged in by certain kinds of people, while excluding other forms engaged in by other people" (Berman 2004, 5). This is equally valid for the contemporary law of armed conflict and the laws of regular war.

[23] LN III.164, 568, and see III.231 on the fundamental importance of strict hierarchy within a state's military apparatus. G. F. von Martens systematically documented and defended the use of regular forces and noted that the laws of war "have been observed with greater punctuality since war has been carried on by the means of regular troops" (Martens and Cobbett 1795, VIII.3.1, 279).Vattel's model may have been Frederick II of Prussia, whose army famously operated like the works of a watch, "the wheels of which by artful gearing produce an exact and regular movement" (Robson 1966, 176). On the crucial importance of discipline and sovereign control for the legitimacy of armed force during the Enlightenment, see further Scheipers 2015, 51–3.

[24] JG §784, 405.

private agents should never be allowed to take the initiative to use "offensive force" because this ran contrary to the imperatives of reason of state.[25] In his words,

> Reasons of state (*ratio civilis*) stand in the way of allowing any chance individual to arm ships, on account of the abuse readily to be apprehended, since, influenced by the desire for gain, they may attack friends or those who are not enemies . . . and it is always a dangerous thing for anything to be done in war under private auspices.[26]

To prevent the abuse of military power, only force authorized and overseen by sovereign powers should be recognized as lawful.

Regular war at its most limited involves regular troops or well-disciplined militia as the sole agents of violence. Regular troops were expected to follow the conventions of pitched battles; conduct orderly requisitions among peasants and town-dwellers; allow for negotiated capitulations during sieges; respect the immunity of prisoners of war; respect neutral trade; and submit to the stipulations of peace treaties.[27] These limiting practices were certainly indebted to Old Regime aristocratic culture and the pressures of social standing, as historians have often noted, but Wolff and Vattel were keen to give them a rational foundation in the theory of state authority.[28]

Historically, aristocratic codes of conduct in war evolved not from state laws or the law of nations, but rather within a more or less independent and self-contained professional ethos, which got its legal articulation already in late medieval times from pan-Europeanist civil jurists.[29] Wolff and Vattel criticized the vanity and backwardness of such aristocratic codes of conduct and suggested ways to rationalize them. Wolff condemned the excessive worry for the "vanity of titles" in Prussia and argued that the higher "excellence" of a

[25] JG §§909–11, and similarly Vattel in LN III.223.

[26] JG §910, 467.

[27] For a historically rich discussion of the limiting effects of pitched battles in eighteenth-century European warfare, see Whitman 2012. This chapter shows that the principles of limited war applied beyond the convention on pitched battles.

[28] According to David Bell, aristocratic culture was pervaded by an "obsession with honor" that fits remarkably well with the *ius in bello* ethos of regular wars. Just as regular war theorists made *in bello* rights and obligations independent of the justice of the cause of war, honor was "more concerned with form, process, and appearance than with cause and right," which made it possible to "fight honorably for a bad cause or dishonorably for a good one" (Bell 2007, 50, 36). On the importance of aristocratic culture for eighteenth-century warfare, see further Howard 1979; Anderson 1988, 131–5; and cf. Whitman 2012, 12–15, 135–47.

[29] On the pan-European history of the legal articulation of the aristocratic warrior ethos, see Lesaffer 2007b, 197; Keen 1965, 19–22.

ruler over another was only "accidental," and could not alter the equal honor of *being* a sovereign. True honor or "renown" depends on the quality of political rule, not on the "excellence" of title.[30] Vattel condemned in particular aristocratic dueling for being socially destructive and manifesting misplaced and archaic notions of honor. He proposed the creation of a special criminal jurisdiction to oversee and rationalize dueling: states should regulate injuries to one's good name, just as it did for private property.[31]

Rather than frame the laws of regular warfare in terms of Aristocratic honor and virtue, they sought to subject long-standing chivalric and aristocratic codes of conduct to the disciplining force of centralized statehood and reason of state. In their accounts of regular forces, the rationality of legal limitations are emphasized, and long-standing customary protections that used to apply only to the warrior nobility are extended to all regular soldiers.

The faith of these Enlightenment theorists of the law of nations on the limiting power of well-disciplined and rationally organized regular armies stands in marked contrast to the positions of other Enlightenment figures, including Montesquieu, Rousseau, and Kant, who feared that the growing power of regular troops would cause the whole enterprise of limited war to collapse. Montesquieu deemed the spread and growth of regular troops in Europe a "contagious disease" that would eventually lead to the "common ruin" of Europe.[32] Rather than embodying a form of limited war, regular troops were threats that would force all states to follow suit and invest heavily on regular armies. Most alarmingly for Rousseau, regular troops were "the plague and depopulators of Europe," "good for only two purposes, to attack and conquer neighbors, or to shackle and enslave citizens."[33] The worry of these Enlightenment thinkers is that the power unleashed by well-trained and disciplined regular troops, and the strategic dynamic of arms races and security dilemmas, would cause military life to spill over uncontrollably into all areas of society and eat away economic production and trade.

This was neither Wolff's nor Vattel's (nor Marten's) worry. Well-trained and disciplined citizen militia could well substitute for regular armies as apt

30 JG §§249–50.

31 I.176.

32 Montesquieu et al. 1989 [1748], XIII.17, 224–5.

33 Rousseau in "Considerations on the Government of Poland" (Rousseau and Gourevitch 1997, 232–239). His advice to Polish republicans was to set up citizen militia following the Swiss model, instead of investing in a regular army and attempting to fight their surrounding great powers. Kant famously called for the abolition of standing armies in *Perpetual Peace*, as "they constantly threaten other states with war by the very fact that they are always prepared for it." Instead of regular standing armies, states should create and regularly train voluntary citizen militia (Kant and Reiss 1970, 94). Also Vattel suggested that a republican citizen militia, like the Swiss, was a model to follow by all states (III.50).

embodiments of ideals of limited war, and presumably states would not be so foolish as to allow themselves to collapse under the weight of their own regular armies. More troubling to them was the temptation of states to enlist all sorts of poorly trained and undisciplined irregulars to oppose their enemies, as a result of which war would fall into brigandage, unbridled cruelty, and wasteful brutality. Vattel noted that in the practice of European warfare, authorizations to use force were usually confined to regular troops, but conceded that sovereign rulers could also authorize irregulars to fight their wars—in fact they often did—and it was their sovereign prerogative to do so.[34] Privateers, resisters to occupation, partisans, and civil warriors could all lawfully use force if authorized explicitly or implicitly by their rulers.[35]

It is somewhat odd that neither Wolff nor Vattel deemed unlawful the use of irregulars by states, but they were pragmatic enough to realize that this would be an over-demanding legal requirement. It would not only diverge too widely from the actual practices of state violence, but also contradict the deference to state authority they were so keen to defend. Their position reflected a rather formidable strategic obstacle for the project of limited war, as enlisting irregulars could be tactically advantageous for states but also lead to the unraveling of limitations. States may share long-term interests in limiting the destructiveness of war, but they also have narrower, short-term interests in resorting to irregulars and half-organized citizen militia to oppose their enemies. Correspondingly, the standing of irregulars in the law of nations, and in particular the determination of how they may or should be treated in war, has been perhaps the most heatedly disputed element in the construction of the modern laws of war.[36]

In the eighteenth century, officers in regular armies often relied on irregulars because of their high mobility, efficiency, and ferocity. Irregular troops were often seen as an indispensable complement to regular armed forces, both in intra-European and colonial wars. During the Seven Years War, France and Britain recruited—or rather brought as allies—American Indian tribes to fight in North America. Arguably France would have fared much worse than it did in the war without its American Indian allies, but irregular warriors were barely under effective French command and rarely played by the rules of

[34] III.228; also Wolff in JG §911.

[35] LN III.224–9, III.292.

[36] See Benvenisti and Lustig 2020; Scheipers 2015, 99–102; Best 1980, 156–7. The figure of the irregular does not entail the negation of regular war principles but rather results from the complex strategic practices associated with these principles. Contrast in this respect Carl Schmitt's commentary in his theory of the partisan, which treats irregulars as an anomaly and contradiction for the Enlightenment theory of regular war (Schmitt 2007 [1963], 6, 24, *passim*; Schmitt 2003, 152–71).

regular warfare.[37] The Russians likewise brought Cossack, Tartar, and Kalmyk fighters to the War. They were deployed against other irregular forces—Poles, Turks, Tartars—but also against European regular forces and noncombatants. They attacked and preyed upon Prussian farmers and townspeople for their resistance and refusal to give supplies.[38]

In response to this conundrum—the aspiration to articulate and defend the project of limited war while at the same time deferring to the state practice of resorting to irregulars—Vattel distinguished three types of agents of violence: regular forces, authorized irregulars, and non-authorized irregulars. Different legal norms apply to each, but the overall orientation of this threefold distinction is to favor and privilege regularity.

Regular forces and *state militia*, as we have already seen, enjoyed distinct privileges. Once they surrendered, they could not be killed nor harmed deliberately. They could be held as prisoners and exchanged for ransom, but they were immune to punishment, except possibly for serious violations of the rules of regular warfare, and only when this clearly served a deterring purpose.[39]

Authorized irregulars, on the other hand, are agents of violence that are neither regular troops nor trained militia but are commissioned (explicitly or implicitly) by the sovereign to engage in hostilities. The most important case is that of "partisans," which Vattel discussed in the context of foreign occupations.[40] In the case of spontaneous uprisings against occupying powers, which in general could be presumed to be authorized by the displaced sovereign, "if the peasants of themselves commit any hostilities," then "the enemy . . . hangs them up as he would so many robbers or banditti."[41] Organized resistance to foreign

[37] Steele 1990; Ward 2012; Witt 2012, 88–93. The famous massacre of Fort William Henry in 1757 occurred after North American Indian fighters did not comply with the regular procedure of capitulation in sieges. In his offer of capitulation to the British garrison, the French commander declared that, "I have it yet in my power to restrain the savages, and oblige them to observe a capitulation, as hitherto none of them has been killed, which will not be in my power in other circumstances." It is unclear whether he ever had such power, as the turn of events revealed (Steele 1990, 99, 84–90, 110–23). The mythology of American Indian savagery that sprang from this event contributed later to justify the unlimited massacring of American Indian tribes.

[38] Prussian officers advised their Russian counterparts that permitting such destruction would ultimately be self-defeating and only cause a degradation of the war, which it eventually did in Eastern Prussia. Whether Russian officers could have controlled the irregulars is an open question; they may have been more a strategic liability than an asset (Füssel 2012).

[39] LN III.140–1, III.149.

[40] The term "partisan" appears in III.224, 612. Arguably privateers are another case of authorized irregulars, but Vattel treated them essentially as regular forces. Privateers are private agents authorized by a ruler to "[fit] out private ships to cruise against the enemy" in naval warfare (III.229, 614). They operated as *ad hoc* navies for states lacking strong standing navies. In addition to the right to use force, Vattel recognized the right in privateers to capture enemy goods and persons, and immunity to punishment (see respectively III.132 and III.229).

[41] LN III.226, 613.

occupation was legally permissible, but the occupier had a right to "call in the aid of terror to a certain degree" against those who resisted.[42] Martens similarly held that citizen militia could permissibly be treated more harshly than standing troops, notably denied prisoners of war privileges, as this was the only way to achieve the ideal of war as a contest between regular forces.[43]

Paradoxically, then, given their adherence to the project of limited war and deference to state authority, Vattel and Martens held that in order to preserve the limitations of regular war, authorized irregulars could be counteracted by "very severe treatment from the enemy," a treatment that exceeded what was lawful among regular forces, and could eventually exceed virtually all limitations. In the case of belligerent occupations, since both irregular resistance to occupation and terror to suppress it were lawful, violence could escalate out of all bounds, without there being any actual breaches of law nor legal mechanisms that contributed to restoring limitations.[44]

Unauthorized irregulars, finally, are agents of violence that lack authorization from a sovereign. They include "predatory expeditions" and "armies of banditti," the sole purpose of which is to obtain "spoil and plunder" during land warfare, as well as pirates and buccaneers in naval wars.[45] Properly speaking, the violence caused by non-authorized irregulars is not part of hostilities but rather constitutes "depredations," lacking as it does any right or apparent cause, and consequently any lawful effects. A nation attacked by such enemies is under no obligation to observe the rules of regular warfare, on the contrary, should treat them as criminals and punish them harshly.[46]

In addition to bandits and pirates, Vattel included in the class of unauthorized irregulars "barbarians" and "savage nations" (*nations féroces*), in particular the expeditions of "Barbary corsairs," the "nation of the Usbecks," the Turks and Tartars, Genghis-khan, and Tamerlane.[47] While in some cases such irregulars could formally be presented as privateers under commission of their

[42] LN III.228, 614.

[43] Martens 1801, 271.

[44] On the specific challenges of governing belligerent occupations in the eighteenth and nineteenth centuries, see Nabulsi 1999, 19–65.

[45] LN III.67, 507.

[46] LN III.68, 508.

[47] See respectively III.141, III.67, II.78, III.34. Wolff did not discuss what kind of violence was permissible against barbarians, but he did note that nations have an obligation to cultivate themselves and become civilized (JG §§52–7). Vattel's position here was in fact novel. As Walter Rech has shown, his treatment of the Barbary states was inconsistent both with customary practice and with the bulk of authors in the modern tradition of the law of nations, including Bodin, Grotius, Pufendorf, Samuel von Cocceji, and Bynkershoek (Rech 2013, 46–7, 112–25).

rulers, in fact they always lacked any presentable cause or pretext to justify their actions, and could safely be presumed to have no other motive than "the lust of plunder."[48] For Vattel, the irregularity of savage nations consists both in their failure to observe the rules of warfare and in their lack of genuine authorization, which results from their lack of proper war declarations and plausible reasons for war.

By far the most extensive breakdown of limitations in Vattel's account of regular war came when dealing with these "savage" or "barbarian" agents of violence, against whom he defended the harshest possible forms of treatment. Having made the point that punishment and the use of punitive language in regular wars should in general be minimized, he made an exception for the case of "savages" and "barbarians," who could be permissibly denied quarter and indiscriminately bombed as form of collective punishment:

> When we are at war with a savage nation, who observe no rules, and never give quarter, we may punish them in the persons of any of their people whom we take (these belonging to the number of the guilty), and endeavor, by this rigorous proceeding, to force them to respect the laws of humanity.[49]

Savagery for Vattel justifies the punitive targeting of any enemy subject, regardless of his capacity and will to use force, or his responsibility in a violation of the laws of war.

In these cases, there appears to be at least some expectation that vicarious punishment could motivate the "savage nation" to eventually abide by the laws of war. In other cases not even that seems tenable. Vattel argued that in the case of "African sea towns" (*villes maritimes de l'Afrique*), it was permissible to "totally ravage a country," to sack towns and villages, and deliver them to "fire and sword." Nobody would deny to Spain and Italy the right to "utterly destroy" such barbarous nations—"those nests of pirates, that are continually molesting their commerce and ruining their subjects." The object of state violence in such limit cases is extermination, not punishment or reformation toward civilized statehood and rule compliance.[50]

[48] III.67, 507.
[49] III.141, 544, and against the use of punishment and punitive language in regular wars, see III.141, III.162, III.173.
[50] III.167, 570.

4.3 Immunity of noncombatants and neutrals

It may be somewhat misleading and anachronistic to speak of "noncombatants" in the context of the laws of war in the eighteenth century. Wolff and Vattel were far from the contemporary humanitarian legal principle of distinction and its associated mandate to take all feasible measures to keep civilians and protected objects out of hostilities. However, they did distinguish legally between those who actively engaged in hostilities and those who did not, and articulated various legal protections for the latter. For present purposes, noncombatants may be defined with Wolff as those who "refrain from all violence, and do not show an intention to use force" during war.[51] Combatants, on the other hand, are those who use or are ready to use force.

Arguing against Grotius's theory of solemn war, Wolff held that "the right against persons in war is not the right of the promiscuous slaughter of those who are in the category of enemies." In particular, those too young to bear arms, "children, boys, girls, those weakened by age, the sick, those who are weak, bodily or mentally," as well as soldiers who surrender and depose arms, cannot be attacked.[52] What makes enemies legitimate targets is their will and capacity to resist one's prosecution of one's right through war. When no resistance is to be expected, no right to use force exists.[53]

If the ideals of limitation in regular war were perfectly put into practice, noncombatants would be free to continue their everyday lives undisturbed, as hostilities would take place only among regular forces. Vattel's evocation of this ideal is worth quoting in full:

> at present, war is carried on by regular troops: the people, the peasants, the citizens, take no part in it, and generally have nothing to fear from the sword of the enemy. Provided the inhabitants submit to him who is master of the country, pay the contributions imposed, and refrain from all hostilities, they live in as perfect safety as if they were friends: they even continue in possession of what belongs to them: the country people come freely to the camp to sell their provisions, and are protected, as far as possible, from the calamities of war. A laudable custom, truly worthy of those nations who value themselves on their humanity, and advantageous even to the enemy who acts with

[51] JG §792, 409; similarly Vattel in LN III.140.

[52] JG §792, 409--10, §795; likewise Vattel in LN III.140, III.143.

[53] Grotius was mistaken when he attributed to the external law of nations the permission to kill indiscriminately. Such practices, Wolff argued, belong rather to the customary laws of barbarous nations, are unlawful, and must cease (JG §793).

> such moderation. By protecting the unarmed inhabitants, keeping the soldiery under strict discipline, and preserving the country, a general procures an easy subsistence for his army, and avoids many evils and dangers.[54]

In reality, in the eighteenth century the two key provisos on which this ideal state of affairs depends—submitting to an occupying power and paying contributions—were often unmet in practice, as Vattel knew well. As a result, the limitations of regular war broke down, often in ways that the laws of regular war were unfit to contain. And yet this passage reveals eloquently both the fragility and the strategic logic behind the immunity of noncombatants. Before discussing how this immunity played out in three war contexts—sieges, property requisitions, and neutrality—it is important to be clear on how it differs from the contemporary principle of civilian protection.

Like Grotius in the case of solemn wars, Wolff and Vattel held that all subjects of enemy states are themselves enemies. They may not be deliberately attacked, but their property and food stock could be deliberately destroyed as a means of weakening enemy forces.[55] They could also be taken hostages and held for ransom in exchange for money or political concessions.[56] They could also be starved to death during sieges because, as Vattel put it, "if there are hopes of reducing by famine a strong place of which it is very important to gain possession, the useless mouths are not permitted to come out."[57] Furthermore, the bombing of "whole towns," not just of their "ramparts and defenses," was permissible in virtue of military necessity or as a form of reprisal.[58]

However, even though entire populations could be permissibly "terrorized" during war in these and other ways, it was categorically prohibited to do so by rape or by killing those already under enemy control. Furthermore, when no military setback was to be expected from an enemy, his life had to be respected.[59] In addition to these general prohibitions, Vattel and Wolff discussed other areas of regular warfare in which restrictions protective of noncombatants applied.

In the case of *sieges*, the laws prior to the eighteenth century were extremely harsh for noncombatants. Once the siege works were set, or artillery fired, capitulations offered did not have to be accepted, and if the town was taken,

54 III.147, 550–1.

55 JG §§725–6, 824, 830; LN III.69–77.

56 JG §§811–13; LN III.148; Martens 1801, 424–6. For the history of the practice of ransoming in eighteenth-century warfare, see Contamine 2000.

57 III.148, 551.

58 LN III.169, 572.

59 JG §§792, 802, 876; LN III.148.

the lives and property of all town dwellers, along with the garrisons, were at the besiegers' disposal.[60] In the eighteenth century, Vattel observed, siege war had become more "prudent and humane" in Europe, as more restrictive rules progressively became customary.[61] Besiegers had an obligation to offer or accept reasonable terms of capitulation at all times, and had to abstain from killing or harming noncombatants if the town was stormed, except possibly as punishment for violations of the laws of warfare. Once a town was taken, it was not at the discretion or mercy of the occupying force, as it used to be in earlier practice.[62]

The strategic logic behind these constraints is simple yet powerful. Rather than forcing towns to hold out until the bitter end—if you will be killed or worse, you might as well be killed while fighting—a conventional procedure was made available to commanders through which, upon assessment of the tactical value of further resistance, agreements on capitulation could be reached. This avoided the complete destruction of besieged cities and the unnecessary waste of military resources.[63] And while norms on capitulation had protective and humane effects, these were not the driving force in Vattel's presentation, as his validation of starving and harsh reprisals against noncombatants reveals.

An analogous economy of violence can be found in Vattel's discussion of the regulation of *requisitions of private property* during war. In this case, the relevant historical background is the long-standing principle according to which all enemy property could be freely captured. As we saw in Chapter 2, Grotius registered this principle in his discussion of solemn warfare when he held that enemy nations could treat each other's property and territory as *res nullius*. Vattel did not flatly reject this nullification principle, but introduced some restrictions.[64] He echoed the evolving practice of requesting contributions in centralized and disciplined fashion, instead of pillaging at each commander's discretion. He deemed the practice of Louis XIV a "very commendable" instance of "humanity and moderation," as the king's competent administrators

[60] Keen 1965, 119–33, Lesaffer 2007b, 177–83.

[61] III.143, 548; JG §825.

[62] Vattel condemned the use of punitive force for "obstinate defense" during sieges (III.143). In eighteenth-century practice, sometimes the besieging army actually paid honors to the surrendering force for their brave resistance (Robson 1966, 167–8; Steele 1990, 109–10).

[63] LN III.147. The logic applies to all forms of surrender, not only in sieges. During the American Independence War, "the fact that every American soldier could legally be hanged as a traitor to his king surely induced some Americans to fight harder and longer" (Selesky 1994, 76). The flip side of capitulation procedures in siege war is that commanders could be tempted to surrender too easily, in response to which states implemented domestic regulation punishing treason (Lesaffer 2007, 188–90).

[64] III.161, III.173; similarly Martens 1801, 412–13, and Wolff in JG §856. Grotius discusses *res nullius* in RWP III.vi.8.

brought the exploitation of enemy villagers to unprecedented levels of efficiency.[65]

The strategic logic behind Vattel's proposal of limited requisitions is again straightforward. Instead of pillaging indiscriminately, each belligerent should negotiate "contribution treaties" in enemy territory, which stipulate sustainable amounts to be paid in exchange for security and restraint. By so doing, the belligerent actor "obtains a part of what is due to him; and the enemy's subjects, by consenting to pay the sum demanded, have their property secured from pillage, and the country is preserved."[66] It was vital for regular forces that contributions be "supportable," as they were often forced to live off the land in occupied territories for long periods of time. The interest of belligerents to sustain their campaigns, and of peasants and villagers to minimize the harm they could suffer, underwrote the efficacy of contributions treaties.

Contribution treaties are creatures of the law of nations, and while not mandatory, they embodied sensible policy and had humanitarian effects. Humanity is again not central to Vattel's discussion. In the case of Louis XIV, Vattel knew well that it was not out of the king's heart that a system of sustainable contributions was set up. It was indispensable for France to secure a constant source of revenue, foodstuff, and forage to sustain his prolonged wars, which had the desirable effect that peasants and villagers were better off than when freebooting was allowed.[67]

For all its relative restraint, the practice of mandatory contributions was nonetheless brutal by any peacetime standards. Villages that failed to contribute were usually burned to the ground; security from pillaging by own or enemy forces was rarely guaranteed; and in the best possible case, money and goods were handed over to a foreign and hostile power under the threat of the harshest possible force. It was robbery indeed, as Rousseau denounced, if performed under the legitimizing mantle of the laws of war. Pillaging and requisitions also ran against the fundamental principle that war be left exclusively to regular forces designated by public powers, while the lives and

[65] The practice of rational requisitioning seems to have emerged during the Dutch Revolt against Spanish rule (Parker 2004, 120–3; Piceu 2014) but during the Thirty Years' War it became systematic, indeed the main source of revenue (Redlich 1959). Louis XIV and his ministers took the practice to unprecedented levels of administrative competence (Lynn 1993).

[66] LN III.165, 569.

[67] As John Lynn remarks, "for contributions to produce money reliably over time, they had to function like a well-evolved parasite and draw sustenance from the host, not kill it" (Lynn 1993, 297). In addition to enabling a system of centralized war taxation in foreign lands, the rationalization of pillage was also motivated by the need to keep discipline within the ranks and avoid desertions. Soldiers often left the army after a good "harvest," or could take advantage of being let loose to pillage in order to escape (Contamine 2000, 181–2; Robson 1966, 168–9).

property of private individuals are left out. According to Rousseau, allowing the taking of private property during war would amount to the degeneration of war into "brigandage," and the degradation of enemies and warriors into tyrants and thieves.[68] His remarks correspond to a more ambitious and demanding ideal of limited war, one which Vattel and Wolff did not find feasible enough to include in the law of nations. For all its horrors and instability, contribution treaties could be sustained in a self-enforcing equilibrium, and as such were a more viable instrument of limited warfare than Rousseau's general prohibition to take private property.[69]

Finally, there is the limiting regulation of the relationship between belligerents and *neutral states* during naval wars. The concept of neutrality, as was clear already in Grotius's discussion of solemn wars, was introduced in order to contain the spread of war to other countries and their commercial relations. A central objective of the laws of neutrality in regular wars was to set limits to hostilities so that, in Vattel's words, "the commerce of neutral nations may subsist in as great a degree of freedom as is consistent with the laws of war."[70]

In the interest of limiting war and respecting the commercial freedom of sovereign states, a privilege must be recognized in states to declare themselves neutral relative to an ongoing war.[71] Such declaration implies, on the one hand, an obligation in neutrals to behave impartially vis-à-vis belligerents, in particular to abstain from giving any assistance that would directly advance their war efforts, notably carrying weapons and other war materials. On the other hand, belligerents have an obligation to keep their hostilities outside of neutral territory, persons, and goods, and to leave undisturbed commerce in non-military goods. When the status of neutrality works, neutrals can "make the advantage of the state still serve as her rule of conduct in her negotiations, her friendly connections, and her commerce," while belligerents go on fighting their war.[72]

Underlying this fundamental bargain there is, again, a tension between general long-term interests and particular short-term interests. Generally

[68] "The State of War" in Rousseau and Gourevitch 1997, 175.

[69] On the contrasting views of Rousseau and Vattel on this matter, see further Best 1980, 55–67. Rousseau's principle is reflected in the contemporary law of armed conflict, which considers pillaging and wanton destruction of private property international crimes. The only object of lawful taking during war is now military equipment and public property that could be used for military purposes. The one aspect in which contemporary law retains a trace of the old contributions regime is in the permissibility of "requisitions" or "contributions in kind and services" during belligerent occupations (Henckaerts and Doswald-Beck 2007, 173–85).

[70] LN III.111, 529; compare Grotius in RWP III.i.5.

[71] LN III.106.

[72] LN III.104, 524.

speaking, all states have an interest in preserving and strengthening commercial relations, and each has an interest in having the power to effectively declare its territory off limits for the conduct of hostilities in a foreign war. Short-term, however, belligerents have an interest in depriving their enemy "of every thing which may enable her to resist or injure," in particular to block access to any form of commerce, while themselves enjoying full access to foreign trade.[73] Neutral states, on the other hand, have an interest in maximizing the profits of their trade, in particular by shipping highly priced goods that sustain the belligerents' war efforts. Not only are these short-term interests of neutrals and belligerents in conflict with the long-term interests of all states, but they are also in conflict between themselves. A belligerent's first preference is to block all trade with its enemy and have full trade for itself, while a neutral's first preference is to engage in all sorts of trade with belligerents, as wars typically brought large increases in freight and commercial rates.[74]

Against the background of these conflicting interests, Vattel introduced a series of rules. It is imperative to distinguish clearly between trade in "ordinary goods" and "contraband goods," which are "particularly subservient to war," including "arms, ammunition, timber for ship-building, every kind of naval stores, horses."[75] Belligerents have a right to inspect all ships leaving or going to enemy ports, and to capture all enemy property and contraband in neutral ships. On the other hand, neutral goods found in enemy ships had to be returned to their owners, as well as neutral ships even if they carried enemy goods.[76]

Other norms were possible, and Vattel's were in fact harsher against neutrals than the rules that crystallized around 1780. The latter were the rules associated with the principle of "free ships, free goods," which mandated that both enemy and non-enemy goods on board of neutral ships be immune from taking, except if they were contraband. Sometimes the harsher policy of "enemy goods, enemy ships" was followed, which meant that neutral ships carrying enemy goods were captured along with all their cargo (this was Napoleon's policy). In the eighteenth and early nineteenth centuries, the cooperative norm of "free ships, free goods" often collapsed into the non-cooperative rule of "enemy goods, enemy ships," or into a complete interdiction of trade by the great sea

[73] LN III.111, 528.
[74] For some striking estimates, see Kulsrud 1936, 322–3.
[75] III.112, 529–30.
[76] III.113–16.

powers, in which case wars ended up extensively undermining the flow of commercial goods.[77]

The legal restrictions associated with neutral status could unravel when the naval power of one of the belligerents ended up overriding the rights of neutrals, or when the conflict between neutrals and belligerents itself became violent. This was the case of the "armed neutralities" of the eighteenth and nineteenth centuries, in which armed convoys escorting fleets of traders came themselves to the brink of, or into war.[78] If a belligerent targeted a neutral trader doing legitimate trade, this could lead to a boycott and consequent reduction of his access to goods, which in turn could eventually drag the neutral state into war. Alternatively, if a belligerent took an expansive policy against neutral trade with its enemy, this could undercut both the rights of neutral traders and the credibility of the neutrality regime as a whole.

In the nineteenth century, an important factor in the unraveling of the limitations of neutrality was the unequal distribution of power among European states, particularly the British and Dutch hegemony on the seas. Claims of neutral rights to maritime trade were most often raised against them by weaker states, but the inequality of naval power made the use of retaliatory enforcement difficult or ineffective. The best chance of defense for weaker neutrals was to set up "neutrality alliances," but they were plagued with collective action problems. Nonetheless, neutrality alliances were sometimes effective, and neutral rights against belligerents successfully upheld with defensive force short of war.[79] Retaliatory measures were applied in defense of neutral rights, including

[77] The free ships, free goods principle governed the various treaties of friendship negotiated by Benjamin Franklin and several European powers at the end of the eighteenth century (Witt 2012, 44–6). Agreement on the 1780 norm was short-lived, as the sieges undertaken by the British during the Napoleonic Wars shattered virtually all respect for neutral commerce. The legal status of neutrality was reinstated on a firmer footing after 1814 and strengthened later on (Grewe 2000, 381–4; Best 1980, 99–100). According to Best, "the prolonged and bitter controversies that marked the development of the law of war at sea from the middle of the eighteenth century well into the twentieth century were more on account of rights of neutrals than anything else" (Best 1980, 70).

[78] Kulsrud 1936, 309–10. The 1812–1814 war between the British navy and the United States was fought over neutrals' rights. According to Best, "it was a vicious little war, with enough instances of misconduct and destruction early committed by both sides to set going a nasty spiral of vindictive reprisals as there has ever been" (Best 1980, 111; and see further Witt 2012, 59–66).

[79] The most famous neutrality alliance was made in 1780 by Russia, Denmark, and Sweden with the aim of protecting their neutral rights in the United States' war of independence, which had Britain on one side and France and Spain on the other as allies of the United States. According to Grewe, this alliance "formed a serious impediment to British naval warfare. During the entire period of the American Revolution the British were compelled to operate with greater caution and reserve vis-à-vis neutrals than had been the case in previous wars" (Grewe 2000, 386). France in particular had an interest in upholding neutral rights because of her own need of securing an inflow of basic goods from her colonies (Kulsrud 1936, 333–4).

the deployment of counter-blockades and the seizure of belligerent merchant ships in retaliation for belligerents' unlawful seizures.

Overall, however, the historical record in the eighteenth century is filled with shortsightedness, self-serving standards, and norm shifting.[80] The big profits that neutrals could reap from trade—particularly in contraband—as well as the tactical advantage of confiscating all ships carrying enemy goods, often proved too tempting for belligerent powers.[81]

4.4 Law enforcement

We saw in Chapter 1 that the distinctive orientation of the scholastic doctrine of *ius in bello* in just wars is to oversee the good moral conscience of rulers, soldiers, and others actively involved in a war. The efficacy of its norms is therefore tied to the individual religious aspiration to lead a Christian life and avoid mortal sin. Correspondingly, the priests and theologians who articulated the doctrine of just war or brought it into military practice took themselves to be custodians of the observance of the laws governing the conduct of just wars. Grotius's solemn wars, on the other hand, are eminently external and public affairs, and as such formally unmoored from matters of Christian good conscience and spiritual salvation, in fact contrary to them in multiple respects. And yet Grotius did not address the question of what mechanisms could underwrite the rules of conduct of solemn wars if not moral scruple.

Wolff and Vattel did discuss the motivational bases of compliance with the rules of regular warfare, as we have seen. In addition to enlightened state interests, they discussed both punishment for legal breaches and the use of what is now called belligerent reprisals. These disciplining mechanisms show the autonomy and systemic character of the legal regime governing the conduct of regular war, which contains not only first-order rules of conduct but also second-order rules for the enforcement of first-order rules.

[80] For instance, in 1691 Sweden and Denmark signed an alliance treaty with the purpose of enforcing the "free ships, free goods" rule against the seizure policies of England and France. In 1721, when Sweden and Denmark fought each other in the Great Northern War, Sweden announced that it would follow the rule of "enemy goods, enemy ship." Similarly, Russia followed a harsh policy against neutrals during the Seven Years' War (1756–1763) but later, as a member of the Armed Neutrality alliance of 1780, sought to defend a more protective status of neutrality. In 1793, in the context of its war against Napoleon, Russia returned to its 1756 anti-neutrality policies. As Kulsrud remarks of Sweden and Denmark, "their immediate commercial interests was their motive, not the advancement of international law" (Kulsrud 1936, 318, *passim*).

[81] Grewe 2000, 535–42.

Regular wars are in principle less punitive affairs than just wars. However, Wolff noted, punishment could be exacted in the context of regular wars when "special offenses" were committed by soldiers or noncombatants.[82] What these "special offenses" are Wolff did not fully spell out, but they include violations of the rules governing the conduct of regular war.

Ideally, punitive responses to violations of the laws of regular war should fall only on those directly responsible, but they could also be applied vicariously, as when villages or orchards were destroyed in response to offenses committed by the sovereign power.[83] Along similar lines, Vattel wrote that when the enemy "has been guilty of some enormous breach of the law of nations, and particularly when he has violated the laws of war," then quarter could be denied and capitulations during sieges refused.[84] In the extreme cases of a "savage nation, who observes no rules, and never gives quarter," any enemy individual could be the target of collective punishment.[85]

Vattel defended in general terms the use reprisals (*réprésailles*) as disciplining responses to legal breaches.[86] To make *ius in bello* legally actionable, he submitted, force that would normally be unlawful must be treated as permissible if used as a proportionate and disciplinary response to violations of the laws of war. In the case of prisoners of war,

> If the hostile general has, without any just reason, caused some prisoners to be hanged, we hang an equal number of his people, and of the same rank, notifying to him that we will continue thus to retaliate (*lui rendre ainsi la pareille*), for the purpose of obliging him to observe the laws of war. It is a dreadful extremity thus to condemn a prisoner to atone, by a miserable death, for his general's crime . . . Nevertheless, as a prince or his general has a right to sacrifice his enemies' lives to his own safety and that of his men, it appears that, if he has to do with an inhuman enemy who frequently commits such enormities, he is authorized to refuse quarter to some of the prisoners he takes, and to treat them as his people have been treated.[87]

82 JG §825, 427, §804.

83 JG §825; also Vattel in LN III.166–9. By contrast, Grotius included the proscription of vicarious punishment in his *temperamenta belli* on the grounds that "nature does not sanction retaliation except against those who have done wrong" (RWP III.xi.16, 741).

84 III.141, 544.

85 III.167, 570.

86 III.142. In his classic study of belligerent reprisals in international law, Frits Kalshoven dates their origin in international law to the nineteenth century, but they can be traced back at least to Vattel and Martens in the second half of the eighteenth century (cf. Kalshoven 2005, 4–5).

87 III.142, 545. The Dutch rebellion in the late sixteenth century provides an important historical precedent and illustration of this harsh logic (discussed by Vattel in III.140, 544n and Martens 1795, 283). In the United Provinces, the duke of Alba's initial policy was to deny quarter to rebel towns and

The strategic logic behind reprisals is transparent in this passage. All nations have an interest in protecting the lives of their soldiers, which directs them to consent to norms limiting the right to kill them. In the eighteenth century, professional soldiers were relatively scarce and expensive to recruit and train, and so generals did all they could to keep them alive.[88] The difficulty, however, is that while all nations can benefit from the immunity of war prisoners, each has an incentive to violate it—have its own soldiers protected while denying quarter or killing enemy captives—because eliminating trained soldiers is a straightforward way to weaken the enemy, plus keeping prisoners safe could be onerous for their keepers in the midst of war, as Vattel noted.[89] Reprisals are a mechanism to add weight to the general interest in preserving soldiers and to counter the short-term temptation to defect from the norm.

Vattel conceded that reprisals were a dreadful recourse. Non-threatening soldiers are killed on the basis of breaches for which they are blameless. Also noncombatants could suffer from reprisals in the form of denial of quarter in sieges and indiscriminate bombing of cities.[90] However, for the sake of own subjects' life and safety, which are undermined by enemy breaches of law, it is permissible to take collective measures against innocent enemies. The requirements of proportionality and public notification make it a disciplinary measure: reprisals are meant to signal to enemy officials the seriousness and cost of violations of the laws of war. Morally repugnant as they are, no alternative mechanism exists to enforce the legal constraints of regular enmity. Moreover, if belligerents are enlightened enough and capable of retaliating, they will eventually abstain from breaches and retaliation will never happen. To use game theoretical language, reprisals if effective are "off the equilibrium path."

Reprisals are nonetheless highly imperfect enforcement mechanisms. They could escalate into spirals of reprisals and counter-reprisals, either because of vindictiveness or because belligerents disagreed on the lawfulness of

hang all captured fighters. As warriors in both sides could expect to face each other at war repeatedly, Spain's unrestrained policy was successfully checked by reprisals. After the Dutch began responding in kind, prisoner exchanges became standard and even formalized in conventions that were subsequently reproduced in other wars (Parker 1994, 49–55). The shadow of reciprocity also sustained moderation toward prisoners during the American War of Independence, the Napoleonic Wars, and the German occupation of France during the Second World War (see respectively Selesky 1994, 82–4; Scheipers 2015, 42–6; Walzer 1977, 208–9).

[88] Bell 2007, 45–6; Howard 2001, 70–1.

[89] III.151.

[90] III.141, III.169. For contemporary moral and legal arguments condemning the use of reprisals, see Walzer 1977, 207–16; Kalshoven 2005, 43–4.

war actions. One party's lawful action is another's breach; consequently one side's lawful reprisal is another's breach, which in turn merits counter-reprisals. Vattel took this danger seriously and proposed to narrow down the scope of valid retaliation:

> [W]ith respect to hostilities against the enemy's person, the voluntary law of nations only prohibits those measures which are *in themselves unlawful and odious*, such as poisoning, assassination, treachery, the massacre of an enemy who has surrendered, and from whom we have nothing to fear . . . on the other hand, it permits or tolerates every act which in itself is naturally adapted to promote the object of the war, without considering whether such act of hostility was unnecessary, useless, or superfluous, in that particular instance, unless there be the clearest evidence to prove that an exception ought to have been made in the case in question.[91]

Only manifestly unlawful actions are suitable for the use of reprisals, that is, tactics and means of war that are categorically unlawful, "*totalement inadmissibles*" under all circumstances, and which as such cannot be justified by appeal to military necessity.[92] For virtually all other acts of war—indiscriminate bombing of towns, denial of capitulation during sieges—military necessity could be offered as justification. In effect, Vattel distinguished between absolute and conditional prohibitions in the laws of war. The rule prohibiting the destruction of private property, for instance, is conditional on military necessity. Villages should be spared except if burning them to the ground was the only way to delay an advancing enemy. But the use of poison, killing those who have surrendered, and rape in war are categorically prohibited.[93]

[91] III.173, 574, emphasis added.

[92] The French expression appears in Martens 1801, 399; see also Vattel III.155, III.173.

[93] LN III.137; also Wolff in JG §783. Interestingly, Vattel argued that Louis XIV's ravage of the Palatinate was an exception to this understanding of military necessity (III.167). While scorched-earth tactics could be lawful—for instance in order to "cover our frontier against an enemy whose incursions we are unable to check by any other means"—he denied that the French could justify their actions in the Palatinate on that basis: "the whole proceeding exhibited nothing to the eyes of mankind but the revenge and cruelty of a haughty and unfeeling minister" (III.167, 571). And yet this is debatable, as in 1689 Louis XIV arguably had no means to defend Alsace against the growing power of Austria and the League of Augsburg other than to create a buffering "artificial desert" in the Palatinate region (Lynn 2002). By contrast, absolute prohibitions are neither debatable nor justifiable by necessity. This Vattelian conception of necessity may be contrasted with that of nineteenth-century Prussian war theorists, who argued that military necessity could trump all legal constraints on war (Best 1980, 166–79; Witt 2012, 341–2, and below section 5.5).

4.5 Peace treaties and *post bellum* rights

We have seen that regular war theorists assumed that in regular wars rulers pursue limited goals with limited means. The goal of regular war is not to exterminate the enemy but only to force him to concede one's terms in the negotiation of peace.[94] The faster such concession is made, and the lesser destruction it takes, the better. As Wolff repeatedly said, the rules of regular war should always facilitate, never undermine, the conclusion of war.[95]

Peace treaties are the most important instrument to realize this imperative of expedite termination. However, as was the case for Grotius's theory of solemn war, peace treaties generated moral dilemmas for the theorists of regular war. On the one hand, a strong reason to recognize that the terms of peace treaties bring closure to a war is that they reduce its destructiveness, in particular by allowing the losing side to negotiate peace before the point of unconditional surrender. Much destruction can be avoided in this way.[96] On the other hand, peace treaties typically run against two principles of justice. The first belongs to corrective justice and holds that rightful claims derived from *ius ad bellum* and *ius in bello* should be redressed; the second belongs to procedural fairness, and holds that the consent of the parties must be free for contracts, in particular treaties, to be binding.

It will often be the case that in a peace treaty one of the parties agrees to its terms only because it is threatened with further violence. But if duress could be used to invalidate the treaty later on, then the very institution of peace treaties would unravel.[97] Vattel added that even in war contexts some amount of genuine consent must exist, because when one of the belligerents agrees to negotiate peace, a choice to stop the fight has been made.[98] However, peace treaties should not be recognized as valid if they impose "hard, ignominious, and insupportable conditions," "conditions which are equally offensive to justice and

[94] Martens 1801, 398. This assumption reflected European practice. As Robson's summary of eighteenth-century European inter-state warfare puts it, "in theory and in practice, eighteenth-century wars were wars of limited liability—about something concrete, rather than the earlier wars of righteousness and moral purpose—clashes between rulers, between dynastic States in limited wars fought with limited means for limited objectives, which ended with the drawing up of a balance sheet" (Robson 1966, 165).

[95] E.g. JG §§887, 892.

[96] Vattel in LN IV.18; cf. Grotius RWP III.xix.11.

[97] So Grotius argued in RWP III.xix.11. See similarly Wolff in JG §408, and Vattel in LN IV.37.

[98] As he wrote, "it was her own free choice to prefer a certain and immediate loss, but of limited extent, to an evil of a more dreadful nature, which, though yet at some distance, she had but too great reason to apprehend" (IV.37, 672).

to all the duties of humanity."[99] This extreme case aside, virtually anything could be included in, or excluded from, peace treaties, in particular claims derived from *ius ad bellum* and *ius in bello*. As Vattel explained, "were the rules of strict and rigid justice to be observed, so that each party should precisely receive every thing to which he has a just title, it would be impossible ever to make a peace." It is consequently assumed that territorial and property claims made at the outset or in the course of war are extinguished, unless the treaty explicitly disposes otherwise.[100]

In the case of property rights, Wolff and Vattel endorsed Grotius's nullification principle, in virtue of which enemy property stands to enemies as *res nullius*.[101] Goods taken in war become rightfully owned by the sheer fact of having been seized and put under the enemy's effective control, unless the peace treaty stipulates otherwise. If Grotius justified this principle by reference to the imperative to reduce the occasions of conflict during and in the aftermath of war, Vattel emphasized its effects on international trade: "there would be no stability in the affairs of mankind, no safety in trading with nations engaged in war, if we were allowed to draw a distinction between a just and an unjust war, so as to attribute lawful effects to the one which we denied to the other."[102] On its face, however, this argument is problematic, for while nullification may cut short disputes about the pedigree of titles, it also creates incentives for wars of acquisition and conquest. Cutting short commercial disputes by excluding pedigree may facilitate the short-term flow of goods, but it also makes property rights generally insecure.

Neither Grotius nor Wolff addressed this worry but Vattel suggested that the mechanism of the balance of power could be a solution. The most effective disincentive for war operates before its onset. The threat of military counter-response is more effective than the threat of a post-war refusal of recognition of property titles. If a state has given signs of an excessive acquisitive appetite, then those who are endangered by this behavior should form an alliance to counterbalance it, and the interest in counterbalancing should also inform the contents of peace treaties.[103]

[99] Vattel IV.37, 672. As Geoffrey Best puts it, the peace which Enlightenment publicists contemplated is "a just peace in the sense of being bearable to the vanquished" (Best 1980, 50). For valuable historical overviews of the practice of peace treaty-making in the eighteenth century, see Lesaffer 2005 and Duchhardt 2004, and specifically on Vattel's contribution to the theory of peace treaties, Lesaffer 2011.

[100] IV.18, 662. In Vattel's words, in peace treaties "no decision is pronounced on the original cause of the war, or on those controversies to which the various acts of hostility might give rise; nor is either of the parties condemned as unjust . . . but a simple agreement is formed, which determines what equivalent each party shall receive in extinction of all his pretensions" (IV.18, 663).

[101] JG §861; LN III.195–6; Grotius RWP III.vi.8, 670, and for discussion, see above section 2.3.

[102] III.196, 595.

[103] III.47–9. On the role of power-balancing considerations in peace and other treaties, see Lesaffer 2005, 37–40; Duchhardt 2004, 56–7.

Things are somewhat more complicated when it comes to territorial rights. As we saw in Chapter 2, Grotius defended a version of the nullification principle for territorial rights. Since in solemn wars all members of the belligerent state can be lawfully targeted, they can also be held under slavery or whatever form of rule the conqueror saw fit to impose, because when faced with the choice between life under the conqueror's rule and death, they could be presumed to prefer life.[104] Given the paramount interest in preserving life, those who might suffer defeat at war must be ready to accept whatever terms the victor imposes.

Wolff's short discussion on this matter is closer to Hobbes's "commonwealth by acquisition" than to Grotius's right of conquest. Like Hobbes, Wolff argued that public authority ceases once a ruler "can no longer defend his subjects," as a result of which the victor can come to have authority over subjects formerly under the defeated power.[105] For Hobbes, fear of the victor at the end of war should prompt members of the vanquished commonwealth to enter into a covenant with him, but this covenant is valid only insofar as the victor is able preserve the lives and the "liberty of body" of the vanquished. There can be no covenant with slaves, "for such men have no obligation at all; but may break their bonds, or the prison; and kill, or carry away captive their master, justly."[106] Similarly for Wolff, while a conqueror's rule could take the form of patrimonial right—war could be the source of "patrimonial kingdoms"—it could never be a "slave-kingdom," except on account of serious wrongs and then only temporarily.[107]

Vattel, by contrast, produced a more nuanced and detailed account of the reconstitution of territorial rights in the aftermath of war. He did defend conquest as a legitimate source of territorial rights, but not on whatever terms the conqueror chose to impose. His discussion contains two lines of argument, which sometimes pull in different directions. There is, first and most visibly, Vattel's adherence to popular sovereignty and republican freedom, on the basis of which he condemned Grotius in language strikingly similar to Rousseau's. But there is also, secondly, the imperative of ending war, which could take priority over popular sovereignty.

Vattel considered separately the case of a whole state falling under the control of a belligerent power, and that of what may be called territorial fragments, which were occupied and became detached from the whole state as a result of

[104] See above section 2.3, and RWP III.iv.6, III.vii.5.

[105] JG §869, 447.

[106] *Leviathan*, chapter XX (Hobbes and Tuck 1991, 141).

[107] JG §874, 448–9. For Wolff, Grotius had mistakenly confused patrimonial rule and slave-kingdoms, the latter is a contradiction in terms.

the dynamics of war. In the first case, when the appointed sovereign could no longer rule in any part of its former territory, the occupier,

> acquires no other rights by his conquest than such as belonged to the sovereign whom he has dispossessed: and, on the submission of the people, he is bound to govern them according to the laws of the state. If the people do not voluntarily submit, the state of war still subsists.[108]

Contrary to Hobbes and Wolff, for Vattel the people or nation, which is the constituent power that appoints the sovereign ruler, is not dissolved through war but retains its sovereignty, in particular the right to use force despite its appointed ruler having been deposed. The terms of the political association, which bound the previous ruler, now bind the conqueror. Moreover, the conqueror's right to rule on those terms is provisional and conditional on the eventual consent of the occupied nation, which is also necessary if the conqueror seeks to undertake constitutional changes.

The key question, of course, is what counts for Vattel as "voluntary submission." His discussion makes clear that the last sentence in the quote above is conceptual: consent is absent if and only if the nation actively resists the conqueror. If armed resistance continues, the state of war continues between a beheaded nation and the enemy sovereign. Active resistance is celebrated by Vattel with Rousseauian eloquence: "men of spirit, to whom life is nothing, less than nothing, unless sweetened with liberty, will always conceive themselves at war with that oppressor, though actual hostilities are suspended on their part through want of ability."[109] Failure to resist, on the other hand, either because of exhaustion, incapacity, or because of genuine sympathy for a conqueror, can be read as consent and as such settle territorial rights after war.

Not only is Vattelian republicanism inconsistent in principle with Grotius's hypothetical consent to enslavement, it also delivers conflicting prudential assessments. In the case of republics, if the victor took to exercise the full array of Grotian rights, and proceeded to enslave the vanquished, the state of war *will* continue. An inherent resilience and resistance to give up a republican constitution should be expected in the occupied republic. If the law of nations creates an expectation in the victor that he could freely oppress and enslave the vanquished, this will only contribute to the prolongation of war, not to the

[108] III.201, 599.

[109] III.201, 600. Compare Rousseau's "Considerations on the Government of Poland" (in Rousseau and Gourevitch 1997, 178, 183).

minimization of violence or the preservation of life. Rulers should learn from history and experience how bloody and unwise it is to try to control a nation without genuine support.[110]

It is important to note, finally, that for Vattel the right of resistance to foreign occupiers belongs not to individuals but to constituted political societies, either "whole nations" or constituted "towns and provinces" under suzerain control. Territorial fragments, that is, areas whose inhabitants do not constitute a self-governing political association but are "simply integrant parts" of a larger nation, could be bargained away in peace treaties as "compensation," and incorporated into a conquering state without constitutional constraints or mediating consent from their members.[111] Those in the incorporated territory could of course be made worse off by the incorporation—for instance if they transitioned from a republican constitution to an absolute monarchy—but, according to Vattel, "this is a misfortune which [they] must wholly impute to the chance of war."[112] That this "misfortune" had to be endured nearly as a natural catastrophe seems to follow as much from the value of national preservation as from the stabilizing orientation of the law of nations. Partial territorial alienation could be necessary to redraw the balance of power in a peace treaty, and for that reason it could not be made to depend on the inhabitants' active consent.[113]

[110] LN III.203, III.296. It should be noted, however, that Vattel distinguished between wars fought against duly constituted nations and wars fought "to subdue a fierce and savage people" (III.201, 599). In such civilizing wars, the occupier did have the right to govern vanquished subjects despotically, and could even, "if necessary, keep them for some time in a kind of slavery. But this forced condition ought to cease from the moment the danger is over—the moment the conquered people are become citizens" (III.201, 599).

[111] III.199, 597–8, I.264, 241. On the practice of compensations in peace treaties, see Morgenthau 1948, 135–6.

[112] III.199, 597.

[113] IV.11, 658. Of course, the successive alienation of territorial fragments could eventually dissolve whole nations. Vattel did not live to see how Poland disappeared after three rounds of dismemberment.

5
Humanizing War in the Nineteenth Century

Contemporary international lawyers often depict the laws of war as requiring a balance between the fundamental principles of military necessity and humanity.[1] While the humanity principle asserts the inviolability of the human person, and correspondingly proscribes actions such as killing, maiming, and harming civilians, the principle of necessity waives such proscriptions under some circumstances. If humanity stands for the protection of fragile individuals in war contexts, necessity stands for the tactical and strategic imperatives that sometimes make such protection impossible.

Even though it may now appear constitutive of the laws of war, humanity as a distinct *legal* category in fact entered the laws and customs of war only in the late nineteenth century, when the project of international legal codification got under way. It was only then that considerations of humanity became integrated into an existing corpus of law, legal concepts, and doctrines produced by defenders of the practice of regular warfare in the Enlightenment.

This chapter looks at the uneasy integration of the humanity concept, along with its associated imperatives and norms, into the Enlightenment theory and doctrine of regular war, which constitutes its intellectual and historical background. The chapter's main contention is that the channeling of humanitarian concerns through the law of nations produced a law of war that was understood to have two fundamental principles in tension—necessity and humanity—and that this duality has obscured our moral appraisals of the law up to the present. The chapter examines the deep changes in legal theory that enabled this transformation in the laws of war, and reconstructs in particular some of the dilemmas that the introduction of the humanity concept produced in the project of codifying the laws and customs of war at the end of the nineteenth century. Unlike in previous chapters, here I will focus nearly exclusively on matters of *ius in bello*, the only exception being a brief commentary on the humanitarians' fraught relationship with the pacifist movement, which touches on aspects of *ius ad* (or rather *contra*) bellum. This focus is a reflection

[1] See e.g. Schmitt 2010, Melzer 2010.

The Laws of War in International Thought. Pablo Kalmanovitz, Oxford University Press (2020). © Pablo Kalmanovitz.
DOI: 10.1093/oso/9780198790259.001.0001.

of the humanitarians' own preoccupations, and of the emerging separation in legal doctrine between the three periods of war.[2]

My sources in this chapter include the writings of some of the lawyers and publicists who helped draft or promoted the first positive legal instruments governing the conduct of war. Foremost among these are Francis Lieber (1800–1872), who famously drafted Lincoln's "General Orders No. 100" during the American Civil War; his friend and Swiss colleague Johann Caspar Bluntschli (1808–1881), one of the foremost international legal publicists of the second half of the nineteenth century, founding member of the *Institut de Droit International*, and member of the German delegation at the Brussels diplomatic conference of 1874; and the Swiss jurist Gustave Moynier (1826–1910), co-founder of the International Committee of the Red Cross, also founding member of the *Institut*, and active participant in the drafting and ratification of the first positive documents of the laws of war, including the first Geneva Convention (1864).

This remarkable group of jurists and their followers had considerable influence in the production and promotion of the first codified instruments of the laws of war, which provided the basis for the great codifications carried out in The Hague in 1899 and 1907. A crucial forum for their endeavors was the *Institut de Droit International*, the first professional association of international lawyers, and arguably the founding institution of the emerging field of professional international law.[3] I look both at their published writings and at their deliberations within the most influential outlet of the emergent international legal profession, the *Revue de Droit International et de Legislation Comparée*.

5.1 Regular war in the nineteenth century

We saw in the previous chapter how for Wolff, Vattel, and Martens the laws and customs of war were essentially maxims of good statesmanship. They were underwritten by "civil prudence" and in particular by a general interest in avoiding total war and the obstruction of the transition to peace. The imperative to keep war violence within certain agreed conventional limits—in particular,

[2] For a valuable discussion of the law and practices of *ius ad bellum* in the nineteenth century, which shows a great deal of continuity with the eighteenth century, see Verdebout 2014.

[3] On the *Institut* and its founding role for the international legal profession, see Koskenniemi 2002a, 11–97; Yakemtchouk 1973. On the connections between Lieber and Bluntschli, see Holquist 2015; Baker-Röben 2002, 250–6; Witt 2012, 342–5. On Moynier and the founding of the Red Cross, see Hutchinson 1996, 20–4.

that wars be fought only by regular forces and that noncombatants and private property be spared as much as possible—was presented as imperatives of enlightened rule. Military actions that unnecessarily or excessively devoured valuable resources were both unlawful and bad policy. For the Enlightenment defenders of regular war, the laws and customs of war embodied a political economy of violence according to which destruction in war should be limited, ideally only as much as necessary to narrowly pursue limited claims against recognized public enemies. The law of nations should be the "handmaid of diplomacy" also in war contexts.[4]

We also saw that the contemporary way of speaking of a tension, opposition, or balance in the laws of war between military necessity and humanitarian protection is alien to the Enlightenment conception of the laws of war. For Vattel and other regular war theorists, military necessity is an eminently constraining principle, indeed arguably the foremost constraint on belligerents. Vattel thought that sound state policies in war and the principle of humanity converged in practice, so that pursuing the former would always lead to protecting the latter. When he invoked states' obligations to discharge the "offices of humanity," it was usually in reference to supererogatory actions, the magnanimity or charity of which made them stand out against the customary but harsher rules of state conduct. They belonged to natural law or charity, not to the voluntary law of nations.[5]

This Enlightenment conception of the laws of war was highly influential throughout the nineteenth century, as were Vattel's writings on the law of nations more broadly. Its influence can be detected in several of the first positive legal instruments of the laws of war, beginning with the 1856 Declaration of Paris, as well as in the work of Francis Lieber, whose Code of 1863 is probably the most influential document of the laws of war in the nineteenth century. Lieber is arguably the most important intellectual figure extending the regular war concept into the nineteenth century.[6]

There are certainly important innovations in Lieber's Code—not least the fact that it was meant to be a portable set of rules for officers in the field—but they were articulated in the language of regular war and very much in keeping with fundamental principles of regular war doctrine.[7] Lieber was a dedicated

[4] To paraphrase Koskenniemi 2002a, 20.

[5] LN III.201, III.158. The "offices of humanity" include providing assistance to relief in cases of famine, natural catastrophes, and military attacks (II.1–10).

[6] For valuable histories of the Code and its influence, see Witt 2012, 229–50, passim; Baxter 2013 [1963]; Giladi 2012; Best 1980, 155–6, 169–72; Scheipers 2015, 71–87.

[7] Recently John Fabian Witt has argued that Lieber departed from Vattel and the Enlightenment project of regular war by restoring the connection between *ius ad bellum* and *ius in bello* and fundamentally re-conceiving the principle of military necessity, but it is unclear that Lieber did either of these things

student of the tradition of natural law and the law of nations, and the influence of the regular war tradition specifically—particularly of Cicero, Gentili, Grotius, Pufendorff, Bynkershoek, and Vattel—is manifest in his early discussion of war in his *Manual of Political Ethics* (first published 1838, with a revised edition prepared and published posthumously in 1881). This book, together with a series of lectures delivered at Columbia University in 1861 and 1862, was the main source of the 157 articles that made it into the final version of the Code.[8]

Lieber's endorsement of the regular war paradigm is explicit in the Code, as when it states that the law of nations "admits of no rules or laws different from those of regular warfare," or when it cites the "modern regular wars of the Europeans" as the model to follow in the American Civil War.[9]

In a line that captures a great deal of the spirit of Enlightenment regular war theory, Lieber observed that inter-state wars are only instruments in the pursuit of legitimate and limited state goals which are outside the war itself, and consequently, "unnecessary or revengeful destruction of life [during war] is not lawful." "Neither destruction nor killing," he emphasizes often in *Political Ethics*, "is the object of war."[10] As was the case already in Grotius's account of solemn wars, the moral force of Lieber's Code is underwritten by a profound conviction in the value of state sovereignty. Echoing a defense of state authority prominent in the natural law tradition, the Code sweepingly—and oddly for a legal code—asserts that, "it is a law and requisite of civilized existence that men live in political, continuous societies, forming organized units, called states or nations, whose constituents bear, enjoy, and suffer, advance and retrograde together, in peace and in war."[11]

Even more than his Enlightenment predecessors, Lieber was an enthusiastic believer in the necessity of recourse to force as a means to preserve a state's existence and "to obtain great ends of state."[12] If for Vattel war is a regrettable

(cf. Witt 2012, 182–5, 218, elsewhere Witt underlines important continuities, e.g. 2, 232–4). My reading of the Code is in line with Geoffrey Best's overall assessment, according to which Lieber was "a representative man, doing his best to summarize the relevant wisdom of his age, and conscious of no great difference between it and the wisdom of a hundred years before" (Best 1994, 378).

[8] The lines of continuity between *Political Ethics*, the Columbia lectures, and the Lieber Code are carefully reconstructed in Baxter 2013 [1963], 123–5.

[9] See respectively art. 67 and art. 25, and similarly art. 155.

[10] Lieber 1881a, 665, and compare Lieber Code art. 68.

[11] Lieber Code art. 20. In *Political Ethics*, Lieber offered a neo-naturalist account of the nation-state. The state exists, he writes, "of necessity, and is the natural state of man," and it is "a form and faculty of mankind to lead the species towards greater perfection" (Lieber 1881b, 162). This close affinity of Lieber's to the metaphysical branch of the German natural law tradition may not be surprising, given his early education in Berlin and doctorate from Jena.

[12] Lieber Code art. 30.

but necessary feature of international political life, and for Rousseau and Kant a deplorable but constitutive defect of the international system, for Lieber it is a morally virtuous activity, among other things because it helps cultivate or restore a nation's moral vitality. His *Political Ethics* goes to great lengths in justifying and indeed celebrating war against pacifist, Christian, and rationalist objections. According to Lieber, by being a source of moral strength, selflessness, and virtuous patriotism, wars have produced "the choicest pages of history, testifying to every glowing bosom the nobleness of human nature." Protracted peace, by contrast, "frequently beget[s] sordid selfishness and degrading submissiveness, increasing with each generation."[13]

It was not Lieber's task in the Code to produce a doctrine of *ius ad bellum*, but the Code is premised on a conception of the laws of war as a set of constraints on the pursuit of valuable state goals that apply equally to all sides in war.[14] Upon a formal war declaration, belligerents tacitly recognize that certain usages and customary obligations enter into force, which among other things grant enemies certain basic entitlements. As he wrote in *Political Ethics*, "wars are undertaken under the silent acknowledgment of certain usages, which, therefore, must be kept; both on common grounds of honor, and because they are necessary, either for mitigating the evils of war and bringing it within the sphere of civilization, or for the obtaining of the end of peace."[15]

Like his Enlightenment predecessors, Lieber's Code holds that in regular warfare it is necessary to distinguish between "combatants" and "noncombatants."[16] Even though all subjects of a "hostile country" are in a sense enemies—they may all be "subjected to the hardships of the war"—only combatants can be directly attacked, and noncombatants should be spared "in person, property, and honor, as much as the exigencies of war will admit."[17] Like Vattel and more famously Rousseau, Lieber conceived of regular war as a clash between conflicting public powers, not private individuals, which should be limited in its destructiveness, and the outcome of which should determine

[13] Lieber 1881a, 633, 645. The full case for war appears at 632–50.

[14] To be justified, he wrote in *Political Ethics*, a war must be pursued "in order to obtain right," but injustice does not carry the loss of belligerent privileges (Lieber 1881a, 643). Overall, Lieber's treatment of *ius ad bellum* in *Political Ethics* is unsystematic and not juridical, more an extension of his ethical nationalism than an account of what the enforcement of state rights might look like in international law (his account of just causes of war appears in Lieber 1881a, 653–7). Revealingly, Lieber rejected international adjudication on grounds similar to those of Vattel and Wolff (see above, sections 3.1 and 3.2). It was likely to revive the old threat of universal monarchy, as it was co-opted by strong monarchical states to the detriment of smaller republics (Lieber 1881a, 650–3).

[15] Lieber 1881a, 664.

[16] Lieber Code art. 155.

[17] Lieber Code arts. 15, 21–22. Compare section 4.3 above.

how their dispute is settled.[18] In a statement that could have come from Vattel, the Code states that, "in modern regular wars . . . protection of the inoffensive citizen of the hostile country is the rule." Also like Vattel, Lieber conceded that under some circumstances noncombatants could permissibly be harmed, in particular starved during sieges and killed or maimed in surprise bombings; their property could be destroyed; and they could be captured and held for ransom.[19]

Regarding combatants, Lieber endorsed the fundamental regular war principle according to which the norms of *ius in bello* are independent from considerations of *ius ad bellum*. Soldiers designated by sovereign governments can permissibly use force—consistent with the law of nations—regardless of the justice of their cause: their "killing, wounding, or other warlike acts, are no individual crimes or offenses."[20] Soldiers must recognize enemy soldiers as public not private enemies, and consequently, "so soon as an enemy is rendered harmless by wounds or captivity, he is no longer my enemy, for he is no enemy of mine individually," and therefore can no longer be lawfully attacked.[21] Soldiers must be given quarter, and the legal protections of prisoners of war must be observed when they are captured. In particular, captured soldiers cannot be punished for participation in lawful hostilities, and they "shall be fed upon plain and wholesome food whenever practicable, and treated with humanity." Of great significance in the context of the American Civil War, race cannot be a reason to deny captured soldiers the status of war prisoners, nor is enslavement of captured soldiers permitted in the law of nations.[22]

Also in line with Enlightenment accounts of regular war, Lieber defended the use of reprisals ("retaliation") as valid means to dissuade an enemy from committing outrages, and warned that they should be used with caution and only as a last resort, as there is always a risk of escalation.[23] He deemed the use of poison and torture to be categorically prohibited, as well as perfidy and the breach of agreements made during war; invocations of military necessity did not waive these prohibitions.[24] Finally, echoing Wolff and more famously Kant, Lieber stated that military acts that would make "the return to peace

[18] Lieber Code arts. 29, 32, 153.
[19] Lieber Code arts. 25, 15, 17–19.
[20] Lieber Code art. 57. Cf. Witt 2012, 182–5, 218.
[21] Lieber 1881a, 659. For similar reasons, means of force that would "cruelly afflict [a soldier] after he has ceased to be an enemy" had to be avoided (Lieber 1881a, 661).
[22] Lieber Code arts. 49, 56, 58, 60–66, 76.
[23] Lieber Code arts. 28–29.
[24] Lieber Code arts. 11, 16, 68-70.

unnecessarily difficult" are unlawful and cannot be justified on grounds of military necessity either.[25]

Lieber's Code turned out to be enormously influential in Europe. It provided the first blueprint for subsequent national military codes, as well as for some of the first multilateral treaties that codified various areas of the laws of war in the late nineteenth century.[26] Caspar Bluntschli translated the Code into German and produced on its basis a code that was used by the Prussian army in the Austro-Prussian war of 1866. Lieber's Code also provided a blueprint for the draft document that Fedor Martens prepared for the 1874 Brussels Convention, which aimed to codify existing customary laws of land warfare in Europe.[27]

But Lieber's Code was not the only channel through which the Enlightenment project of regular war made its way into codified instruments in the nineteenth century. The 1856 Paris Declaration "Respecting Maritime Law," which is the first open-for-accession multilateral treaty in history, was devoted to neutrality in naval warfare and follows fundamental principles of regular warfare. The Declaration originated in a formal statement by France and Great Britain regarding the terms in which they would enter the Crimean War (1853–1856), but it was also included in the final terms of peace in the hopes that it would be observed in subsequent wars.[28] It upholds the rule of free ships, free goods, as it grants immunity from capture to both neutral goods in enemy ships and enemy goods in neutral ships, except for war contraband.[29] The Declaration also prohibited privateering in naval warfare, that is, the commissioning of private ships to attack enemy forces and prey on enemy commerce, thus restricting the use of lawful force in naval warfare to regular navies. On both counts, the Declaration sought to advance ideals of limitation

[25] Lieber Code art. 16. This, Lieber argued in *Political Ethics*, is the main reason why perfidy and other breaches of faith in the context of hostilities were categorically proscribed in the law of nations: they erode the minimal trust among belligerents without which transitions to peace become impossible (Lieber 1881a, 661–663).

[26] Best 1980, 155–6; Witt 2012, 327–8, 342–5; Baxter 2013 [1963], 146–8.

[27] On the close similarities between Bluntschli's and Lieber's codes, see Schindler 2007, 440–3. While the Brussels Conference produced only a "project of an international declaration," it was widely taken to reflect settled customs in Europe, and was influential in the drafting of the 1899 Hague Convention (Giladi 2014). It may be noted that disagreement over the definition of regular forces constituted an insurmountable obstacle to treaty-making in Brussels (Benvenisti and Lustig 2020; Scheipers 2015, 99–102; also Witt 2012, 344–5, Best 1980, 156–7).

[28] Eventually 51 state parties acceded to the Declaration (Roberts and Guelff 2000, 5, 47–51; Witt 2012, 133–6).

[29] The Declaration defines the immunity of neutrals in more protective terms than those proposed by Vattel, but is in line with Enlightenment ideals of limited war. According to Vattel, it was not permissible to capture neutral goods in enemy ships, but enemy goods in neutral ships could be captured (see section 4.3 above).

in regular warfare by minimizing the impact of war on international commerce, limiting the legally permissible scope of hostilities, and narrowing the set of lawful agents of violence.

Principles of regular warfare can also be found in the second international instrument of the laws of war, the 1868 Saint Petersburg Declaration "Renouncing the Use, in Time of War, of Explosive Projectiles under 400 Grammes Weight." The one single norm in the Declaration is enunciated in its title, and in practice consists in the prohibition of attacking enemy soldiers with explosive bullets (explosive heavy artillery was neither prohibited nor meant for direct use against individual soldiers).[30] In its preamble, the Declaration contains what may well be the most succinct expression of regular war's core ideal: "the only legitimate object which States should endeavour to accomplish during war is to weaken the military forces of the enemy." For this purpose, the preamble continues, "it is sufficient to disable the greatest number of men," a purpose which "would be exceeded by the employment of arms which uselessly aggravate the suffering of disabled men, or render their death inevitable." The Declaration is a natural extension of the customary prohibitions of denial of quarter, attacking soldiers *hors de combat*, and killing prisoners of war. These are all superfluous forms of harm, which do not advance legitimate state interests and as such violate the economy of violence that underpins the norms and principles of regular war.

References to humanity are nearly absent in these early codified documents. They make no appearance at all in the Paris Declaration, but the 1868 Declaration does state in its preamble that the use of the banned projectiles would be "contrary to the laws of humanity," in addition to alien to the pursuit of any legitimate tactical aim. Lieber's Code famously held that "the more vigorously wars are pursued, the better it is for humanity," and also, less famously, that "humanity induces the adoption of the rules of regular war toward rebels."[31] And yet, in both Lieber and the Saint Petersburg Declaration, references to humanity are marginal and complementary to the instrumental logic of the distinction between necessary and superfluous harm, which does have a central role in both texts. Implicitly, they concur with the Vattelian postulate of convergence between sound policy and humanity. The concept of

[30] Roberts and Guelff 2000, 53–5.

[31] Lieber Code arts. 29 and 152 respectively. The claim that "intense wars are of short duration," and therefore better for humanity, can also be found in Lieber's *Political Ethics* (Lieber 1881a, 660–1). Contrary to a common and widespread misunderstanding, Lieber made patently clear that this was not meant as a justification of unlimited war, but rather as an exhortation to fight wars decisively *within the limits recognized by civilized nations.*

humanity does no independent work, but it appears as a valuable byproduct of sound state policy.[32]

It is nonetheless significant that this particular language would be included in these documents, marginal as their inclusion may be. They reflect the growing influence of the emerging humanitarian movement, which began to gain traction at the same time that Lieber produced his Code.[33] Within this movement, and eventually as its centerpiece, the International Committee of the Red Cross was created in 1863, and soon after it scored its first treaty-making victory by leading the diplomatic negotiations that produced the first Geneva Convention "for the Amelioration of the Condition of the Wounded in Armies in the Field" in 1864.

The 1864 Geneva Convention is consistent with regular war ideals of limiting the destructiveness of war, but its approach to limitation is novel and not quite in line with Enlightenment views on regular war. The Convention's distinctive strategy consists in reformulating and extending the category of neutrality, so that it covers not only third-party states and international trade but also medical and religious personnel and private humanitarian rescuers operating in battlefields. This extension of the neutrality concept gave humanitarian rescue an altogether novel legal standing in the midst of hostilities.[34] The Convention granted neutral status not only to the Red Cross and other duly recognized relief societies, but also to *any noncombatant* who cared for wounded soldiers. As article 5 radically has it,

> Generals of the belligerent Powers shall make it their duty to notify the inhabitants of the appeal made to their humanity, and of the neutrality which humane conduct will confer. The presence of any wounded combatant receiving shelter and care in a house shall ensure its protection. An inhabitant who has given shelter to the wounded shall be exempted from billeting and from a portion of such war contributions as may be levied.

[32] The term "humanity" in Lieber may also denote a different concept from that advocated by the humanitarians in the late nineteenth century, to be discussed below (Giladi 2012). It does independent work in the Code only to the extent that it is said to motivate the application of rules of inter-state war in the American Civil War (art. 152).

[33] Valuable general discussions of humanitarianism, to which I am indebted, include Barnett 2011; Fassin 2012; Hutchinson 1996.

[34] As Geoffrey Best puts it, the neutralization of those involved in helping wounded soldiers was "a radically new approach," as it "proclaimed the supremacy of the humanitarian ideal and purpose above immediate military considerations and intruded boldly into the military's normal territory" (Best 1980, 150).

If Vattel and other Enlightenment regular war theorists appealed to the good sense and prudence of military commanders to make the practice of billeting and contributions moderate and sustainable (see above, section 4.3), the Geneva Convention introduced an obligation in commanders to grant immunity to humane noncombatants in recognition of their humanitarian endeavors.

As could be expected, this attempt to fundamentally reorganize the conduct of hostilities around firmer humanitarian rights and obligations was resisted by military officers and eventually diluted in the revised 1906 Geneva Convention.[35] The 1906 Convention restored the full authority of military commanders in the battlefield and set military necessity as a potentially countervailing consideration to the obligations of care for the sick and wounded.[36] Already in 1906, then, jurists seem to have understood that implicit in that language was a call for a *balance* between military necessity and the imperatives of humanity. To explain the intellectual origins and significance of this deep transformation in the laws of war is the purpose of the following sections.

5.2 Civilization, progress, and legal cosmopolitanism

The jurists who began introducing humanitarian considerations into the laws and customs of war operated in a cultural context that differed markedly from that of their eighteenth-century predecessors. While there are several important contrasts, the most relevant for present purposes is a deeply-rooted belief in historical progress, and the jurists' corresponding self-image as beacons of progress and impersonated consciences of civilized mankind. For the international jurists of the nineteenth century, it was a matter of course that Europe was at the vanguard of historical progress, and their historical mission, indeed that of the emerging profession of public international law, was to help Europeans and non-Europeans—especially colonial subjects—achieve progress and civilization.[37]

Beginning in the late eighteenth century, and largely in support of the European project of colonial expansion, the law of nations became the nearly exclusive province of European states. There is virtually no trace of Leibniz and Wolff's admiration for Eastern civilizations in the international legal writings

[35] The strategic abuse of the 1864 Convention during the Franco-Prussian war (1870–1871) was decisive in this regard, on which see Benvenisti and Lustig 2020; Best 1980, 150–5.

[36] See e.g. arts. 1, 12, and 17.

[37] Koskenniemi 2002a, 11–97; Pitts 2007; Sylvest 2007.

of the nineteenth century.[38] In tandem with this increasingly affirmative euro-centralization, there was a profound transformation in how the international legal profession saw itself as a historical and cultural phenomenon. While Enlightenment writings on the law of nations portray it as predominantly state-centric and rationalist, in the late nineteenth century international law was pan-European, teleological, and historicist. Under the towering influence of Savigny's historical jurisprudence, international lawyers came to understand international society not as the expression of a form of rationality that "created constraint out of pure self-regard," as Vattel did, but rather as a historical and cultural formation, of which international law was one important organic development.[39] For this cultural, historicist, and teleological conception of international law, degrees of culture and progress had a great deal of practical weight and legal significance.

Furthermore, if Enlightenment jurists conceived of the law of nations as the "handmaid of cultivated European diplomacy," in the nineteenth century the role of handmaid came to be seen as below international law's dignity.[40] The distinctive mission of international law was to give voice to cosmopolitan public opinion and to promote and preserve civilization. In this capacity, international law was bound to speak truth to power. It had to mobilize the public conscience of mankind against the crude and sometimes barbaric practices of European *realpolitik*, not to mention non-European savages. This "gentle civilizing" was one of the constitutive tasks of the *Institut de Droit International*. Its members understood their historical task to be that of articulating the progressive public conscience of initially European but eventually universal civilization, and to denounce state practices and societies that ran contrary to their universalistic moral conscience.

This pan-European and supranational orientation of nineteenth-century international law created unprecedented doctrinal space, relative to the eighteenth century, for legal invocations of humanity and human rights in the regulation of warfare. Even though Europe lacked a common sovereign, it constituted a legally integrated political entity. Emphasis on the European character of international law allowed jurists to take critical distance from state sovereignty and created space for such invocations.

This is not to say that nineteenth-century international law was cosmopolitan *rather than* state-centric. State sovereignty continues to be the core

[38] Becker Lorca 2014, 40–140; Anghie 2004, 32–114.
[39] Koskenniemi 2002a, 43–6.
[40] Koskenniemi 2002a, 20.

articulating concept in international legal doctrine and practice. But as many scholars have documented, the familiar characterization of nineteenth century international law as positivistic and state-centric is off the mark, really a distortion produced by the legal reformers of the League of Nations and the enormous influence of Lassa Oppenheim in the twentieth century, which became established historiography.[41] A moral aspiration is unmistakable among some influential nineteenth-century international jurists to make international law less state-centric and more protective of the rights and interests of private persons, in particular private property rights, rights to liberty, physical integrity, and life, the right not to be arbitrarily detained, and freedom of religious practice.[42]

For Bluntschli, humanity was a "pillar" of international law, in fact the ultimate source of its legitimacy and the engine of its dynamism and progressive effect. This assertion of the humanity principle implies no denial of the reality, value, or authority of state sovereignty. Both Lieber and Bluntschli were still mindful of the threat of universal monarchy that troubled eighteenth century publicists so much, and thought of nationalism and state sovereignty as valuable counter-forces to monarchical domination. But the ultimate aspiration of international law should be to eventually become a law for humanity, directly protective of individual human rights, not solely of state rights.[43]

This simultaneous affirmation of cosmopolitanism and sovereignty generated deep tensions and pervasive ambivalences. Bluntschli praised state diplomacy for its contributions to international legal progress and deemed the diplomatic corps of European capitals the very "personification of international law." While ambassadorships had been created out of sheer state interest, they had undeniably contributed to the growing influence of international law, and as such had value.[44] On the other hand, however, while statesmen were directly in charge of improving international law, the law's main "lever of progress" was public opinion. The efficacy of international law depended ultimately not on the alignment of state interests but on the existence of adequate public sentiments and of a public conscience supportive of the progressive principles of international law.[45] The more mankind developed an enlightened common

[41] Koskenniemi 2002a; Pitts 2007; Kennedy 1996.

[42] See notably Bluntschli 1895 [1868], 21–7. It goes without saying that what they considered to be human rights was far from the large catalogue of rights included in the human rights treaties of the second half of the twentieth century. Not implausibly, Bluntschli himself considered the inclusion of human rights and the humanity concept in his treatise on international law to be his most original contribution to juridical science (Schindler 2007, 443–4).

[43] Baker-Röben 2002, 250, 264; Koskenniemi 2002a, 52–4, 63–7; Holquist 2013, 37–9.

[44] Bluntschli 1895 [1868], 24.

[45] Bluntschli 1895 [1868], 56.

conscience, the more efficacious and comprehensive international law would become. Eventually, international law should become a "law of humanity" that directly protected interests shared universally by individual human beings.[46]

In sum, for Bluntschli state sovereignty and diplomacy, on the one hand, and public opinion, on the other, are the two fundamental forces that sustain progress in international law, but they could come into conflict. State diplomacy produced and advanced international law, but enlightened public opinion brought humanity and civilization to bear in state practice and international legislation. Enlightened public opinion could and should be critical of diplomatic practice, but diplomatic practice could forcefully oppose the social forces that sought to undermine archaic forms of dynastic power. The two forces behind international legal progress should be expected to conflict.

Clearly aware of this conflict, Bluntschli acknowledged that in the nineteenth century the project of turning international law into the law of humanity was more aspiration than reality. Attempts to directly protect "individual rights common to all humanity" in international law were still feeble and rare. Deference to state sovereignty when it came to the protection of individual rights remained firmly in place. But in the future and progressively, international law was bound to become less timid. It would come to authorize foreign interventions when human rights were "insufficiently respected," and eventually become like the constitutional law of a federation which directly protected individual rights.[47] Bluntschli listed as marks of progress toward a true law of humanity—and pointers to the future of international law—the elimination of the slave trade and slavery, the protection of religious freedoms, for which some states had already shown readiness to take arms, and the protection of private property during war.[48]

5.3 Sovereignty and human rights in war

The tension between cosmopolitan aspiration and state sovereignty impacted directly on the project of regulating inter-state wars in nineteenth-century international law. War is the first and foremost prerogative of state sovereignty, and yet it unleashes destructive forces that cause massive setbacks on individual rights. The nineteenth-century re-orientation of international law in a

[46] Bluntschli 1895 [1868], 20–1, 27, 36.
[47] Bluntschli 1895 [1868], 20–1.
[48] Bluntschli 1895 [1868], 21–7.

more cosmopolitan and progressive direction had important implications for the laws of war as they entered their modern phase of codification. Nineteenth-century jurists who followed Bluntschli came to see humanity as a source of distinctive legal claims *against* states in war contexts. States were deemed to have a legal obligation to respect certain individual rights, which Gustave Moynier described in strikingly modern terms as "the inviolability of the human person."[49] This, however, put humanitarian jurists in a seemingly untenable position. On the one hand, they conceded in traditional fashion that war should be decided in the cabinets of diplomats and following the dictates of enlightened reason of state. But, on the other hand, it was a matter of huge concern to them that war undermined the "rights of humanity." Notwithstanding their recognition of state authority to declare and wage war, these jurists expected or hoped that statesmen, diplomats, and military officers would be moved by claims of humanity in ways that effectively restrained their use of force.

Humanity was brought to bear on the regulation of hostilities through a recognizably modern notion of human rights. If during the French and American revolutions the "rights of man" had been asserted as internal conditions of state authority, and central elements in the construction of national forms of citizenship, for these nineteenth century jurists supranational human rights could be *opposed* to state conduct, and not only to one's own state but to any belligerent state. Human rights as they understood them were cosmopolitan, not necessarily constitutional, and as such were brought to bear in diplomatic conferences and raised against state policies and actions.[50] In this way, humanity and human rights could become the basis for a juristic critique of reason of state. It was the humanitarian jurists' distinctive task, as they understood it, to raise claims of humanity against actions undertaken by states, particularly in the battlefield.[51]

[49] Moynier 1895, 53, 1870, 2; similarly Bluntschli 1895 [1868], 68.

[50] I follow here an important distinction introduced by Samuel Moyn between Enlightenment "rights of man" and post-1940 human rights. In the eighteenth and nineteenth centuries, Moyn argues, individual rights were predicated on membership in a political community and "achieved through the construction of spaces of citizenship in which rights were accorded and protected." By contrast, "the central event in human rights history is the recasting of rights as entitlements that might contradict the sovereign nation-state from above and outside rather than serve as its foundation" (Moyn 2010, 13). Moyn locates this fundamental shift in the emergence of the human rights regime after the Second World War but, as my discussion shows, influential humanitarian jurists in the late-nineteenth century already drew individual rights from outside and above the state and in opposition to state practice.

[51] The applicability of human rights during armed conflict has been much debated in recent legal scholarship (see e.g. Ohlin 2016; Alexander 2015). Opposing a common narrative that situates the emergence of these debates in the late 1960s, it has been shown that such debates were important during the deliberations that produced the Geneva Conventions in 1949 (van Dijk 2018). They actually go further back to the first humanitarian jurists at the beginning of the project of codifying the laws of war.

The emergence of philanthropies devoted to battlefield relief, and the turn to cosmopolitanism in late-nineteenth-century international legal theory, together brought into the laws of war supranational invocations of humanity, which were foreign to the logic of state interest and enlightened reason of state. This insertion of cosmopolitan humanitarian considerations produced a fracture in the inherited construction of the laws and customs of war. If in the eighteenth century the laws of war could essentially be justified entirely from the internal logic of legitimate state interests—for Vattel, as we have seen, humanity and sound policy always went together—in the late nineteenth century jurists articulated *legal* claims of humanity as conditions of legitimacy on the use of force, and demanded that they be weighed *against* statist considerations of military necessity. This provided the ideological background for the emergence of the legal problem of balancing necessity and humanity.

It was the nineteenth-century jurists' aspiration that the laws of war would encompass both statist and cosmopolitan elements. Bluntschli and Moynier gave resolutely affirmative answers to the question whether human rights apply during armed conflict, even if they qualified this by saying that the hard necessities of war could justify some infringement of rights. Indeed, the project of "humanizing war," as they conceived of it, was precisely about bringing human rights and the "law of humanity" to bear legally and progressively on the use of state force.[52]

Moynier celebrated the historical novelty and progressiveness of this project in his 1895 study of the history of the laws of war. Comparing the 1856 Paris Declaration with the 1864 Geneva Convention and the 1868 Saint Petersburg Declaration, he argued that the latter two constituted a whole new "point of departure for new propositions" in international law. The Paris Declaration, which culminated over two centuries of diplomatic and military disputes over the rights of neutral shipping in naval warfare, was for Moynier merely an "agreement of wills" among state representatives, while Geneva and Saint Petersburg rested on human rights imperatives which were profoundly moral and valid regardless of conventional agreements.[53] While delegates in Paris 1856 created a legal situation that would at best remain static for a long time, those of 1864 in Geneva "opened the floodgates of humanitarianism" and showed the path toward future humanitarian progress.[54] "While in 1856 diplomats were concerned above all to avoid great disruptions to the game

[52] Bluntschli 1895 [1868], 301; Moynier 1895, 52–3.
[53] Moynier 1895, 56.
[54] Moynier 1895, 107–9.

of international exchange . . . in 1864 material interests played no role," he concluded.[55]

The historical accuracy of this rendering is questionable, but for present purposes its importance lies in what it reveals about how one of the foremost humanitarian jurists of the nineteenth century undestood his movement in the long history of the laws of war. In fact there were state interests also at play in Geneva 1864 and Saint Petersburg 1868, and surely there were also humanitarian dividends in Paris 1856. But Moynier's point had to do with what he perceived as the contrasting guiding spirits of these diplomatic events. In Paris, when delegates agreed that destroying a state's foreign trade should not be a legitimate war strategy, they acted old style, out of sheer state interest. In Geneva and Saint Petersburg, when delegates agreed on measures to ameliorate the suffering of soldiers in the battlefield, and to prevent it by banning the use of explosive projectiles, they were motivated by charity and respect for the involability of the human person.

Moynier was keen to emphasize the contrast between these two orientations. Interests at diplomatic conferences were contingent and morally indifferent or worse, but human rights had an "absolute and universal character" and their violation "shocked the human heart" in ways that breach of interests could not.[56] The language of 1864 Geneva and 1868 Saint Petersburg was distinctively humanitarian: amelioration, relief of suffering, avoidance of superfluous injury; that of Paris—trade, neutrality, effective blockade, free pasage—was not.[57]

5.4 The humanitarians' dilemma

The humanitarians' simultaneous regard for human rights and recognition of state authority made them characteristically ambivalent about the legitimacy of war. Bluntschli denounced war for its destructiveness and horrors in the most emphatic terms, yet asserted that it was "regrettably still today an indispensable means for assuring the progress of humanity."[58] Even more vehement in their denunciations, if also ambivalent, were Moynier and his philanthropist colleague, medical doctor, and co-founder of the International Committee of

[55] Moynier 1895, 21–2. On the material interests at play in Geneva 1864, see however Hutchinson 1996, 30–2, 55–6.
[56] Moynier 1895, 56, 52.
[57] Moynier 1895, 21–2.
[58] Bluntschli 1895 [1868], 10–11.

the Red Cross, Louis Appia. Humanitarian ambivalence is in full display in the concluding words of Appia's final report to the 1864 Geneva Conference:

> What, gentlemen, is the essence of all our work? To reduce, to mitigate the sufferings of war by works of charity. Everyone understands that in our era war is not fought to make the enemy suffer, but only to put him beyond being able to inflict damage, and that consequently, the means of relieving [suffering] must be accorded a large place; but, on the other hand, no matter how much good one would wish to see philanthropy accomplish, the exigencies of politics do not permit us to interfere, for humanitarian reasons, with the success of war, once it has broken out. To humanize war—if it is not a contradiction to bring such things together—that is our mandate. Let us proclaim loudly our deep regret, our sorrow that we cannot do more; let us protest against the great collective iniquity called war, an iniquity which is only one of the forms of evil in the world; but after this unequivocal protest, taking war for what it is, let us unite our efforts to relieve its distress; let us openly and energetically demand that above the flag of victory shall be flown the white flag and red cross of charity![59]

Two elements are worth highlighting in this remarkable statement. On the one hand, there is Appia's reference to the point of war being to disable rather than harm one's enemy, which is in line with core principles of eighteenth-century regular war doctrine. Furthermore, his recognition of the "exigencies of politics," and his readiness to stop humanitarian action where it began to influence the outcome of hostilities, signal his deference to state authority. He located humanitarian work in a space of indifference to belligerents—when soldiers no longer pose a threat, humanitarian rescue can proceed. In fact, belligerents have an interest in having their own wounded soldiers be rescued and cared for, which historically helped the humanitarian project gain acceptance among militarymen. Humanitarian actors, Appia admits, must operate at the margins of political conflict, relative to which they are neutral, as the 1864 Geneva Convention stipulates in its first article.

On the other hand, Appia's reference to the basic tenets of regular war, and his declared deference to sovereign belligerence privileges, were subsequently belied by his emotive denunciation of war and all the suffering and distress it causes. If Appia's battlecry to humanitarian action was succesful, and the flag of charity prevailed over that of victory at the end war, then presumably

[59] Cited in Hutchinson 1996, 65.

belligerents would soon realize that charity, humanitarian sympathy, and cosmopolitan fraternity, rather than national arms and reason of state, should govern human affairs. Peace among nations would be the ultimate outcome.

A similar two-fold rhetorical move can be found in Moynier. He began his study of the 1864 Geneva Convention by condemning war emphatically: it is barbarous and contrary to civilization, a "terrible expression of the old barbaric prejudice that the reason of the stronger is always the best."[60] His personal faith was that the progress of civilization would bring war to an end, yet in that gradual process, philanthropic endeavors of relief and succor had to be prioritized. In his later work, however, Moynier asked forcefully how it could be that those who sought to "make law prevail over force"—which of course included himself and his colleagues at the *Institut*—could work together with military officers and diplomats in crafting regulations for their appalling business. Instead of standing strong for human rights, humanitarians seemed to objectionably accept the arbitrary imposition of force by the stronger. The concept of civilized or humane war is nonsense, and humanitarian neutrality in the face of war deeply troubling.[61]

In these moving passages, Moynier agonized over what may be called the humanitarians' dilemma. On the one hand, humanitarians could participate in the production and implementation of norms that sought to mitigate the horrors and suffering of war. To do so, they had to be willing to operate at the margins of the politics driving hostilities. They had to defer to military officers and diplomats, for it was them who were in charge of the conduct of hostilities and of disciplining soldiers to act in line with legal obligations. Being a very pragmatic man, Moynier understood this well, and the pitfalls of actual implementation of the Geneva Convention in the 1870s showed it all too clearly.[62]

On the other hand, humanitarian deference to state authority facilitated and could be perceived as validating the actions of military men and diplomats. By failing to denounce war forcefully, humanitarians could end up being co-opted into sustaining and facilitating its course. Instead of providing a stepping-stone on the way to international peace, they would become aiders and abettors of endless if humane war. Worse still, their calls for humanizing war could be a trap for pacifists, who under the never-materialized promise of peace through humanization could end up condoning humane but endless war.[63]

60 Moynier 1870, 3.

61 Moynier 1895, 44–5.

62 Moynier 1895, 24, 37, 40, 43, 48; and see also Hutchinson 1996, 48–53.

63 On the complex relationship between pacifism and humanitarianism in the nineteenth century, and for this pacifist critique of humanitarianism in particular, see Moyn 2021, chapters 1 and 3; Witt 2012, 341–2; Best 1980, 130–140. Moyn shows that Moynier considered the scenario of endless war but

Such is the humanitarians' dilemma. To have practical effect, they had to defer to military officers and reason of state and operate at the margins of their decisions. In that process, they could legitimize military actions and in this way contribute to perpetuate war. This is precisely how some prominent pacifists came to see them on the eve of the Hague Peace Conference.[64] On the other hand, if they denounced war forcefully as the appalling evil it is, and highlighted its arbitrariness, injustice, and horrors, the cost would be to become irrelevant in practice. If humanitarians took the path of high-minded idealism, they would be sidelined by events and in the process lose the chance of ameliorating and succoring suffering in war. This was essentially the warning that the Prussian Field Marshal Helmuth von Moltke gave to Bluntschli upon receiving the 1880 Oxford Manual.[65]

Humanitarians followed the first horn of the dilemma, but the dilemma continued to haunt them in various ways. Very importantly, it structured their attitudes toward legal codification, which was a central element in the nineteenth-century humanization of war project.[66] In an 1875 symposium dedicated to the Brussels Declaration and held at the *Institut de Droit International*, the director Gustave Rolin-Jaequemyns perceptively identified a fundamental predicament in the codification effort. On the one hand, a codified instrument would have to reflect faithfully the actual state of the laws and customs being codified. States were typically wary of introducing new norms in such instruments, and correspondingly instructed delegates at diplomatic conferences—a majority of whom were military officers—to abstain from creative legislation.[67] On the other hand, however, legal codification should also be about improving international law, and consequently reflect the most progressive notions reached by the public conscience of civilized mankind. The challenge, as Rolin saw it, was that codification had to be *both* progressive and

thought it was too improbable to be taken seriously. The conflict between humanitarians and pacifists played out starkly around the Hague Peace Conference of 1899, which originally had the ambitious goal of institutionalizing international peace and arbitration, and as such mobilized hundreds of thousands in the peace movement, but at the end produced the most comprehensive war regulations to date.

64 Moyn 2021, chapter 3. The Red Cross leadership was well aware of this perception (ICRC 1901).

65 In response to von Moltke's observation that humanitarian philanthropists were misguidedly seeking perpetual peace, Bluntschli clarified that the *Institut* was well aware of the necessity of war as an instrument of state (*Institut de Droit International* 1881, 79, 82).

66 It is remarkable how in the late nineteenth century, it was thought that international law itself was a philanthropic endeavor. Moynier thought there was no criterion of progress more transparent than the very idea of law (*l'idée juridique*): the more refined it became, the more the rule of force was weakened (Moynier 1870, 1). An equally striking, nearly magical thinking about the inherent compulsive power of international law can be found in Bluntschli: the very "consecration" of a general principle in international law was thought to exert moderating effects (*Institut de Droit International* 1881, 83).

67 For an illuminating historical account of these instructions, see Holquist 2015.

conservative: humanitarian codifiers had to "reconcile" (his word) progressive and conservative forces when writing down applicable law.[68]

This reconciliation was not a purely intellectual or abstract problem. Beginning precisely with the 1874 Brussels conference, professional jurists became active participants at diplomatic conferences as *jurisconsults*, and their presence and influence only increased thereafter. As mentioned before, Bluntschli was part of the German and Martens of the Russian delegations in Brussels 1874. As a jurisconsult, Bluntschli declared at the Brussels conference, "one must hold not only a diplomatic point of view or a military point of view—but also a legal point of view, a point of view which has its own value. All three groups ought to be able to participate, as appropriate, in the deliberations. At the discretion of states, a legal advisor should be able to take the place of a diplomat or a military man, and vice versa."[69] The value of the juristic point of view, as he saw it, was no less than expressing the public conscience of mankind. In this way, the international legal profession, "presumed not only to offer advise to the military but also to advise government on how to control the military," which "evidently gave the generals much cause for concern."[70]

Furthermore, if not as direct participants at conferences, jurists could have a wide influence as public commentators, or could produce documents that, although not legally binding, influenced the drafting of future binding international instruments or of national legislation. The 1880 Oxford Manual was produced by members of the *Institut* in the hopes that it would be adopted in national legislation and eventually contribute to regulate land warfare, and with that purpose it was sent to governments all over the world.[71] Its preamble is careful to assert that "the Institute has not sought innovations in drawing up the Manual; it has contented itself with stating clearly and codifying the accepted ideas of our age so far as this has appeared allowable and practicable." Some years before, Bluntschli had a produced a codification in a similar spirit. His case for the authority of such single-handed legislation was not so much that it constituted a faithful statement of existing law, but rather that it was the product of true juridical science and a reflection of the conscience of civilized

[68] *Institut de Droit International* 1875, 465. Moreover, jurists could in the process of codification give legal sanction to the particular legal views of strong states, as Martens skillfully did with his famous clause during the Hague Peace Conference (Giladi 2014). The rule of the stronger could become rule of law in the hands of skilled jurists.

[69] Cited in Holquist 2015, 25.

[70] Best 1980, 144. On the complex role of the legal profession in this context, see further Hull 2014, 16–50; Giladi 2014.

[71] *Institut de Droit International* 1881, 79.

humanity.[72] Reflection of practice and aspiration to progress coexisted in tension in the production of such non-binding instruments.

Hence the predicament for humanitarian codifiers and quasi-legislators. If they were too conservative and merely tried to reflect settled practice, they would betray their cosmopolitan vocation as advocates for progress and spokespersons of civilized conscience, which demanded a more restraining law. But if they were too progressive, they would no longer be in the business of codifying the rules and customs of actual war, and their rules would probably fail to guide action. Commenting on the Brussels Declaration for the *Revue de droit international et de législation comparée*, Moynier warned that being too progressive—"succumbing to an excess of sentimentality"—would be counterproductive, as it would produce rules alien to military practice.[73] Similarly, in the summary of its deliberations about the Brussels Declaration, the *Institut* warned against "utopianism" and "misguided philanthropy."[74]

This deep dilemma made the humanitarians' philanthropic endeavors in the nineteenth century inherently unstable. On the one hand, national Red Cross societies, which had been created following cosmopolitan ideals of rescue and Christian charity in the 1860s, became absorbed by the growing militarism of the late nineteenth century. They became "wedded to their countries' war machines and highly valued parts of them," as their "efficient and total integration" with their national armies pushed them away from the original cosmopolitan ideals of the humanitarian lawyers.[75] On the other hand, prominent international humanitarians became either professed pacifists (Dunant) or crypto-pacifists. Moynier tried to dissolve the humanitarian dilemma by appealing to a heroic (and in hindsight patently misplaced) faith in the progress of the civilizing mission, which would lead inexorably from humanitarianism to pacifism. His argument is remarkably straightforward: once the obligation to care for wounded enemy soldiers became firmly entrenched in military discipline, soldiers would start questioning the appropriateness of wounding enemies in the first place. If succor for wounded enemy soldiers was a virtue, how could killing or maiming them be virtuous as well? The progress of the laws of humanity would necessarily sow doubts in soldiers' hearts; the laws of war were "secret agents of pacification."[76]

[72] Bluntschli 1895 [1868], 6–7.
[73] *Institut de Droit International* 1875, 454–5.
[74] *Institut de Droit International* 1875, 285.
[75] Best 1980, 141–2.
[76] Moynier 1895, 94–101.

We now know how mistaken Moynier was about the pacifying effects of humanitarianism, but the relevant point here is that this was his way to come to terms with the humanitarians' dilemma. It was only because the laws of war could operate as secret agents of pacification when infused with the principles and laws of humanity—however fraught that infusion might be—that the "unnatural alliance" (*alliance contre nature*) of philanthropy and war could be justified.[77] Of course, once the Victorian faith in the inexorable progress of humanity is no longer professed, Moynier's solution vanishes. The contemporary regime of international humanitarian law seems to have lost sight both of the humanitarians' dilemma and of the profound moral ambivalence of the whole project of "humanizing war" through law in the late nineteenth century. In this sense, contemporary humanitarians may have failed one of their most revered founding fathers.

5.5 The two faces of the laws of war

Leaving aside the humanitarians' dilemma and its suppression, this last section looks more closely at how the introduction of the humanity concept changed the character of the laws of war by introducing the perceived need of balancing the principles of necessity and humanity.

One may doubt the existence of any major transformation in the laws of war if one accepts the Vattelian postulate of a necessary convergence of humanitarian principles and sound state policies. The legal duty to avoid "superfluous injury" is the best example. Superfluous injury is both an inefficient use of state resources and contrary to individual rights; it runs against both the political economy of violence articulated by Enlightenment theorists and the human rights protections demanded by nineteenth century humanitarians. Historically, humanitarian proposals that could be justified "in both pietist and utilitarian terms" were particularly well received by state diplomats and military officers at the beginning of the Red Cross movement.[78] Furthermore, the legal doctrines produced by nineteenth-century jurists associated with the *Institut de Droit International* also acknowledged that war could be a legitimate and rational pursuit of legitimate state interests, and as such should be limited, not wasteful, cruel, or personal.[79] The postulate of convergence would seem to imply that no balancing is needed.

[77] Moynier 1895, 99.
[78] Hutchinson 1996, 30.
[79] Koskenniemi 2002a, 83–8.

However, this apparent convergence is only superficial and misleading, as it hides from view the distinctive character and moral ambivalence of the nineteenth-century humanitarian project. As we have seen, the humanitarians condemned war-making for being uncivilized and pushed for legal measures in a language that was alien to the logic of state interests and reason of state. In addition to the set of rights we encountered in section 5.2, they pressed (unsuccessfully) for making obligations to respect human rights independent of reciprocal compliance; for banning the practice of taking noncombatants as hostages for ransom; and for making compensation for requisitions mandatory in international law.[80] Furthermore, nineteenth-century humanitarians mobilized public opinion in distinctive ways, indeed were early precursors of contemporary strategies of public naming and shaming in human rights promotion. By invoking charity, empathy, and the shame of being uncivilized, the humanitarians tried to mobilize broad political and social forces to limit the use of violence during war.[81] More than ever before, war became in the nineteenth century a public spectacle, reported regularly and in detail by the growing mass media and discussed in public commentary, not least by international lawyers. The humanitarian lawyers hoped that their public denunciations, and the emotional shock caused by widely publicizing the calamities of war, would shape public opinion and ultimately contribute to moderate and effectively constrain the use of military force.[82]

The humanitarian mobilizations of public opinion and associated legal proposals were often framed as limitations on the scope of military necessity and reason of state. In this very way of framing, they contributed to transform the character of the laws of war. They came to be understood as entailing a confrontation with sovereign decisions, and consequently necessitating a balance between the opposing principles of necessity and humanity. In the debates over the Brussels Declaration at the *Institut*, the British jurist Travers Twiss suggested that the old reason of state maxim *salus populi suprema lex* should be incorporated as a principle of the laws of war, to which Rolin's exasperated response was that the whole problem in formulating the laws of war was precisely how to simultaneously take into account necessity and humanity, conflicting principles as they were. *Salus populi suprema lex* was already part of the laws of war, indeed only another name for military necessity, and hence only one side in the difficult balance sought.[83]

[80] See Moynier 1895, 56–61; and Bluntschli 1895 [1868], 44–6, 341.
[81] See e.g. Moynier 1870, 12, and Moynier 1895, 71–2.
[82] Hutchinson 1996, 26–8; Best 1980, 138–9. Nationalist public media, however, could have precisely the opposite effect, as Geoffrey Best documents (Best 1980, 138–9).
[83] *Institut de Droit International* 1875, 467. Similarly Moynier 1895, 40.

No analogous opposition is to be found in Vattel, Wolff, or Lieber. For them, reason of state and necessity were constraining principles (also permissive, of course, as the language of privilege reveals). The good of the people, as well as the good of the international order, were understood to generate specific limitations for political rulers and military officers. As we saw in Chapter 4, the laws of war in the Enlightenment essentially encapsulated maxims of political prudence in the context of hostilities. And while long-term state interests often came into conflict with short-term interests, and did so in ways that could well unravel all legal limitations, there were no interests outside and above states—no interests of humanity—against which state interests ought to be balanced.

For the humanitarians, by contrast, necessity operates as an eminently permissive principle and humanity as an external constraint on state action. Furthermore, necessity appears to have no moral valence at all for them. It stands as a regrettable reality, the concrete form of an international order with which they had to deal and to which they reluctantly had decided to defer. The *moral* content of reason of state, which was exploited to such great lengths by the Enlightenment regular war theorists, and also to a lesser extent by Grotius in the seventeenth century, is all but gone. It is therefore hardly surprising how, devoid of any moral valence, military necessity in late nineteenth-century German military thought became radicalized to become a complete exception to all legal norms—*kriegsrason* trumps all form of *kriegsmanier*. Military necessity appears then not so much as a distinct legal principle, but rather becomes decoupled from all legality, amounting to the suspension of law in the conduct of hostilities.[84]

It is clear, then, that military necessity in the late nineteenth-century came to be something very different from what earlier thinkers had in mind. Vattel would have protested that taking exception from all legality threatened to unravel all limitations in war, a development that should be avoided at all costs *as a matter of good statesmanship*. Somewhat ironically, nineteenth-century humanitarians may have contributed to eroding the restraining aspects of the necessity principle. By articulating necessity and humanity as opposites, they contributed to set the stage in which one side in the opposition could overtake

[84] This radicalization can be traced back to the early 1870s but its most devastating impact can be seen in the conduct of the First World War (Hull 2008, 365; Hull 2014; also Best 1980, 135–46, 173–7). Hull reconstructs in detail a complex constellation of elements that contributed to this radicalization, but reaction to the humanitarians and to the peace movement may have been one of them, as Best suggests (Best 1980, 144).

the other. Conversely, if humanity is singled out as the distinctive principle of the laws of war—as in the term "international humanitarian law," which nowadays is the most frequent mode of reference to the laws of war—then there is the danger of presenting the laws of war as embodiments of rescue, amelioration, and humanity. From that optic, we lose sight of the perennial presence of reason of state in the operation of the laws of war.

Epilogue

We have seen in the preceding chapters how the modern laws of war evolved historically from largely self-enforcing customary norms and practices in European inter-state warfare. In Vattel's account of regular war, belligerent states comply to the extent that they take it to be in their best interest to do so. The most important interest is to keep the destructiveness of war within certain limits, but also important is the anticipation of onerous consequences from legal breaches, either in the form of direct reprisals or from developing a reputation for savagery that could be harmful in the future.

As many commentators have noted, this old normative logic no longer seems to hold.[1] Non-international armed conflicts, by far the most prevalent form of warfare in contemporary politics, do not seem to sustain the reciprocity dynamics that historically made the laws of war a largely self-enforcing project. Furthermore, in contrast to the conception of war on the basis of which the laws of war developed historically, the contemporary law of armed conflict does not treat all armed forces as equals in legal privileges and obligations, and virtually proscribes belligerent reprisals as an instrument of legal compliance. Typically only one side in war has sovereign standing, while the other not only lacks belligerent privileges but is also liable to punishment by its enemy. Neither international law nor the contemporary dynamics of armed conflict appear to sustain the logic of reciprocity that was essential for the laws of war during most of their existence.[2]

Unmoored from its original and relatively stabilizing conditions, the laws of war appear to be drifting. As noted in the Introduction, for some critics this drift has been alarming, as the law threatens to become a predominantly authorizing and permissive regime, oriented more toward sanctioning and

[1] On the obsolescence of the normative logic of reciprocity, see e.g. Clark et al. 2018; Lamp 2011; Benvenisti 2010.

[2] On the proposition that belligerent privileges apply only to state forces, not to non-state actors, see Henckaerts and Doswald-Beck 2009, 11. For contrasting assessments of the importance of reciprocity in contemporary armed conflicts, see Morrow (2014, 62, *passim*), for whom reciprocity remains important, "an unstated but necessary norm underlying the laws of war," as well as Posner 2013; Peeler 2019.

The Laws of War in International Thought. Pablo Kalmanovitz, Oxford University Press (2020). © Pablo Kalmanovitz.
DOI: 10.1093/oso/9780198790259.001.0001.

legitimating than limiting state force.[3] To others, the drift amounts to the end of the laws of war as a viable international project.[4] Yet for others, such drift is a positive development, as it heralds the progressive "humanization of the laws of war" through the "convergence" of several international legal regimes, the common purpose of which is to protect civilians and ultimately to safeguard the dignity of the human person.[5] For these last commentators, there is not so much a drift in the foundations of international humanitarian law but rather the progressive realignment and convergence of international humanitarian, human rights and criminal law, which can impose progressively greater limitations on the use of force by strengthening the protective and constraining dimensions of the law of armed conflict.

The thesis of convergence reflects important institutional developments in international law. Regional human rights courts, notably the Inter-American Court of Human Rights but also the European Court, have become actively involved in monitoring compliance with the law of armed conflict. The courts' original mandate of human rights protection during peacetime has been leveraged by expansive rulings that follow the convergent interpretation, according to which human rights law applies "concurrently" with the laws of war during an armed conflict.[6] Alongside these developments, criminal investigations by international courts, notably the International Criminal Tribunal for the former Yugoslavia, the International Criminal Tribunal for Rwanda, and the International Criminal Court, have produced a considerable amount of jurisprudence applicable to the regulation of hostilities beyond the traditional instruments of the laws of war, a development which stands in marked contrast to the dearth of criminal provisions in the traditional instruments.

Of course, this epilogue cannot settle the debate about the future of the laws of war, but it can highlight the remarkable persistence in time of several important and characteristic elements of the modern laws of war. Their persistence may not be as evident as it should be, particularly if one is attached to the image of legal convergence. But in order to better understand the nature of any such convergence, and the complex interplay between human rights, international criminal law, and the law of armed conflict in the present, it is necessary to have a clear sense of the historical origins and distinctive orientation of the laws of war.

[3] Kennedy 2006; Koskenniemi 2002b, 167–71.

[4] Lamp 2011; Clark et al. 2018.

[5] E.g. Teitel 2011; Walzer 2004, 3–22; Meron 2000; Cançado Trindade 2001.

[6] On the Inter-American Court of Human Rights an the law of armed conflict, see e.g. Burgorgue-Larsen and Ubeda de Torres 2011; Ibánez Rivas 2016. On the European Court of Human Rights, see Milanovic 2012.

We have seen how Enlightenment jurists conceived of war as the result of a political conflict among legally equal parties, which dispute each other's claims largely non-punitively and pursue limited political goals through limited military means. A central legal construct in this normative conception is the "state of war," which opens with a war declaration and concludes with a peace treaty, and in which a special legal regime governing the use of force applies. In Chapter 2 we saw that this legal construct can be found already in early modernity—from which it can be traced back to Roman law—but it continues to be part of the constitutive fabric of the contemporary laws of war. Since the practice of war declarations has fallen into desuetude, the politics of legal classification of violence has become all the more important. The "state of war" construct has been reaffirmed in important rulings by the International Court of Justice, according to which the law of armed conflict constitutes a *lex specialis* relative to human rights law, and as such contains exceptions to obligations derived from human rights.[7] It is also manifest in the common use of the vernacular of "operational theater," "zone of operations," "area of hostilities," etc. which signal the endurance of a "normative project whose goal it is to make sure that the battlefield, or something as close as possible to it, remains a central notion to the pursuit of warfare."[8]

The International Committee of the Red Cross (ICRC) made an important doctrinal update to this normative logic when it produced its recent interpretive guidelines on the concept of "direct participation in hostilities."[9] The ICRC in effect updated the definition of irregular combatancy, a central concern for both Vattel and Lieber. The ICRC guidelines posit a two-fold functional criterion that serves to designate which agents can be lawfully targeted in war, namely, members of "dissident armed forces" and civilians who directly participate in hostilities. While this criterion is meant to apply in contexts of irregular warfare, and those designated lack any belligerent privileges, the ICRC guidelines draw a conventional distinction between battlefield and peace zones very much in the spirit of Vattel and Lieber, who were also keen on articulating criteria on how irregular and unprivileged fighters could be lawfully treated.

Another persistent element of the laws of war has to do with punishment. We saw in Chapters 2 and 4 how central to the modern laws of war is the postulate of certain privileges of belligerence, which include the immunity of state

[7] See in particular *Legality of the Threat or Use of Nuclear Weapons*, Advisory Opinion, 1996 ICJ REP. 226, §§ 24–25; *Legal Consequences of the Construction of a Wall in the Occupied Palestinian Territory*, Advisory Opinion, 2004 ICJ REP. 136, §§102–13.

[8] As pointed out by Mégret 2011, 137.

[9] ICRC 2009.

soldiers to being punished by their enemies, except possibly for war crimes. State soldiers can kill and maim with impunity, as long as it is in the context of hostilities and their target is lawful; if they surrender or are made prisoners, they are not only immune to punishment but also entitled to certain special protections associated with their status as prisoners of war.

Furthermore, both historically and in contemporary law, amnesties have been deemed necessary to facilitate transitions from war to peace. The ICRC has recognized as part of customary international humanitarian law a rule according to which, "at the end of hostilities, the authorities in power must endeavor to grant the broadest possible amnesty to persons who have participated in a non-international armed conflict," with the exception of acts that constitute war crimes.[10] This rule is motivated by the valuable role of amnesties in facilitating transitions from war to peace, and hence limiting the duration of war, a justification that can be found in Grotius, Wolff, Vattel, and even Kant. And yet, while this old element in the laws of war persists, it is now in tension with the "anti-impunity agenda" in human rights and international criminal law, which in the spirit of convergence has come to denounce and reject amnesties in transitions from war to peace.[11]

By getting a clearer sense of the intellectual foundations of the laws of war and of the persistence of some of its constitutive elements, we are in a better position to identify the limitations that the convergence of legal regimes must necessarily face. We can also better appreciate the ethical dilemmas and conflicts of value that the convergence thesis may elicit, and be mindful of the striking echoes and contrasts between the contemporary aspiration to humanize war and its late-nineteenth century predecessors.[12]

In this process, it is crucial not to lose sight of the characteristic permissiveness of the law of war, and of the role that state sovereignty and reason of state have in activating and giving sanction to its permissions. The intellectual history of the laws of war reveal and display their crucial importance unmistakably. But one can lose sight if this if one imagines or expects that human rights can progressively merge with the laws of war and virtuously humanize war. It is part of the very concept of a state of war that states have wide powers to kill and

[10] Henckaerts and Doswald-Beck 2009, 614–8.

[11] For a valuable overview of the anti-impunity agenda and some of its problems, see Engle 2016. The practical dilemma between peace and punshment in transitions from war to peace has been discussed extensively in the transitional justice literature, but for a recent rich theoretical discussion see Freeman and Orozco 2020.

[12] Valuable recent discussions of the convergence thesis and its problems in the context of *ius in bello* include Modirzadeh 2010 and Bohrer, Dill, and Duffy 2020. I discuss some of the morally problematic aspects of eroding the distinction between states of war and peacetime from a *ius post bellum* perspective in Kalmanovitz 2016.

cause deliberate harm. Reason of state, now in the legal guise of military necessity and tactical advantage, continues to be an active element in the laws of war, and for as long as there are laws of war, it will continue to do so.

The contrast with Gustave Moynier is illuminating. As we saw in Chapter 5, he was aware of the moral danger for humanitarians of giving ideological cover to, and thus prolonging, the horrors of war. Instead of denouncing war for what it is, humanitarians could misguide the public by making it appear humane and in the process become abettors of its continuation. Moynier eased his moral conscience with the thought that humanitarianism in war would inexorably lead to pacifism, but we now know that this is by no means the case. On the contrary, history has shown that Moynier's fears but not his hopes were well founded.

References

Alexander, Amanda. 2015. "A Short History of International Humanitarian Law." *The European Journal of International Law* no. 26(1):109–38.

Alexandrowicz, Charled Henry. 1958. "The Theory of Recognition in Fieri." *British Yearbook of International Law* no. 34:176–98.

Anderson, Matthew Smith. 1988. *War and Society in Europe of the Old Regime, 1618–1789*. New York: St. Martin's Press.

Ando, Clifford. 2010. "Empire and the Laws of War: A Roman Archaeology." In *The Roman Foundations of the Law of Nations: Alberico Gentili and the Justice of Empire*, edited by Benedict Kingsbury and Benjamin Straumann. Oxford; New York: Oxford University Press.

Anghie, Anthony. 2004*Imperialism, Sovereignty and the Making of International Law*. Cambridge: Cambridge University Press.

Anghie, Antony. 2011. "Vattel and Colonialism: Some Preliminary Observations." In *Vattel's International Law in a XXIst Century Perspective*, edited by Vincent Chetail and Peter Haggenmacher. Boston: M. Nijhoff.

Aquinas, Thomas, and R.W. Dyson. 2004. *Aquinas: Political Writings*. Cambridge: Cambridge University Press.

Armitage, David. 2012. *Foundations of Modern International Thought*. Cambridge: Cambridge University Press.

Armitage, David. 2017. *Civil Wars: A History in Ideas*. New York: Alfred A. Knopf.

Ayala, Balthazar, and John Westlake. 1912. *Three Books on Law of War and on the Duties Connected to War and on Military Discipline*. Washington D.C.: Carnegie Institution of Washington.

Bain, William. 2013. "Saving the Innocent, then and now: Vitoria, Dominion and World Order." *History of Political Thought* no. 34(4):588–613.

Baker-Röben, Betsy. 2002. "The Method Behind Bluntschli's 'Modern' International Law." *Journal of the History of International Law* no. 4:249–92.

Barnett, Michael N. 2011. *The Empire of Humanity: A History of Humanitarianism*. Ithaca, N.Y.: Cornell University Press.

Baugh, Daniel A. 2011. *The Global Seven Years War, 1754–1763: Britain and France in a Great Power Contest*. 1st ed. Harlow, England; New York: Longman.

Baumgartner, Frederic J. 2011. *Declaring War in Early Modern Europe*. 1st ed. New York: Palgrave Macmillan.

Baxter, Richard. 2013 [1963]. "The First Modern Codification of the Law of War: Francis Lieber and General Orders No. 100." In *Humanizing the Laws of War: Selected Writings of Richard Baxter*, edited by Detlev F. Vagts, Theodor Meron, Stephen M. Schwebel, and Charles Keever. Oxford: Oxford University Press.

Beaulac, Stéphane 2003. "Emer de Vattel and the Externalization of Sovereignty." *Journal of the History of International Law* no. 5:237–92.

Becker Lorca, Arnulf. 2014. *Mestizo International Law: A Global Intellectual History 1842–1933*. Cambridge: Cambridge University Press.

Béguelin, Ed. 1929. *En Souvenir de Vattel*. Neuchatel: Universtié de Neuchatel.
Belissa, Marc. 1998. *Fraternité Universelle et Intérêt National (1713–1795)*. Paris: Éditions Kimé.
Bélissa, Marc. 2004. "Peace Treaties, Bonne Foi and European Civility in the Enlightenment." In *Peace Treaties and International Law in European History*, edited by Randall Lesaffer. Cambridge: Cambridge University Press.
Bell, David A. 2007. *The First Total War: Napoleon's Europe and the Birth of Warfare as We Know it*. Boston: Houghton Mifflin.
Bellamy, Alex. 2006. *Just Wars: From Cicero to Iraq*. Cambridge: Polity.
Bellamy, Alex. 2018. "Francisco de Vitoria (1492–1546)." In *Just War Thinkers: From Cicero to the 21st Century*, edited by Daniel Brunstetter and Cian O'Driscoll. London and New York: Routledge.
Bély, Lucien. 1992. *Les relations internationales en Europe: XVIIe–XVIIIe siècles*. Paris: Presses Universitaires de France.
Benner, Erica. 2013. "Nationalism: Intellectual Origins." In *The Oxford Handbook of the History of Nationalism*, edited by John Breuilly. Oxford: Oxford University Press.
Benton, Lauren A. 2010. *A Search for Sovereignty: Law and Geography in European Empires, 1400–1900*. Cambridge: Cambridge University Press.
Benvenisti, Eyal. 2010. "The Law on Asymmetric Warfare." In *Looking to the Future: Essays on International Law in Honor of Michael Reisman*, edited by Mahnoush Arsanji, Jacob Katz Cogan, Robert Sloane, and Siegfried Wiessner. Leiden: Martinus Nijhoff.
Benvenisti, Eyal, and Doreen Lustig. 2020. "Monopolizing War: Codifying the Laws of War to Reassert Governmental Authority 1856–1874." *European Journal of International Law* no. 31.
Berman, Nathaniel. 2004. "Privileging Combat? Contemporary Conflict and the Legal Construction of War." *Columbia Journal of Transnational Law* no. 43(1):1–72.
Best, Geoffrey. 1980. *Humanity in Warfare*. New York: Columbia University Press.
Best, Geoffrey. 1994. *War and Law since 1945*. Oxford, England: Clarendon Press.
Bhuta, Nehal. 2017. "State Theory, State Order, State System—*Jus Gentium* and the Constitution of Public Power." In *System, Order, and International Law*, edited by Stefan Kadelbach, Thomas Kleinlein, and David Roth-Isigkeit. Oxford: Oxford University Press,
Black, Jeremy. 1999. *From Louis XIV to Napoleon: The Fate of a Great Power*. London: UCL Press.
Bluntschli, Caspar. 1895 [1868]. *Le droit international codifié*. Paris: Guillamin et Cie Editeurs.
Bohrer, Ziv, Janina Dill, and Helen Duffy. 2020. *The Law Applicable to Armed Conflict*. Cambridge: Cambridge University Press.
Brett, Annabel. 1997. *Liberty, Right and Nature: Individual Rights in Later Scholastic Thought*. Cambridge: Cambridge University Press.
Brett, Annabel. 2002a. "Natural Right and Civil Community: The Civil Philosophy of Hugo Grotius." *The Historical Journal* no. 45(1):31–51.
Brett, Annabel. 2002b. "What is Intellectual History Now?" In *What Is History Now?*, edited by D. Cannadine. London: Palgrave Macmillan.
Brett, Annabel. 2011. *Changes of State: Nature and the Limits of the City in Early Modern Natural Law*. Princeton: Princeton University Press.
Brett, Annabel. 2016. "The Space of Politics and the Space of War in Hugo Grotius's *De iure belli ac pacis*." *Global Intellectual History* no. 1(1):33–60.
Brett, Annabel. 2019. "The Subject of Sovereignty: Law, Politics and Moral Reasoning in Grotius." *Modern Intellectual History*: 1–27.

Brierly, J. L., and Andrew Clapham. 2012. *Brierly's Law of Nations: An Introduction to the Role of International Law in International Relations*. 7th ed. Oxford: Oxford University Press.

Brunt, Peter Astbury. 1990. *Roman Imperial Themes*. Oxford: Oxford University Press.

Bull, Hedley. 1966. "The Grotian Conception of International Society." In *Diplomatic Investigations: Essays in the Theory of International Politics*, edited by Herbert Butterfield and Martin Wight. Cambridge: Harvard University Press.

Bull, Hedley. 1990. "The Importance of Grotius in the Study of International Relations." In *Hugo Grotius in International Relations*, edited by Hedley Bull, Benedict Kingsbury, and Adam Roberts. Oxford: Oxford University Press.

Burgorgue-Larsen, Laurence, and Amaya Úbeda de Torres. 2011. "'War' in the Jurisprudence of the Inter-American Court of Human Rights." *Human Rights Quarterly* no. 33:148–74.

Bynkershoek, Cornelis van, and Tenney Frank. 1930 [1737]. *Quaestionum juris publici libri duo*. Oxford: Clarendon Press.

Cançado Trindade, Antônio Augusto. 2001. "Derecho Internacional de los Derechos Humanos, Derecho Internacional de los Refugiados y Derecho Internacional Humanitario: Aproximaciones y Convergencias." *CODHEM* no. Mayo/Junio:62–97.

Capozzi, Mirella, and Gino Roncaglia. 2009. "Logic and Philosophy of Logic from Humanism to Kant." In *The Development of Modern Logic*, edited by Leila Haaparanta. Oxford: Oxford University Press.

Carlyle, Thomas. 1864. *History of Friedrich the Second, Called Frederick the Great*. Vol. III. New York: Harper & brothers.

Cavallar, Georg. 2002. *The Rights of Strangers: Theories of International Hospitality, the Global Community, and Political Justice since Vitoria*. Burlington: Ashgate.

Christov, Theodore. 2013. "Vattel's Rousseau: *Ius Gentium* and the Natural Liberty of States." In *Freedom and the Construction of Europe: Religious and Constitutional Liberties*, edited by Quentin Skinner and Martin van Gelderen. Cambridge; New York: Cambridge University Press.

Christov, Theodore. 2015. *Before Anarchy: Hobbes and his Critics in Modern International Thought*. Cambridge: Cambridge University Press.

Cicero, Marcus Tullius, M.T. Griffin, and E.M. Atkins. 1991. *On Duties*. Cambridge: Cambridge University Press.

Clark, Ian, Sebastian Kaempf, Christian Reus-Smit, and Emily Tannock. 2018. "Crisis in the Laws of War? Beyond Compliance and Effectiveness." *European Journal of International Relations* no. 24(2):310–43.

Contamine, Philippe. 2000. "The Growth of State Control. Practices of War, 1300–1800: Ransom and Booty." In *War and Competition between States*, edited by Philippe Contamine. New York: Oxford University Press.

Craven, Matthew 2007. "Introduction: International Law and Its Histories." In *Time, History and International Law*, edited by Matthew Craven, Malgosia Fitzmaurice, and Maria Vogiatzi. Leiden: Martinus Nijhoff Publishers.

Crawford, Neta C. 2013. *Accountability for Killing*. Oxford: Oxford University Press.

Devetak, Richard. 2011. "Law of Nations as Reason of State: Diplomacy and the Balance of Power in Vattel's Law of Nations." *Parergon* no. 28(2):105–28.

Dill, Janina. 2015. *Legitimate Targets? Social Construction, International Law and US Bombing*. Cambridge: Cambridge University Press.

Duchhardt, Heinz. 2004. "Peace Treaties from Westphalia to the Revolutionary Era." In *Peace Treaties and International Law in European History*, edited by Randall Lesaffer. Cambridge: Cambridge University Press.

Edelstein, Dan. 2008. “War and Terror: The Law of Nations from Grotius to the French Revolution.” *French Historical Studies* no. 31(2):229–62.

Elster, Jon. 1999. *Alchemies of the Mind: Rationality and the Emotions*. Cambridge; New York: Cambridge University Press.

Engle, Karen. 2016. “A Genealogy of the Criminal Turn in Human Rights.” In *Anti-Impunity and the Human Rights Agenda*, edited by Karen Engle, Zenaida Miller, and D.M. Davis. Cambridge: Cambridge University Press.

Fabre, Cécile. 2012. *Cosmopolitan War*. Oxford: Oxford University Press.

Fassbender, Bardo, and Anne Peters. 2012. *The Oxford Handbook of the History of International Law, Oxford Handbooks*. Oxford: Oxford University Press.

Fassin, Didier. 2012. *Humanitarian Reason: A Moral History of the Present*. Berkeley: University of California Press. http://dx.doi.org/10.1525/california/9780520271166.001.0001.

Fazal, Tanisha M. 2018. *Wars of Law: Unintended Consequences in the Regulation of Armed Conflict*. Cornell: Cornell University Press.

Fenwick, Charles G. 1913. “The Authority of Vattel I.” *The American Political Science Review* no. 7(3):395–410.

Fernández-Santamaría, J. A. 1977. *The State, War and Peace: Spanish Political Thought in the Renaissance 1516–1559*. Cambridge; New York: Cambridge University Press.

Forde, Steven. 1998. “Hugo Grotius on Ethics and War.” *American Political Science Review* no. 92(3):639–48.

Foucault, Michel. 1981. *Omnes et Singulatim: towards a Criticism of ‘Political Reason.’ The Tanner Lectures on Human Values*. Utah.

Fraga Iribarne, Manuel. 1947. *Luis de Molina y el Derecho de Guerra*. Madrid: Consejo Superior de Investigaciones Científicas.

Freeman, Mark, and Iván Orozco. 2020. *Negotiating Transitional Justice: Firsthand Lessons from Colombia and Beyond*. Cambridge: Cambridge University Press.

Füssel, Marian. 2012. “‘Féroces et Barbares’? Cossacks, Kalmyks and Russian Irregular Warfare during the Seven Years’ War.” In *The Seven Years’ War: Global Views*, edited by Mark H. Danley and Patrick J. Speelman. Boston: Brill.

Geuss, Raymond. 2001. *History and Illusion in Politics*. Cambridge; New York: Cambridge University Press.

Geuss, Raymond. 2010. *Politics and the Imagination*. Princeton: Princeton University Press.

Gierke, Otto von, and Ernest Barker. 1934. *Natural Law and the Theory of Society, 1500 to 1800*. Cambridge: The University Press.

Giladi, Rotem. 2012. “A Different Sense of Humanity: Occupation in Francis Lieber’s Code.” *International Review of the Red Cross* no. 94(885):81–116.

Giladi, Rotem. 2014. “The Enactment of Irony: Reflection on the Origins of the Martens Clause.” *The European Journal of International Law* no. 25(3):847–69.

Goering, Joseph. 2008. “The Internal Forum and the Literature of Penance and Confession.” In *The History of Medieval Canon Law in the Classical Period, 1140–1234: from Gratian to the Decretals of Pope Gregory IX*, edited by Wilfried Hartmann and Kenneth Pennington. Washington D.C.: The Catholic University of America Press.

Grewe, Wilhelm Georg. 2000. *The Epochs of International Law*. Berlin; New York: Walter de Gruyter.

Grotius, Hugo, and Richard Tuck. 2005. *The Rights of War and Peace*, edited by Richard Tuck. Indianapolis: Liberty Fund.

Haakonssen, Knud. 1985. “Hugo Grotius and the History of Political Thought.” *Political Theory* no. 13(2):239–65.

Haakonssen, Knud. 2006. "German Natural Law." In *The Cambridge History of Eighteenth-Century Political Thought*, edited by Mark Goldie and Robert Wokler. Cambridge; New York: Cambridge University Press.

Haggenmacher, Peter. 1983. *Grotius et la doctrine de la guerre juste, Publications de l'Institut universitaire de hautes études internationales, Genève*. Paris: Presses universitaires de France.

Haggenmacher, Peter. 1990. "Grotius and Gentili: A Reassessment of Thomas E. Holland Inaugural Lecture." In *Hugo Grotius in International Relations*, edited by Hedley Bull, Benedict Kingsbury, and Adam Roberts. Oxford: Oxford University Press.

Haggenmacher, Peter. 1992. "Just War and Regular War in Sixteenth Century Spanish Doctrine." *International Review of the Red Cross* no. 290:434–45.

Haggenmacher, Peter. 2011. "Le Modèle de Vattel et la Discipline du Droit International." In *Vattel's International Law in a XXIst Century Perspective*, edited by Vincent Chetail and Peter Haggenmacher. Boston; Leiden: Martinus Nijhoff Publishers.

Hamilton, Bernice. 1963. *Political Thought in Sixteenth-Century Spain*. Oxford: Clarendon Press.

Hanke, Lewis. 1949. *The Spanish Struggle for Justice in the Conquest of America*. Philadelphia: University of Pennsylvania Press.

Haque, Adil Ahmad. 2016. "Human Rights in Armed Conflict." Available at <https://www.justsecurity.org/34631/human-rights-armed-conflict-part/> (published November 21, 2016, accessed July 1, 2020).

Haque, Adil Ahmad. 2017. *Law and Morality at War*. Oxford: Oxford University Press.

Haque, Adil Ahmad. 2019. "Indeterminacy in the Law of Armed Conflict." *I nternational Law Studies* no. 95:118–60.

Hathaway, Oona, and Scott Shapiro. 2017. *The Internationalists: How a Radical Plan to Outlaw War Remade the World*. New York: Simon & Schuster.

Henckaerts, Jean-Marie, and Louise Doswald-Beck. 2007. *Customary International Humanitarian Law*. Vol. 1. Cambridge: Cambridge University Press.Henckaerts, Jean-Marie, and Louise Doswald-Beck. 2009. *Customary International Humanitarian Law*. Vol. 1. Cambridge: Cambridge University Press.

Hinsley, F. H. 1963. *Power and the Pursuit of Peace: Theory and Practice in the History of Relations between States*. Cambridge: Cambridge University Press.

Hobbes, Thomas, and Richard Tuck. 1991. *Leviathan*. Cambridge; New York: Cambridge University Press.

Hochstrasser, T. J. 2000. *Natural Law Theories in the Early Enlightenment, Ideas in Context*. Cambridge; New York: Cambridge University Press.

Holmes, Robert. 1992. "Can War Be Morally Justified? The Just War Theory." In *Just War Theory*, edited by Jean Bethke Elshtain. New York: New York University Press.

Holquist, Peter. 2013. "Fedor Martens (1845-1909) and the Crystallization of International Law in Russia." Paper presented at the Russian History Seminar, Washington DC.

Holquist, Peter. 2015. "Codifying the "Laws of War": Brussels 1874." Paper presented at the "History of the Laws of War" conference, European University Institute, Florence.

Holsti, Kalevi. 1991. *Peace and War: Armed Conflicts and International Order, 1648–1989*. Cambridge; New York: Cambridge University Press.

Hont, Istvan. 2005. *Jealousy of Trade: International Competition and the Nation-State in Historical Perspective*. Cambridge: Harvard University Press.

Höpfl, Harro. 2004. *Jesuit Political Thought: The Society of Jesus and the State, c. 1540–1630*. Cambridge: Cambridge University Press.

Höpfl, Harro. 2006. "Scholasticism in Quentin Skinner's Foundations." In *Rethinking the Foundations of Modern Political Thought*, edited by Annabel Brett, James Tully, and Holly Hamilton-Bleakley. Cambridge: Cambridge University Press.

Howard, Michael. 1979. "Temperamenta Belli: Can War Be Controlled?" In *Restraints on War: Studies in the Limitation of Armed Conflict*, edited by Michael Howard. Oxford: Oxford University Press.

Howard, Michael. 2001. *War in European History*. Oxford; New York: Oxford University Press.

Hull, Isabel. 2008. ""Military Necessity" and the Laws of War in Imperial Germany." In *Order, Conflict, and Violence*, edited by Stathis Kalyvas, Ian Shapiro, and Tarek Masoud. Cambridge: Cambridge University Press.

Hull, Isabel. 2014. *A Scrap of Paper: Breaking and Making International Law during the Great War*. Ithaca: Cornell University Press.

Hunter, Ian. 2001. *Rival Enlightenments: Civil and Metaphysical Philosophy in Early Modern Germany*. Cambridge; New York: Cambridge University Press.

Hunter, Ian. 2010. "Vattel's Law of Nations: Diplomatic Casuistry for the Protestant Nation." *Grotiana* no. 31:108–40.

Hunter, Ian. 2013. "The Figure of Man and the Territorialisation of Justice in 'Enlightenment' Natural Law: Pufendorf and Vattel." *Intellectual History Review* no. 23(3):289–307.

Hurrell, Andrew. 1996. "Vattel: Pluralism and its Limits." In *Classical Theories of International Relations*, edited by Ian Clark and Iver B. Neumann. Basingstoke; New York: Macmillan; St Martin's Press.

Hutchinson, John. 1996. *Champions of Charity: War and the Rise of the Red Cross*. Boulder: Westview Press.

Ibánez Rivas, Juana Mar̂ia. 2016. "El Derecho Internacional Humanitario en la Jurisprudencia de la Corte Interamericana de Derechos Humanos." *Revista de Derecho del Estado* no. 36:167–98.

ICRC. 1901. "The Croix-Rouge et l'Ouvre de la Paix." *Bulletin International des Societés de la Croix-Rouge* no. 126:74–7.

ICRC. 2009. *Interpretive Guidance on the Notion of Direct Participation in Hostilities under International Humanitarian Law*. Geneva: International Committee of the Red Cross.

Institut de Droit International. 1875. "Examen de la déclaration de Bruxelles." *Revue de droit international et de législation comparée* no. VII:438–552.

Institut de Droit International. 1881. "Les lois de la guerre sur terre—Lettres de M. le Comte de Moltke et de M. Bluntschli." *Revue de droit international et de législation comparée* no. XIII:79–84.

Jo, Hyeran. 2015. *Compliant Rebels*. Cambridge: Cambridge University Press.

Johnson, James Turner. 1975. *Ideology, Reason, and the Limitation of War: Religious and Secular Concepts, 1200–1740*. Princeton: Princeton University Press.

Jouannet, Emmanuelle. 1998. *Emer de Vattel el l'émergence Doctrinale du Droit Internationale Classique*. Paris: Editions A. Pedone.

Hobbes, Thomas, and Richard Tuck. 1991. *Leviathan*. Cambridge: Cambridge University Press.

Kalmanovitz, Pablo. 2015a. "Aggression and the Symmetrical Application of International Humanitarian Law." *International Theory* no. 7(1):1–32.

Kalmanovitz, Pablo. 2015b. "Modern Sources of the Regular War Tradition: Grotius to Vattel." In *Oxford Handbook of the Ethics of War*, edited by Seth Lazar and Helen Frowe. Oxford: Oxford University Press.

Kalmanovitz, Pablo. 2016. "*Ius post bellum* and the Imperative to Supersede IHL." *American Journal of International Law Unbound* no. 110:193–8.

Kalmanovitz, Pablo. 2018. "Sovereignty, Pluralism, and Regular War: Wolff and Vattel's Enlightenment Critique of Just War." *Political Theory* no. 46(2): 218–241.

Kalshoven, Frits. 2005. *Belligerent Reprisals*. Leiden; Boston: Martinus Nijhoff Publishers.

Kant, Immanuel, and Hans Reiss. 1970. *Kant's Political Writings*. Cambridge: Cambridge University Press.

Keen, Maurice. 1965. *The Laws of War in the late Middle Ages*. London; Toronto: Routledge & Kegan Paul.

Kelley, Donald. 1994. "Law." In *The Cambridge History of Political Thought, 1450–1700*, edited by J. H. Burns and Mark Goldie. Cambridge; New York: Cambridge University Press.

Kennedy, David. 1996. "International Law and the Nineteenth Century: History of an Illusion." *Nordic Journal ofInternational Law* no. 65:385–420.

Kennedy, David. 2006. *Of War and Law*. Princeton: Princeton University Press.

Kingsbury, Benedict. 1999. "Grotius, Law and Moral Skepticism: Theory and Practice in the Thought of Hedley Bull." In *Classical Theories in International Relations*, edited by Ian Clark. New York: Palgrave Publishers.

Kinsella, Helen. 2011. *The Image before the Weapon: A Critical History of the Distinction between Combatant and Civilian*. Ithaca: Cornell University Press.

Kinsella, Helen. 2017. "Superfluous Injury and Unnecessary Suffering: National Liberation and the Laws of War." *Political Power and Social Theory* no. 32:205–31.

Kolb, Robert. 1997. "Origin of the Twin Terms Jus ad Bellum/Jus in Bello." *International Review of the Red Cross* no. 320:553–62.

Koselleck, Reinhart. 1988. *Critique and Crisis*. 1st ed. Cambridge, Mass.: MIT Press.

Koskenniemi, Martti. 2002a. *The Gentle Civilizer of Nations: The Rise and Fall of International Law 1870–1960*. Cambridge; New York: Cambridge University Press.

Koskenniemi, Martti. 2002b. "The Lady Doth Protest Too Much: Kosovo and the Turn to Ethics in International Law." *Modern Law Review* no. 65.

Koskenniemi, Martti. 2005. *From Apology to Utopia: The Structure of International Legal Argument*. Cambridge: Cambridge University Press.

Koskenniemi, Martti. 2008. "Into Positivism: Georg Friedrich von Martens (1756–1821) and Modern International Law." *Constellations* no. 15(2):189–207.

Koskenniemi, Martti. 2011. "Empire and International Law: The Real Spanish Contribution." *University of Toronto Law Journal* no. 61:1–36.

Koskenniemi, Martti. 2012a. "A History of International Law Histories." In *The Oxford Handbook of the History of International Law*, edited by Fassbender Bardo and Anne Peters. Oxford: Oxford University Press.

Koskenniemi, Martti. 2012b. "Ius Gentium and the Birth of Modernity." In *Constructing International Law: The Birth of a Discipline*, edited by Luigi Nuzzo and Milos Vec. Frankfurt am Main: Vittorio Klostermann.

Koskenniemi, Martti. 2013a. "Histories of International Law: Significance and Problems for a Critical View." *Temple International and Comparative Law Journal* no. 27(2): 215–40.

Koskenniemi, Martti. 2013b. "International Law and the Emergence of Capitalism: Grotius to Smith." In *The Roots of International Law / Les fondements du droit international*, edited by Pierre-Marie Dupuy and Vincent Chetail. Brill, Nijhoff.

Koskenniemi, Martti. 2014. "Vitoria and Us." *Rechtsgeschichte* no. 22:119–38.

Koskenniemi, Martti. 2019. "Imagining the Rule of Law: Rereading the Grotian 'Tradition.'" *The European Journal of International Law* no. 30(1):17–52.

Kress, Claus, and Frédéric Mégret. 2014. "The Regulation of Non-international Armed Conflicts: Can a Privilege of Belligerency be Envisioned in the Law of Non-international Armed Conflicts?" *International Review of the Red Cross* no. 96(893):29–66.

Kulsrud, Carl J. 1936. *Maritime Neutrality to 1780*. Boston: Little, Brown, and Company.

Lamp, Nicholas. 2011. "Conceptions of War and Paradigms of Compliance: The 'New War' Challenge to Humanitarian Law." *Journal of Conflict and Security Law* no. 16(2): 225–62.

Lauterpacht, Hersh. 1946. "The Grotian Tradition in International Law." *British Yearbook of International Law* no. 23:1–53.

Lauterpacht, Hersch. 1953. "Rules of Warfare in an Unlawful War." In *Law and Politics in the World Community: Essays on Hans Kelsen's Pure Theory and Related Problems in International Law*, edited by George A. Lipsky. Berkeley: University of California Press.

Lavenia, Vincenzo. 2014. "Conscience and Catholic Discipline of War: Sins and Crimes." *Journal of Early Modern History* no. 18:447–71.

Lazar, Seth. 2009. "Responsibility, Risk, and Killing in Self-Defense." *Ethics* no. 119(4):699–728.

Lazar, Seth. 2012. "The Morality and Law of War." In *The Routledge Companion to Philosophy of Law*, edited by Andrei Marmor. London: Routledge.

Lee, Daniel. 2016. *Popular Sovereignty in Early Modern Constitutional Thought, Oxford Constitutional Theory*. Oxford: Oxford University Press.

Leibniz, Gottfried Wilhelm, and Patrick Riley. 1988. *Leibniz: Political Writings*. 2nd ed. Cambridge; New York: Cambridge University Press.

Lesaffer, Randall. 2004. "Peace Treaties from Lodi to Westphalia." In *Peace Treaties and International Law in European History: From the Late Middle Ages to World War One*, edited by Randall Lesaffer. Cambridge; New York: Cambridge University Press.

Lesaffer, Randall. 2005. "Paix et guerre dans les grands traités du dix-huitième siècle." *Journal of the History of International Law* no. 7:25–41.

Lesaffer, Randall. 2007a. "International Law and Its History: The Story of an Unrequited Love." In *Time, History and International Law*, edited by Matthew Craven, Malgosia Fitzmaurice, and Maria Vogiatzi. Leiden: Martinus Nijhoff Publishers.

Lesaffer, Randall. 2007b. "Siege Warfare in the Early Modern Age: A Study on the Customary Laws of War." In *The Nature of Customary Law*, edited by Amanda Perreau-Saussine and James Bernard Murphy. Cambridge; New York: Cambridge University Press.

Lesaffer, Randall. 2010. "Alberico Gentili's Ius Post Bellum and Early Modern Peace Treaties." In *The Roman Foundations of the Law of Nations: Alberico Gentili and the Justice of Empire*, edited by Benedict Kingsbury and Benjamin Straumann. Oxford; New York: Oxford University Press.

Lesaffer, Randall. 2011. "A Schoolmaster Abolishing Homework? Vattel on Peacemaking and Peace Treaties." In *Vattel's International Law in a XXIst Century Perspective*, edited by Vincent Chetail and Peter Haggenmacher. Boston: M. Nijhoff.

Lieber, Francis. 1881a. *Manual of Political Ethics*, edited by Theodore Woolsey. Vol. 1. Philadelphia: J.B. Lippincott &co.

Lieber, Francis. 1881b. *Manual of Political Ethics*, edited by Theodore Woolsey. Vol. 2. Philadelphia: J.B. Lippincott &co.

Linklater, Andrew. 1982. *Men and Citizens in the Theory of International Relations*. New York: St. Martin's Press.

Lloyd, Howell A. 1991. "Constitutionalism." In *The Cambridge History of Political Thought, 1450–1700*, edited by J. H. Burns and Mark Goldie. Cambridge; New York: Cambridge University Press.

Loughlin, Martin. 2010. *Foundations of Public Law*. Oxford: Oxford University Press.

Luban, David. 2013. "Military Necessity and the Cultures of Military Law." *Leiden Journal of International Law* no. 26(2): 315–49.

Lynn, John A. 1993. "How War Fed War: The Tax of Violence and Contributions during the Grand Siècle." *The Journal of Modern History* no. 65(2):286–310.

Lynn, John A. 2002. "A Brutal Necessity? The Devastation of the Palatinate, 1688–1689." In *Civilians in the Path of War*, edited by Mark Grimsley and Clifford J. Rogers. Lincoln: University of Nebraska Press.

Malcolm, Noel. 2007. *Reason of State, Propaganda, and the Thirty Years' War*. Oxford: Oxford University Press.

Malettke, Klaus. 1998. "L'"equilibre" Européen face a la 'monarchia universalis.'" In *L'Invention de la Diplomatie*, edited by Lucien Bély. Paris: Press Universitaires de France.

Mantilla, Giovanni. 2019. "Social Pressure and the Making of Wartime Legal Protections for Civilians." *European Journal of International Relations* no. 26(2): 443–68.

Martens, Georg Frederic de. 1801. *Précis du droit des gens moderne de l'Europe, fondé sur les tratiés et l'usage*. Gottingue: Dieterich.

Martens, Georg Frederic de, and William Cobbett. 1795. *Summary of the Law of Nations*. Philadelphia: Thomas Bradford.

Maryks, Robert. 2008. *Saint Cicero and the Jesuits: The Influence of the Liberal Arts on the Adoption of Moral Probabilism*. Aldershot: Ashgate.

Mavrodes, George I. 1975. "Conventions and the Morality of War." *Philosophy and Public Affairs* no. 4(2):117–31.

May, Larry. 2007. *War Crimes and Just War*. Cambridge: Cambridge University Press.

McMahan, Jeff. 2004. "The Ethics of Killing in War." *Ethics* no. 114(4):693.

McMahan, Jeff. 2008. "The Morality of War and the Law of War." In *Just and Unjust Warriors: The Moral and Legal Status of Soldiers*, edited by David Rodin and Henry Shue. Oxford: Oxford University Press.

McMahan, Jeff. 2009. *Killing in War*. Oxford: Clarendon Press.

Mégret, Frédéric. 2006. "From 'Savages' to 'Unlawful Combatants': A Postcolonial Look at International Humanitarian Law's 'Other.'" In *International Law and its Others*, edited by Anne Orford. Cambridge; New York: Cambridge University Press.

Mégret, Frédéric. 2011. "War and the Vanishing Battlefield." *Loyola University Chicago International Law Review* no. 9(1):131–155.

Mégret, Frédéric. 2016. "Theorizing the Laws of War." In *The Oxford Handbook of the Theory of International Law*, edited by Anne Orford and Florian Hoffmann. Oxford: Oxford University Press.

Melzer, Nils. 2010. "Keeping the Balance between Military Necessity and Humanity." *New York University Journal of International Law and Politics* no. 42(3):831–916.

Meron, Theodor. 1991. "Common Rights of Mankind in Gentili, Grotius, and Suárez." *The American Journal of International Law* no. 85:110–16.

Meron, Theodor. 2000. "The Humanization of Humanitarian Law." *American Journal of International Law* no. 94(2):239–78.

Midgley, E. B. F. 1975. *The Natural Law Tradition and the Theory of International Relations*. London: Elek Books.

Milanovic, Marko. 2012. "Al-Skeini and Al-Jedda in Strasbourg." *The European Journal of International Law* no. 23(1):121–39.

Modirzadeh, Naz. 2010. "The Dark Sides of Convergence." *U.S. Naval War College International Law Studies* no. 86:349–410.

Montesquieu, Charles de Secondat, Anne Cohler, Basia Miller, and Harold Stone. 1989 [1748]. *The Spirit of the Laws*. Cambridge: Cambridge University Press.

Montesquieu, Charles de Secondat, and Charles Porret. 2000 [1734]. *Réflexions sur la monarchie universelle en Europe*. Genève: Droz.

Morgenthau, Hans. 1948. *Politics Among Nations*. New York: Alfred A. Knopf.

Morrow, James. 2014. *Order within Anarchy*. Cambridge: Cambridge University Press.

Moyn, Samuel. 2010. *The Last Utopia: Human Rights in History*. Cambridge, Mass.: Harvard University Press.

Moyn, Samuel. 2021. *Humane: How America Made the World Safe for Endless War*. New York: Farrar, Straus Giroux.

Moynier, Gustave. 1870. *Étude sur la Convention de Genève*. Paris: Librairie de Joël Cherbuliez.

Moynier, Gustave. 1895. *Essai sur les caractères généraux des lois de la guerre*. Genève: Ch. Eggimann & Cie Éditeurs.

Nabulsi, Karma. 1999. *Traditions of War Occupation, Resistance, and the Law*. Oxford; New York: Oxford University Press.

Neff, Stephen C. 2005. *War and the Law of Nations: A General History*. Cambridge; New York: Cambridge University Press.

Ohlin, Jens David. 2016. *Theoretical Boundaries of Armed Conflicts and Human Rights*. Cambridge: Cambridge University Press

Onuf, Nicholas Greenwood. 1994. "Civitas Maxima: Wolff, Vattel and the Fate of Republicanism." *The American Journal of International Law* no. 88(2):280–303.

Onuma, Yasuaki. 1993. "War." In *A Normative Approach to War: Peace, War, and Justice in Hugo Grotius*, edited by Yasuaki Onuma. Oxford: Clarendon Press.

Orford, Anne. 2012. "In Praise of Description." *Leiden Journal of International Law* no. 25(3):609–25.

Orford, Anne. 2013. "On International Legal Method." *London Review of International Law* no. 1(1):166–97.

Pagden, Anthony. 1981. "The Search for Order: The 'School of Salamanca' and the *Ius Naturae*." In *Mediaeval and Renaissance Studies on Spain and Portugal in honour of P.E. Russell*, edited by F. W. Hodcroft, D. G. Pattison, and R. D. F. Pring-Mill. Oxford: Oxford University Press.

Pagden, Anthony. 1982. *The Fall of Natural Man: The American Indian and the Origins of Comparative Ethnology*. Cambridge; New York: Cambridge University Press.

Pagden, Anthony. 1990. "Dispossessing the Barbarian: Rights and Property in Spanish America." In *Spanish Imperialism and the Political Imagination: Studies in European and Spanish-American Social and Political Theory 1513–1830*. New Haven: Yale University Press.

Pagden, Anthony. 2012. "Conquest and the Just War: The 'School of Salamanca' and the 'Affair of the Indies'" In *Empire and Modern Political Thought*, edited by Sankar Muthu. Cambridge; New York: Cambridge University Press.

Parker, Geoffrey. 1994. "Early Modern Europe." In *The Laws of War: Constraints on Warfare in the Western World*, edited by Michael Howard, George Andreopoulos, and Mark Shulman. New Haven; London: Yale University Press.

Parker, Geoffrey. 2004. *The Army of Flanders and the Spanish Road, 1567–1659*. 2nd ed. Cambridge; New York: Cambridge University Press.

Peeler, Bryan. 2019. *The Persistence of Reciprocity in International Humanitarian Law*. Cambridge: Cambridge University Press.

Pereña, Luciano. 1954. *Teoría de la Guerra en Francisco Suarez*. Madrid: Instituto Francisco de Vitoria.

Pereña, Luciano. 1981. "Estudio Preliminar." In *Francisco de Vitoria: Relectio de iure belli o Paz dinámica*, edited by Luciano Pereña. Madrid: Consejo Superior de Investigaciones Científicas

Perreau-Saussine, Amanda. 2011. "Lauterpacht and Vattel on the Sources of International Law: The Place of Private Law Analogies and General Principles." In *Vattel's International Law in a XXIst Century Perspective*, edited by Peter Haggenmacher and Vincent Chetail. Leiden: Martinus Nijhoff Publishers.

Piceu, Tim. 2014. "'Une Oppression Insupportable au Peuple': The Impact of Contributions on Armistice, Peace and Truce Negotiations." In *The Twelve Years Truce (1609): Peace, Truce, War, and Law in the Low Countries at the Turn of the 17th Century*, edited by Randall Lesaffer. Leiden: Brill Nijhoff.

Piirimäe, Pärtel 2010a. "War and Polemics in Early Modern Europe." In *Exploring Cultural History: Essays in Honour of Peter Burke*, edited by Joan Pau Rubiés, Melissa Calaresu, and Filippo de Vivo. Farnham; Burlington: Ashgate.

Piirimäe, Pärtel 2010b. "The Westphalian Myth and the Idea of External Sovereignty." In *Sovereignty in Fragments: The Past, Present and Future of a Contested Concept*, edited by Hent Kalmo and Quentin Skinner. Cambridge; New York: Cambridge University Press.

Pitts, Jennifer. 2007. "Boundaries of Victorian International Law." In *Victorian Visions of Global Order*, edited by Duncan Bell. Cambridge: Cambridge University Press.

Pitts, Jennifer. 2015. "The Critical History of International Law" *Political Theory* no. 43(4):541–52.

Pitts, Jennifer. 2018. *Boundaries of the International: Law and Empire*. Cambridge: Harvard University Press.

Plumer Ward, Robert. 1805. *An Enquiry into the Manner in Which the Different Wars in Europe Have Commenced during the Last Two Centuries*. London: J. Butterworth and J. Stockdale.

Pocock, J. G. A. 1987. "The Concept of a Language and the Metier d'Historien: Some Considerations on Practice." In *The Languages of Political Theory in Early-Modern Europe*, edited by Anthony Pagden. Cambridge: Cambridge University Press.

Pocock, J. G. A. 2001. *Barbarism and Religion* Cambridge: Cambridge University Press.

Posner, Eric. 2013. "Human Rights, the Laws of War, and Reciprocity." *Law & Ethics of Human Rights* no. 6(2):147–71.

Rech, Walter. 2013. *Enemies of Mankind: Vattel's Theory of Collective Security*, edited by Martti Koskenniemi. Vol. 18, *The Erik Castrén Institute Monographs on International Law and Human Rights*. Leiden: Martinus Nijhoff Publishers.

Redlich, F. 1959. "Contributions in the Thirty Years' War." *The Economic History Review* no. 12(2):247–54.

Regout, Robert. 1935. *La doctrine de la guerre juste de Saint Augustin à nos jours, d'après les théologiens et les canonistes catholiques*. Paris: A. Pedone.

Reichberg, Gregory. 2007. "Preventive War in Classical Just War Theory." *Journal of the History of International Law* no. 9:5–34.

Reichberg, Gregory. 2008. "Just War and Regular War: Competing Paradigms." In *Just and Unjust Warriors: The Moral and Legal Status of Soldiers*, edited by David Rodin and Henry Shue. Oxford: Oxford University Press.

Reichberg, Gregory. 2012. "Legitimate Authority: Aquinas's First Requirement of Just War." *The Thomist* no. 76:337–69.

Remec, Peter Pavel. 1960. *The Position of the Individual in International Law According to Grotius and Vattel*. The Hague: M. Nijhoff.

Riggsby, Andrew. 2006. *Caesar in Gaul and Rome*. Austin: University of Texas Press.

Roberts, Adam. 2008. "The Equal Application of the Laws of War: A Principle under Pressure." *International Review of the Red Cross* no. 90(872):931–62.

Roberts, Adam, and Richard Guelff. 2000. *Documents on the Laws of War*. 3rd ed. Oxford: Clarendon Press.

Robson, Eric. 1966. "The Armed Force and the Art of War." In *The New Cambridge Modern History: The Old Regime 1713–1763*, edited by J. O. Lindsay. Cambridge: Cambridge University Press.

Rodin, David. 2004. *War and Self-defense*. Oxford; New York: Clarendon Press.

Rodin, David. 2008. "The Moral Inequality of Soldiers: Why jus in bello Asymmetry is Half-right." In *Just and Unjust Warriors: The Moral and Legal Status of Soldiers*, edited by David Rodin and Henry Shue. Oxford: Oxford University Press.

Rodin, David. 2011. "Morality and Law in War." In *The Changing Character of War*, edited by Hew Strachan and Sibylle Scheipers. Oxford; New York: Oxford University Press.

Rodin, David, and Henry Shue. 2008. *Just and Unjust Warriors: The Moral and Legal Status of Soldiers*. Oxford: Oxford University Press.

Rolfe, John C., and Coleman Phillipson. 1933. *De Iure Belli Libri Tres by Alberico Gentili*. Oxford: Clarendon Press.

Rousseau, Jean-Jacques. 1991 [1761]. "Abstract and Judgement of Saint-Pierre's Project for Perpetual Peace." In *Rousseau on International Relations*, edited by Stanley Hoffmann and David Fidler. Oxford; New York: Oxford University Press.

Rousseau, Jean-Jacques, and Victor Gourevitch. 1997. *Rousseau: The Social Contract and Other Later Political Writings*. Cambridge: Cambridge University Press.

Rousseau, Jean-Jacques. 1997 [1755]. "The State of War." In *Rousseau: The Social Contract and Other Later Political Writings*, edited by Victor Gourevitch. New York: Cambridge University Press.

Ruddy, Francis Stephen. 1968. "International Law and The Enlightenment." *International Lawyer* no. 3(4):839–58.

Ruddy, Francis Stephen. 1972. "The Acceptance of Vattel." In *Grotian Society Papers: Studies in the History of the Law of Nations*, edited by Charled Henry Alexandrowicz. The Hague: Martinus Nijhoff.

Sassòli, Marco. 2019. *International Humanitarian Law: Rules, Controversies, and Solutions to Problems arising in Warfare*. Northampton, Mass.: Edward Elgar Publishing.

Scheipers, Sibylle. 2015. *Unlawful Combatants: A Genealogy of the Irregular Fighter* Oxford: Oxford University Press.

Schindler, Dietrich. 2007. "J.C. Bluntschli's Contribution to the Law of War." In *Promoting Justice, Human Rights and Conflict Resolution through International Law*. Geneva: BRILL.

Schmitt, Carl. 2003. *The Nomos of the Earth in the International Law of the Jus Publicum Europaeum*. New York: Telos Press.

Schmitt, Carl. 2007 [1963]. *Theory of the Partisan: Intermediate Commentary on the Concept of the Political*. New York: Telos Press Pub.

Schmitt, Michael. 2010. "Military Necessity and Humanity in International Humanitarian Law: Preserving the Delicate Balance." *Virginia Journal of International Law* no. 50(4):796–839.

Schneewind, Jerome B. 1998. *The Invention of Autonomy: A History of Modern Moral Philosophy*. Cambridge: Cambridge University Press.

Schröder, Peter. 2010. "Vitoria, Gentili, Bodin: Sovereignty and the Law of Nations." In *The Roman Foundations of the Law of Nations: Alberico Gentili and the Justice of Empire*, edited by Benedict Kingsbury and Benjamin Straumann. Oxford; New York: Oxford University Press.

Schwartz, Daniel. 2013. "Probabilism, Just War and Sovereign Supremacy in the Work of Gabriel Vázquez." *History of Political Thought* no. 34(2):177–94.

Schwartz, Daniel. 2018. "Late Scholastic Just War Theory." In *The Oxford Handbook of Ethics of War*, edited by Seth Lazar and Helen Frowe. Oxford: Oxford University Press.

Scott, James Brown. 1934. *The Spanish Origin of International Law*. Oxford, London: Clarendon Press.

Selesky, Harold. 1994. "Colonial America." In *The Laws of War: Constraints on Warfare in the Western World*, edited by Michael Howard, George J. Andreopoulos, and Mark R. Shulman. New Haven; London: Yale University Press.

Silvestrini, Gabriela. 2010. "Justice, War and Inequality: The Unjust Aggressor and the Enemy of the Human Race in Vattel's Theory of the Law of Nations." *Grotiana* no. 31:44–68.

Skinner, Quentin. 1978. *The Foundations of Modern Political Thought Volume 2: The Age of Reformation*. Cambridge; New York: Cambridge University Press.

Skinner, Quentin. 1998. *Liberty before Liberalism*. Cambridge: Cambridge University Press.

Skinner, Quentin. 2002 [1969]. "Meaning and Understanding in the History of Ideas." In *Visions of Politics: Regarding Method*, edited by Quentin Skinner. Cambridge: Cambridge University Press.

Sonnino, Paul. 1976. "Louis XIV and the Dutch War." In *Louis XIV and Europe*, edited by Ragnhild Marie Hatton. London: Macmillan.

Stanton, Jessica. 2016. *Violence and Restraint in Civil War: Civilian Targeting in the Shadow of International Law*. Cambridge: Cambridge University Press.

Steele, Ian Kenneth. 1990. *Betrayals: Fort William Henry and the Massacre*. New York: Oxford University Press.

Stein, Peter. 1999. *Roman Law in European History* Cambridge: Cambridge University Press.

Straumann, Benjamin. 2015. *Roman Law in the State of Nature: The Classical Foundations of Hugo Grotius' Natural Law*. Cambridge: Cambridge University Press.

Straumann, Benjamin. 2019. "The Energy of Concepts: The Role of Concepts in Long-Term Intellectual History and Social Reality." *Journal of the Philosophy of History* (2019):1–36.

Sylvest, Casper. 2007. "The Foundations of Victorian International Law." In *Victorian Visions of Global Order*, edited by Duncan Bell. Cambridge: Cambridge University Press.

Tadashi, Tanaka. 1993a. "Grotius's Concept of Law." In *A Normative Approach to War: Peace, War, and Justice in Hugo Grotius*, edited by Yasuaki Onuma. Oxford: Clarendon Press.

Tadashi, Tanaka. 1993b. "Temperamenta (Moderation)." In *A Normative Approach to War: Peace, War, and Justice in Hugo Grotius*, edited by Yasuaki Onuma. Oxford: Clarendon Press.

Teitel, Ruti. 2011. *Humanity's Law*. Oxford; New York: Oxford University Press.

Textor, Johann Wolfgang, and John Pawley Bate. 1916 [1680]. *Synopsis Iuris Gentium*. Vol. 2. Washington, D.C.: Carnegie Institution of Washington.

Tierney, Brian. 1997. *The Idea of Natural Rights: Studies on Natural Rights, Natural Law, and Church Law, 1150–1625*. Atlanta: Scholars Press.

Tierney, Brian. 2007. "Vitoria and Suarez on Ius Gentium, Natural Law, and Custom." In *The Nature of Customary Law*, edited by Amanda Perreau-Saussine and James Bernard Murphy. Cambridge: Cambridge University Press.

Todescan, Franco. 2013. "Ius gentium medium est intra jus naturale et jus civile: La 'double face' du droit des gens dans la scolastique espagnole du 16eme siècle." In *The Roots of International Law: Liber Amicorum Peter Haggenmacher*, edited by Pierre-Marie Dupuy and Vincent Chetail. Leiden: Martinus Nijhoff Publishers.

Tourme-Jouannet, Emmanuelle. 2014. "Des Origines Coloniales du Droit International: À propos du droit des gens moderne au 18ème siècle" In *The Roots of International Law: Liber Amicorum Peter Haggenmacher*, edited by Pierre-Marie Dupuy and Vincent Chetail. Leiden: Martinus Nijhoff Publishers.

Tuck, Richard. 1979. *Natural Rights Theories: Their Origin and Development*. Cambridge: Cambridge University Press.

Tuck, Richard. 1993. *Philosophy and Government, 1572–1651, Ideas in Context*. Cambridge; New York: Cambridge University Press.

Tuck, Richard. 1999. *The Rights of War and Peace: Political Thought and the International Order from Grotius to Kant*. New York: Oxford University Press.

Tuck, Richard. 2015. *The Sleeping Sovereign*. Cambridge: Cambridge University Press.

Tully, James. 1993. *An Approach to Political Philosophy: Locke in Contexts*. Cambridge: Cambridge University Press.

Tully, James. 1995. *Strange Multiplicity: Constitutionalism in an Age of Diversity*. Cambridge; New York: Cambridge University Press.

Turner Johnson, James. 1975. *Ideology, Reason, and the Limitation of War: Religious and Secular Concepts, 1200–1740*. Princeton: Princeton University Press.

van Dijk, Boyd. 2018. "Human Rights in War: On the Entangled Foundations of the 1949 Geneva Conventions." *American Journal of International Law* no. 112(4):553–82.

van Ittersum, Martine Julia. 2010. "The Long Goodbye: Hugo Grotius' Justification of Dutch Expansion Overseas, 1615–1645." *History of European Ideas* no. 36:386–411.

Vanderpol, Alfred. 1919. *La doctrine scolastique du droit de guerre*. Paris: A. Pedone.

Vattel, Emer de. 1765. *Amusements de Litterature, de Morale et de Politique*. The Hague: Chez Pierre Gosse Junior et Daniel Pinet.

Vattel, Emer de, and Bela Kapossy. 2008 [1758]. *The Law of Nations*. Indianapolis: Liberty Fund.

Verdebout, Agatha. 2014. "The Contemporary Discourse on the Use of Force in the Nineteenth Century: A Diachronic and Critical Analysis" *Journal on the Use of Force and International Law* no. 1(2):223–46.

Villey, Michael. 2013 [1975]. *La formation de la pensée juridique moderne*. 2nd ed, *Quadrige Manuels*. Paris: Presses Universitaires de France.

Vollenhoven, Cornelis van. 1919. *The Three Stages in the Evolution of the Law of Nations*. The Hague: M. Nijhoff.

Waldron, Jeremy. 2010. "Civilians, Terrorism, and Deadly Serious Conventions." In *Torture, Terror, and Trade-Offs: Philosophy for the White House*, edited by Jeremy Waldron. Oxford: Oxford University Press.

Walzer, Michael. 1977. *Just and Unjust Wars: A Moral Argument with Historical Illustrations*. New York: Basic Books.

Walzer, Michael. 2004. *Arguing about War*. New Haven: Yale University Press.

Ward, Matthew C. 2012. "Understanding Native American Alliances." In *The Seven Years' War: Global Views*, edited by Mark H. Danley and Patrick J. Speelman. Boston: Brill.

Whatmore, Richard. 2010. "Vattel, Britain and Peace in Europe." *Grotiana* no. 31:85–107.

Whelan, Frederick. 1988. "Vattel's Doctrine of the State." *History of Political Thought* no. 9(1):59–90.

Whitman, James Q. 2012. *The Verdict of Battle: The Law of Victory and the Making of Modern War*. Cambridge: Harvard University Press.

Wilenius, Reijo. 1963. *The Social and Political Theory of Francisco Suárez*. Helsinki: Societas Philosophica Fennica.

Witt, John Fabian. 2012. *Lincoln's Code: The Laws of War in American History*. New York; London: Free Press.

Wolff, Christian. 1992 [1730]. "On the Philosopher King and the Ruling Philosopher." In *Moral Enlightenment: Leibniz and Wolff on China*, edited by Julia Ching and Willard Gurdon Oxtoby. Nettetal: Steyler Verlag.

Wolff, Christian, and Joseph Drake. 1934 [1750]. *The Law of Nations Treated According to a Scientific Method*, edited by James Brown Scott, *Classics of International Law*. New York: Oxford University Press.

Yakemtchouk, Romain. 1973. "Les origines de l'Institut de droit international." *Revue générale de droit international* no. 77:373–423.

Zurbuchen, Simone. 2009. "Vattel's Law of Nations and just war theory." *History of European Ideas* no. 35(4):408–17.

Index

For the benefit of digital users, indexed terms that span two pages (e.g., 52–53) may, on occasion, appear on only one of those pages.

adjudication
  enemies of mankind 90–91
  formation of states 22
  partiality 11–12, 36–41
  solemn war 56, 62, 63–64
  sovereignty 8
  Spanish scholasticism 35
  war manifestoes 86
aggression 71, 80, 85, 90–91
Alciatus, Andrea 35, 45, 47–48
ambassadorships 29
amelioration of harm 8–9, 15–16, 68, 142, 145, 150–51
American Civil War 130, 132, 133
American Indians 19, 31, 33, 43–44
American Revolution 140
amnesties 52–53, 156
Appia, Louis 142–44
Aquinas, Thomas 19–21, 24, 25–27, 83
Aristotle 18, 20–21, 64
Austrian Succession, War of 92
Austro-Prussian War of 1866 133
Ayala, Balthazar 45, 47–48

barbarians 108, 110
Barbeyrac, Jean 54–55
battlefield relief 140–41, 142, 144
belligerent equality
  punishment for war crimes 101, 118–20
  regular war 78–86, 100–2, 115
  solemn war 45, 67
  Spanish scholasticism 31–35, 49, 83
belligerent privileges 95, 153, 155–56
  definition 14, 99
  non-international armed conflicts 2
  privilege to kill 8
  regular forces 108
  regular war 14, 99, 155–56
  solemn war 45, 104–5, 155–56
  sovereignty 62–63, 104–5
belligerent status 93–95
bellum solenne ***see*** **Solemn war**
Bluntschli, Johann Caspar 14–15, 128, 133, 138–40, 141, 145–47
Bohemia, invasion of 92–93
Brussels Declaration of 1874 145–46, 147, 149
Brussels Peace Conference of 1874 133, 146

Cicero 33–34
civil law 35, 41–42, 45–46, 63–64
civil war 9, 93–94
civilizing mission 43–44, 136–39, 144, 147
codification 127–28, 134–35, 145–47
  diplomatic conferences 7, 140, 142, 145–47
  humanity, principle of 3, 127–36, 140, 142, 145–47
  laws and customs of war 7
coercive power of states 2
  conscience 25, 56
  divine law 19–20, 25
  functions of state, protection of 74–75
  Grotius on solemn war 77
  legitimization 4–5, 153–54
  monopoly of legitimate coercion 64
  sovereignty 4–5, 8–9, 23–24, 25
  Spanish scholasticism 19–20, 23, 25, 28, 31
combatants ***see also*** **irregular forces; regular forces**
  Additional Protocol to Geneva Conventions 2
  belligerent status 93–95
  designated combatants 103–4
  distinction, principle of 1–2, 5–6, 51–52, 67–68, 131–32, 155
  immunities 108, 155–56
communities, existence of political 20–23
confession, sacrament of 15–16, 18, 19–20, 40

conquest 17, 19, 22, 43–44, 124
conscience
ius in bello 41–42, 118
ius post bellum 41–42
partiality in adjudication 11–12, 36–40
religion 11, 28, 118
solemn war 15–16, 55–56, 67, 118
soulcraft and statecraft 25–26, 56
Spanish scholasticism 11–12, 18, 19, 25–31, 36–40, 41–42
consent
formation of states 22
occupation 31, 125
Spanish scholasticism 22–23, 31
voluntary law of nations 78–79
consequentialism 79–80, 98
contextualism, in historiography 4, 5–6
corrective justice
ius post bellum 43–44
regular war 100, 101–2, 122
solemn war 49, 50, 60–61, 63–64, 67
Spanish scholasticism 39, 43, 44
cosmopolitanism 7–8, 137–42, 147
Crimean War 133–34
customary law 22, 153
Brussels Declaration 1874 145–46, 147, 149
codification 7
humanity, 19th-century principle of 127, 128–29, 131, 133, 134, 136, 141, 145–46, 147
Oxford Manual 1880 145, 146–47
property 29
Spanish scholasticism 27–29
voluntary law of nations 78–86

declaration of war 13, 50–51, 74, 87, 88, 89, 131, 155; *see also* **war manifesto, war publication**
defensive war 24–25
diplomacy 13, 70, 138–39, 141–42
diplomatic conferences 7, 140, 142, 145–47
direct participation in hostilities 106–7, 155
distinction, principle of 1–2, 5–6, 51–52, 67–68, 131–32, 155
divine law 19–20, 25, 50
duels 105–6
Dutch war of 1672 91–92

economy of violence 13, 97, 113–14, 128–29, 134, 148
emancipatory project, laws of war as 9
enemies of mankind 71, 90–93
enforcement *see* **punishment and enforcement**
enlargement of empire 34–35, 39
enmity, Roman doctrine of 35–36, 39, 40, 50, 87
English School of International Relations 47
Enlightenment 70, 97–98; *see also* **regular war, ideals of limitation**
enslavement
Enlightenment ideals of limited warfare 124, 125–26
humanity in 19th century, principle of 139
right to enslave 58, 59, 62
Rousseau 57
Solemn war 58, 59, 62, 125–26
Vattel on regular war 76, 85
equality *see* **belligerent equals**
European Court of Human Rights (ECtHR) 154
evil 28–29, 34
excuses, doctrine of 32
external justice
enforcement powers 55–56, 60–61
internal justice distinguished 55–57, 58–61, 65
Solemn war 55–57, 58–63, 65–66, 67
external law of nations 12–13, 69, 103
natural law 12, 53–57, 64–65
Solemn war 12–13, 53–58, 66–68, 69–70, 78, 103
Vattel and Wolff on voluntary law of nations 69, 78–79, 81
volitional, as 53

faultless wrong, concept of 33
federalism 75, 76, 94
formation of states 22–23
Frederick the Great, King of Prussia 92–93
French Revolution 140
Fulgosius, Rafael 35, 47–48

Geneva Conventions
1864 Convention 7, 128, 135–36, 142
1906 Convention 136
Additional Protocols 2
distinction, principle of 2
humanity, principle of 128, 135–36, 141–42, 143

Gentili, Alberico 35, 45–46, 47–48, 87
good faith 39–40, 41, 80–82
Gratian's *Decretum* 25–26

Hague Peace Conferences 7, 128, 145
Hobbes, Thomas 56–57, 69, 70, 73, 75, 124
honour and standing, contests for 33–34
hors de combat 15–16, 134
human rights
  applicable in war 137, 138, 139–41
  humanity in 19th century, principle of 2–3, 14–15, 137, 138, 139–41, 142–43, 144
  International Humanitarian Law (IHL) 153–54, 155, 156–57
  legal cosmopolitanism 140–41
  lex specialis, IHL as 155
  reciprocity, independence from 148
  regional courts 154
Humanity 67–68, 99; *see also* **temperamenta belli**
  19th-century principle of 127–51
    amelioration of harm 15–16, 68, 142, 145, 150–51
    battlefield relief 140–41, 142, 144
    civilization 136–39, 144, 147
    codifications 3, 68, 127–28, 145–47
    cosmopolitanism 137–41, 147
    diplomacy 138–39, 141–42
    diplomatic conferences 140, 142, 145–47
    Geneva Convention 1864 128, 135–36, 141–42, 143
    human rights 14–15, 137, 138, 139–41, 142–43, 144, 148
    humanity, definition of 127
    Moynier, Gustave 14–15, 128, 139–40, 141–43, 144, 147–48, 157
    sick and wounded on battlefield 135, 136, 143, 147
    succour 15–16, 144
    superfluous injury 148
humanization of the laws of war 2–3, 45–46, 67–68, 99; *see also* **humanity**

IHL *see* **International Humanitarian Law (IHL)**
immunities
  belligerent privileges 115, 155–56
  combatants 108, 111, 155–56
  irregular fighters 155
  necessity 42–43, 112
  neutrals 14, 99, 111–18
  non-combatants 14, 99, 111–18, 136
  prisoners of war 155–56
  qualifications 42–44
  requisitions 14, 99, 113–15
  sieges 14, 99, 112–13
  Spanish scholasticism 29, 42–44
impartiality 11–12, 36–41
impunity 155–56
Institut de Droit International
  Brussels Declaration 1874 145–46, 147, 149
  Humanity, 19th-century principle of 128, 144, 145–47, 148, 149
  Oxford Manual 1880 145, 146–47
  Revue de Droit International et de Legislation Comparée 128
Inter-American Court of Human Rights 154
internal justice
  corrective justice 67
  distinction, principle of 67–68
  external justice 55–57, 58–61, 65
  Solemn war 55–57, 58–61, 65–66
International Committee of the Red Cross (ICRC) 14, 128, 142–43, 147
  amnesties 156
  direct participation in hostilities, interpretive guidelines on 155
  Lieber's Code 135
  Moynier, Gustave 128, 139–40, 141–43, 144, 147–48
  neutrality 135
International Court of Justice 155
International Criminal Law 1–3, 33, 42–43, 102, 153–54
International Humanitarian Law
  convergence with human rights, 153–54, 156–57
  human rights 153–54, 155, 156–57
  International Criminal Law 153–54
  justification for war 66–67
  laws and customs of war 156
  lex specialis, as 155
  use of term 8–9, 150–51
International Relations 4, 6–7, 47
international society 13, 69–70, 73–78
irregular forces
  authorized forces 108
  barbarians 108, 110
  belligerent privileges 155

irregular forces (*Cont.*)
citizens directly participating in hostilities 106–7, 155
dissident armed forces 155
immunities 155
organized resistance to occupation 108
partisans 108–9
pirates and brigands 62–64, 104–5, 110, 133–34
privateers 108–10
regular forces 106–9
savages 109–10
tactical advantages 107
unauthorized forces 108, 110
Isidore's *Eymologies* 25–26
***ius ad bellum* (law of resort of force)** 10–11, 50–53, 97
declarations of war 50–51
excuses, Scholastic doctrine of 32
humanity in 19th century, principle of 127–28, 132
peace and termination of war 52–53, 122–23
regular war 13, 15–16, 97
regular war and resort to force in Enlightenment 70–71, 77–78, 93
Spanish scholasticism 32, 40–41
***ius gentium* (law of nations)** *see also* **external law of nations; voluntary law of nations**
claim rights 31–32
corrective justice 67
declarations of war 50–51
external law of nations 12–13, 53–58, 66–68, 69, 103
natural law 53, 69
regular war 98
Solemn war 12–13, 50–51, 53–58, 66–68, 69, 103
Spanish scholasticism 21–23, 25–31
state-centrism 30–31, 136–37
voluntary law of nations 13, 78–86
***ius in bello* (law governing hostilities)** 10–11, 93, 102
belligerent equality 35, 100–2
competing state interests 14, 97–98
conscience 41–42, 118
corrective justice 100, 101–2
good faith 41
humanity 14, 67–68, 99, 127–51
illegal means 14, 97–98
limitations on force 97–98
natural law 100, 101–2
peace and termination of war 101, 102, 122–23
punishment and enforcement 101, 102, 118
regular war 13–14, 15–16, 100–2, 118
reason of state 13–14
reprisals 101
Spanish scholasticism 35, 40–44
***ius post bellum* (law of transition to peace)** 10–11, 35, 40–44
belligerent status 93
peace and termination of war 122
reason of state 13
regular war 13, 15–16, 97
rule-consequentialism 98
Spanish scholasticism 35, 40–44

Jesuits 19–20, 40
judges, sovereigns as 24, 36
judgment, right of 73, 77
jurisdiction over foreigners 24, 36
just war *see also* ***ius ad bellum* (law of resort of force); *ius in bello* (law governing hostilities); Spanish scholasticism, *ius gentium* and just war**
aggression 71
belligerent status 93
declarations of war 51
enemies of mankind 71
execution of a just war 40–44
natural law 69
regular war 102, 119
regular war and resort to force in Enlightenment 70–71, 97
Solemn war 12–13, 45–50, 51, 65–66, 104–5
Spanish scholasticism 45–48, 49–50
justification for war *see also* **reason of state; war manifestoes** 100, 121, 123
guilty 42
legitimate resort to force, doctrine of 4–5, 9, 13, 153–54
manifestoes 88, 90–91

pretexts (quasi-justifying reasons) for war 13, 88, 89–90, 91, 92–93
regular war 69, 70, 79, 83–84, 86–87, 88–90, 91, 92–93
Solemn war 57–65, 66–67, 69, 123
Wolff on reasons for war 88–89

Kant, Immanuel 106, 130–31, 132–33, 156
Koselleck, Reinhardt 70–71

law of armed conflict 2–3, 5–6, 12–13; *see also* International Humanitarian Law
law of nations *see* ***ius gentium*** **(law of nations)**
League of Nations 137–38
Leibniz, Gottfried Wilhelm 136–37
lesser evil, concept of 12, 13, 19–20, 58, 59, 69, 79
Lieber's Code 14–15, 128–36
American Civil War 130, 132, 133
declarations of war 131
distinction, principle of 131–32, 155
innovations 129–30
Manual of Political Ethics 129–32
military necessity 130–31, 132–33, 150
natural law 129–30
perfidy 132–33
prisoners of war 132, 134
quarter 132
regular war 14, 128–36
reprisals 132–33
rescue 135
Slavery 132
Lincoln's General Orders No 100 *see* **Lieber's Code**
Locke, John 17, 50
long-term state interests 14, 97–98, 99, 150
Louis XIV, King of France 91–92, 113–14
Luther, Martin 19–20

manifestoes *see* **war manifestoes**
Martens, GF von 97–98, 106–7, 108–9, 133, 146
means of war, proscription of 42–43, 52, 121, 134
metaphysics 18–19
Molina, Luis de 36
Montesquieu, Charles de 98, 106
moral conscience *see* **conscience**
Moynier, Gustave 14–15, 128, 139–40, 141–43, 144, 147–48, 157
murder 1–2, 42–43, 102

nationalism 9, 138
natural law 10–11, 17, 69
coercive power of states 19–20, 25
communities, existence of 22
external law of nations 12, 53–57, 64–65
ius in bello 100, 101–2
Lieber's Code 129–30
punishment and enforcement 19, 50, 64, 79
regular war 100, 101–2
reparations 64
Solemn war 12, 45–46, 49, 50, 53–57, 61–63, 64–65, 69
sovereignty 62–63
Spanish scholasticism 11–12, 21–22, 26–27, 28–30, 41–42, 54
civilizing mission 43–44
coercive power of states 19–20, 25
formation of states 23
partiality 36, 39
voluntary law of nations 78–79, 80–81, 82
naval wars
neutrality 115–18, 133–34
privateering 9–10, 133–34
ships, inspection of 116
necessity
Enlightenment 121
Geneva Convention 1906 136
Humanity 127–28, 130–31
balancing humanity and necessity 15, 127–28, 129, 148–51
reason of state 149–50
immunities 42–43
Lieber's Code 130–31, 132–33, 150
punishment and enforcement 121
reason of state 149–50, 156–57
Spanish scholasticism 42–43
neutrality
alliances 117–18
belligerent privileges 115
contraband 116–17
enemy goods, enemy ships 116–17

neutrality (*Cont.*)
Enlightenment 14, 99, 111–18
free ships, free goods 116–17
Geneva Convention 1864 135
humanity in 19th century, principle of 15–16, 144
immunities 14, 99, 111–18
impartially, treating belligerents 52
naval wars 115–18, 133–34
Solemn war 52, 58, 61–62, 115
third parties, effect on 58, 61–62
trade, protection of innocent 52
non-combatants
definition 14
distinction, principle of 1–2, 5–6, 51–52, 67–68, 131–32, 155
hostages 149
humanity 15–16, 128–29, 135, 155
immunities 99, 111–18, 136
Lieber's Code 131–32
ransom 108, 112
reprisals 120
sick and wounded, care for 135
sieges 112, 120, 131–32
non-international armed conflicts 94, 153

occupation 22, 31, 106–7, 108–9, 125
offensive war
aggression 71, 80, 85, 90–91
defensive war distinguished 24–25
Solemn war 50, 104–5
Spanish scholasticism 24–25, 50
Oppenheim, Lassa 137–38
Oxford Manual of the Laws and Customs of War 1880 145, 146–47

pacifism
humanity 14–15, 127–28, 130–31, 144–45, 147–48, 157
Spanish scholasticism 19–20
Paris Declaration 1856 129, 133–35, 141–42
patrimonial rights 124
peace and termination of war *see also* ***ius post bellum*** **(law of transition to peace)**
amnesties 52–53, 156
concessions 123
conquest, right of 124
consent 122–23, 125–26
corrective justice 122
damage to private property 52–53
duress 58, 59–60, 62, 122–23
enslavement 124, 125–26
ius in bello 101, 102, 122–23
manifestoes 87
pirates and brigands 63–64
political compromise 122
procedural fairness 122
property rights 123–26
regular war 13, 99, 122–26
resistance, right to 126
solemn war 52–53, 58, 59–60, 62, 63–64, 122, 123–24, 125–26
sovereignty 62, 124, 125
territorial rights 52–53, 123–26
uti possidetis 52–53, 58
voluntary submission 125
peace zones and battlefields, distinction between 155
perfect rights of states 83–85, 86, 88
perfidy 132–33
pillage 113–15
pirates and brigands 62–64, 104–5, 110, 133–34
Pomponius 50
pre-emption 33–35
preventive force, use of 33–34, 85–86, 91–93
prisoners of war
Enlightenment ideals of limited warfare 119–20
enslavement 132
immunities 155–56
Lieber's Code 132, 134
punishment and enforcement 119–20, 132
race 132
reprisals 120
privateers 9–10, 108–10, 133–34
privileges *see* **belligerent privileges**
progress 136, 139–40, 145–46, 147–48, 153
property
custom 29
destruction 112, 131–32
humanity, 19th-century principle of 128–29, 131–32, 137–38, 139
immunities 121
ius gentium 31
liability for damage 52–53
nullification principle (*res nullius*) 60–61, 113–14, 123, 124

peace and termination of war 52–53, 122–23
pillage 114
regular war 74, 87, 112–15, 116, 121, 122–26
requisitions 14, 99, 113–15
Roman law 34, 43–44
solemn war 49, 52–53, 58, 60–61
territorial rights 52–53, 58, 71, 123–26
theft 29
uti possidetis 58, 60–61
proportionality, principle of 43, 49, 65, 101, 119, 120
public opinion 138–39, 148–49
Pufendorf, Samuel 69, 70
punishment and enforcement
barbarians 110
belligerent status 93, 153, 155–56
criminal punishment 153
divine laws 19, 50
impunity 53, 55, 108, 155–56
ius in bello 101, 102, 118
natural law 19, 50, 64
prisoners of war 119–20, 132
private right to punish 50
regular war 108, 118–21
reprisals 118, 119–21, 153
self-enforcement 2, 153
solemn war 50, 55–56, 60–61, 64–65, 69
Spanish scholasticism 24–25, 41, 50
war crimes 118–19,
vicarious punishment 110, 119

quarter, giving 51–52, 110, 119, 120, 132, 134

rape 42–43, 52, 112, 121
realism 6–7, 47, 80, 98
reason of state
humanity, 19th-century principle 14–15, 145, 148–51
manifestoes 88
necessity 149–50, 156–57
political prudence 14–15, 150
regular war 13–14, 69, 71, 97, 105, 106
solemn war 45–46, 150
Wolff on persuasive reasons 88
reasons for war *see* **justification for war; reason of state; war manifestoes**
Red Cross movement 148; *see also* **International Committee of the Red Cross (ICRC)**
regular forces *see also* **combatants**
barbarians 108, 110
billeting 135–36
citizen militia 106–7
designated combatants 103–4
irregular forces 106–9
occupation 108–9
regular war 103–10
single combat, practice of 103
Regular war 97–126
aristocratic codes of conduct 105–6
barbarians 108, 110
belligerent equality 100–2
belligerent privileges 14, 99, 108, 155–56
breaches and law enforcement 118–21
economy of violence 13, 97, 113–14
illegal means for tactical advantage 14, 97–98
immunities 14, 99, 111–18, 155–56
combatants, definition of 111
neutrality 14, 99, 111–18
non-combatants 14, 99, 111–18
reprisals 112
requisitions 14, 99, 113–15
sieges 14, 99, 112–13
irregular forces 106–9
ius ad bellum 13, 15–16, 97, 122–23
ius gentium 98
ius in bello 13–14, 15–16, 97–98, 100–2, 118, 122–23
ius post bellum 13, 15–16, 97, 98, 122
long-term state interests 14, 97–98, 99
occupation 108–9
peace and termination of wars 13, 14, 99, 101, 102, 122–26
preventive force 85–86, 91–93
prisoners of war 119–20
property 112–15, 116, 121, 122–26
reason of state 13–14, 97, 105, 106
regular forces 103–10
reprisals 14, 99, 101, 112, 118, 119–21, 153
requisitions 14, 99, 113–15
short-term state interests 97–98
sieges 14, 99, 112–13
Solemn war 99, 111
sovereignty 15–16, 125
state interests 14, 97–98, 99
territorial rights 123–26
regular war, doctrine of 68, 127–51; *see also* **regular war**

religion
conscience 11, 28, 118
divine laws 19–20, 25, 50
foro interno 28, 40
freedom of religion 137–38, 139
humanity, 19th-century principle 147
ius gentium 67
Jesuits 19–20, 40
punishment and enforcement 118
solemn war 12–13, 15–16
Spanish scholasticism 17, 18–20, 23, 28, 30, 36–37
wars of religion in Europe 15–16, 70–71
reparations 24–25, 41, 50, 54–55, 64
reprisals
counter-reprisals 120–21
declarations of war 87
Lieber's Code 132–33
necessity 121
prisoners of war 120
punishment and enforcement 118, 119–21, 153
regular war 14, 99, 101, 118, 119–21, 153
republicanism 9, 71, 124, 125–26
requisitions 14, 99, 113–15
res nullius 60–61, 113–14, 123, 124
rescue 15–16, 135, 143, 147
resistance 106–9, 111, 113, 125–26
resort to force in regular war 69–95
aggression 71, 80, 85, 90–91
balance of power 76–77
belligerent equality 78–86
belligerent status 93–95
codification 68
coercive power of states 74–75
collective security 89–93
declarations of war 13, 86–93
diplomacy 13, 70
enemies of mankind 71
judgment, right to 73, 77
just cause 70–71
just war 70–71, 93, 97
moderation 70–71
political judgment 82–83, 86, 97
security, right to 74–75, 77–78, 83–85, 86, 97
sovereignty 70–71, 79–80, 83
supra-national institutions, creation of 75–76
voluntary law of nations 13, 78–86
Rolin-Jaequemyns, Gustave 145–46, 149
Roman law
corpus iuris civilis 25–26
enmity, Roman doctrine of 35–36, 39, 40, 50, 87
solemn war 45–48
sovereignty 7
Spanish scholasticism 41–42, 45–48
Roman wars 34–35
Rousseau, Jean-Jacques
belligerent equality 85–86
consent to peace treaties 125
Grotius, critique of 57–58, 124
necessity 130–31
regular forces 103, 106
property 114–15
public powers, war between 131–32
sovereignty 75, 76
rule-consequentialism 98

Saint Petersburg Declaration of 1868 7, 134–35, 141–42
Saint-Pierre, Abbé de 75–76
Savigny, Friedrich Carl von 136–37
Saxony, invasion of 92–93
Schmitt, Carl 70–71
security, right to 74–75, 77–78, 83–85, 86, 97
self-defence 1, 61
Seneca 67
short-term state interests 14, 97–98, 115–16, 150
sick and wounded 15–16, 134, 135, 136, 143, 147
sieges 99, 112–13
capitulation 105, 112–13, 119
immunities 14, 42
non-combatants 112, 120, 131–32
punishment and enforcement 112–13
Silesia, invasion of 92–93
single combat, practice of 103
slavery *see* **enslavement**
social contract 17, 73–74
Solemn war (*bellum solenne*) 12–13, 15–16, 45–68, 155
adjudication 56, 62, 63–64
amnesties 52–53, 156

belligerent privileges 45, 62–63, 104–5, 155–56
civil law 45–46, 63–64
conquest, right of 124
conscience 15–16, 56, 67, 118
corrective justice 49, 50, 60–61, 63–64, 67
De iure belli ac pacis 12, 46, 49, 51, 53, 54–55, 61, 62–64, 66–67, 103
De iure praedae 46, 49, 62–64
declarations of war 50–51
Enlightenment ideals of limited warfare 99, 111, 115
enslave enemies, right to 58, 59, 62, 124
external justice 55–57, 58–63, 65–66, 67
external law of nations 12–13, 53–58, 64–65, 66–68
humanity 45–46, 67–68, 130
internal justice 12–13, 55–57, 58–61, 65–66, 67–68
ius ad bellum 50–53
ius gentium 12–13, 15–16, 45, 47–48, 50–51, 53, 67, 69
just war 12–13, 45–50, 51, 65–66, 104–5
justification 57–65, 66–67, 69
lesser evil, concept of 12, 58, 59, 69, 79
limitation and management of war 52, 58, 103–5
might can make right, why 57–65
natural law 12, 45–46, 49, 50, 53–57, 61, 62
  external law of nations 12, 53–57, 64–65
  ius gentium 53, 69
  reparations 64
  sovereignty 62–63
neutrality 52, 58, 61–62, 115
peace treaties 52–53, 58, 59–62, 63–64, 122, 123–24, 125–26
property 49, 52–53, 58, 60–61
punishment and enforcement 50, 55–56, 60–61, 64–65, 69
soulcraft 12–13, 56
sovereignty 12, 62–64, 65
Spanish scholasticism, influence of 45–48, 49–50, 54, 56, 58
special privileges 58, 62–63, 69
statecraft 12–13, 56
temperamenta belli (moderation in conduct of war) 65–68, 99
uti possidetis 52–53, 58, 60–61, 62
war manifestoes 87, 88, 91

sovereignty 7–9
  belligerent equality 79–80, 83, 100
  belligerent privileges 62–63, 104–5
  coercive power of state 4–5, 8–9, 23–24, 25
  cosmopolitanism 7–8, 139–40
  emancipatory project, laws of war as 9
  enslave enemies, right to 58
  external justice 62–63
  human rights 139–40
  humanity, 19th century principle 137–38, 139–42
  inherent powers 23–24
  international society 13, 69–70, 73–78
  judgment, right of 73
  justice 63–64
  offensive war 24–25
  peace and termination of war 62, 125
  permissiveness of laws of war 156–57
  regular war 13, 15–16, 69–71, 73–78, 124
  Solemn war 12, 62–64, 65, 70, 104–5
  Spanish scholasticism 20–25

Spanish scholasticism 11–12, 17–44
  American Indians 19, 31, 33, 43–44
  belligerent equality, critique of 31–35, 49
  civil law tradition 35, 41–42
  civilizing mission 43–44
  coercive power of states 19–20, 23, 25, 28, 31
  communities, existence of political 20–23
  confession, sacrament of 15–16, 18, 19–20, 40
  conquest 17, 19, 22, 43–44
  conscience 19, 25–31, 41–42
    ius in bello 41–42
    partiality in adjudication 11–12, 36–40
  consent 22–23, 31
  custom 27–29
  defensive wars 24–25
  divine law 19–20, 25, 50
  dual character of *ius gentium* 30–31
  enlargement of empire 34–35, 39

Spanish scholasticism (*Cont.*)
evil 28–29, 34
excuses, doctrine of 32
execution of a just war 40–44
faultless wrong, concept of 33
formation of states 22–23
gentiles, wars of the 34–35
good faith 39–40, 41
immunities 29, 42–44
ius ad bellum 32
ius in bello 35, 40–44
ius post bellum 35, 40–44
judge, sovereign as 24, 36
jurisdiction over foreigners 24, 36
metaphysics 18–19
natural law 11–12, 21–22, 26–27, 29–30, 41–42
offensive war 24–25, 50
partiality in adjudication and good conscience 11–12, 36–41
political theology 11–12, 17–44
positive law 19, 21–22, 26–27
preventive force 85
punishment and enforcement 24–25, 41, 50
religion 17, 18–20, 23, 28, 30, 36–37
Roman law 41–42, 45–48
sources 25–26, 31
sovereignty 20–25
subjective rights 58, 83
theology 11–12, 18–19
vindication of rights 33–34, 41, 42
starvation, as a means of war 112, 113, 131–32
state interests
competing interests 14, 97–98
humanity, 19th century principle 134, 138–39, 141, 142, 148, 150
ius in bello 10–11, 14, 97–98
long-term interests 14, 97–98, 99, 150
regular war 14, 74–75, 89, 97–98, 99
short-term interests 14, 97–98
Suárez, Francisco 21–22, 23, 27–29, 41
ambassadorships 29
custom 27–28
gentiles, wars of 34–35
immunity of the innocent 42
ius gentium 11, 23–24, 27–31
just war 11, 23–24, 27–31
partiality in adjudication 36, 37–39
sovereignty, inherent powers of 23–24
speculative and practical knowledge, difference between 38
succour 15–16, 144
superfluous injury 148

temperamenta belli* (moderation in conduct of war)** *see also* **Humanity; *ius in bello 65–68 , 99
territorial rights 52–53, 58, 71, 123–26
Terror, use in war 112
Tertullian 19–20
theology 11–12, 18–19

universal monarchy 76, 91, 138
***uti possidetis* (letting things remain as they are)** 52–53, 58, 60–61

Vattel, Emer de 13, 14–16
amnesties 156
barbarians 109–10
belligerent status 93–95
civil prudence 128–29
civil wars, definition of 94
collective security 93
functions of the state 73–74
Grotius, critique of 74–75, 103–5
humanity 129,
Law of Nations 72, 92–93, 99, 103–4
nation, concept of 94
regular war 13, 15–16, 70–79, 81–95, 99, 105
republican freedom 124
resistance, right to 126
Wolff 72
Vitoria, Francisco de 11, 19–22
American Indians 19, 31, 33
coercive power of states, justification of 31
defensive war 25
excuses, doctrine of 32
global commonwealth 30-31
immunity of the innocent 42
jurisdiction over foreigners 24
just war 19–22, 24–28, 36–41, 42–44
natural law 19, 21–22, 27
partiality in adjudication 37–40
theology 19–20, 25–26

voluntary law of nations 13, 78–86
von Moltke, Helmuth 144

War crimes 1–3, 33, 42–43, 101, 102, 118–20, 153–54
war manifestoes 86–93
counter-manifestoes 86
declarations of war, practice of 87, 88, 89
enemies of mankind 90–93
formal state of war 87–88
justifying reasons 88, 90–91
persuasive reasons 88
pretexts (quasi-justifying reasons) 13, 88, 89–90, 91, 92–93
probable reasons 88–89, 90–91
public validation, imperative of 13, 86–93
Wolff, Christian 13, 14–16
belligerent status 93–94
centralized adjudication, absence of 78
ius gentium 69–72, 78–82, 85–86
natural law, suspension of 78
political prudence 14–15, 150
punishment and enforcement 118–19
reason of state 74–75
reasons for war 88, 89–90, 91, 92–93
regular forces 106–7, 109
regular war 13, 15–16, 105, 118–19, 122, 123–24
solemn war, critique of 69, 78, 103–5, 111
voluntary law of nations 78–82, 85–86
war manifestoes 86–89, 91